Reelection

POWER, CONFLICT, AND DEMOCRACY

American Politics Into the Twenty-first Century

POWER, CONFLICT, AND DEMOCRACY:
AMERICAN POLITICS INTO THE TWENTY-FIRST CENTURY
Robert Y. Shapiro, Editor

This series focuses on how the will of the people and the public interest are promoted, encouraged, or thwarted. It aims to question not only the direction American politics will take as it enters the twenty-first century but also the direction American politics has already taken.

The series addresses the role of interest groups and social and political movements; openness in American politics; important developments in institutions such as the executive, legislative, and judicial branches at all levels of government as well as the bureaucracies thus created; the changing behavior of politicians and political parties; the role of public opinion; and the functioning of mass media. Because problems drive politics, the series also examines important policy issues in both domestic and foreign affairs.

The series welcomes all theoretical perspectives, methodologies, and types of evidence that answer important questions about trends in American politics.

JOHN G. GEER, *From Tea Leaves to Opinion Polls: A Theory of Democratic Leadership*

KIM FRIDKIN KAHN, *The Political Consequences of Being a Woman: How Stereotypes Influence the Conduct and Consequences of Political Campaigns*

KELLY D. PATTERSON, *Political Parties and the Maintenance of Liberal Democracy*

DONA COOPER HAMILTON AND CHARLES V. HAMILTON, *The Dual Agenda: Race and Social Welfare Policies of Civil Rights Organizations*

HANES WALTON JR., *African-American Power and Politics: The Political Context Variable*

AMY FRIED, *Muffled Echoes: Oliver North and the Politics of Public Opinion*

RUSSELL D. RILEY, *The Presidency and the Politics of Racial Inequality: Nation-Keeping from 1831 to 1965*

ROBERT W. BAILEY, *Gay Politics, Urban Politics: Identity and Economics in the Urban Setting*

RONALD T. LIBBY, *ECO-WARS: Political Campaigns and Social Movements*

DONALD GRIER STEPHENSON JR., *Campaigns and the Court: The U.S. Supreme Court in Presidential Elections*

KENNETH DAUTRICH AND THOMAS H. HARTLEY, *How the News Media Fail American Voters: Causes, Consequences, and Remedies*

DOUGLAS C. FOYLE, *Counting the Public In: Presidents, Public Opinion, and Foreign Policy*

RONALD G. SHAIKO, *Voices and Echoes for the Environment: Public Interst Representation in the 1990s and Beyond*

Reelection

William Jefferson Clinton as a Native-Son
Presidential Candidate

HANES WALTON JR.

COLUMBIA UNIVERSITY PRESS

NEW YORK

Columbia University Press
Publishers Since 1893
New York   Chichester, West Sussex

Copyright © 2000 Columbia University Press
All rights reserved
Library of Congress Cataloging-in-Publication Data
Walton, Hanes, 1941–
    Reelection : William Jefferson Clinton as a native-son presidential
candidate / Hanes Walton, Jr.
      p.   cm. — (Power, conflict, and democracy)
    Includes bibliographical references and index.
    ISBN 0–231–11552–0 (cloth : alk. paper). — ISBN 0–231–11553–9
(pbk. : alk. paper)
    1. Elections—Arkansas. 2. Voting—Arkansas. 3. Afro-Americans—
Suffrage—Arkansas. 4. Clinton, Bill, 1946–   . I. Title.
II. Series.
JK5192.W35   2000
324.9767'053—dc21   99-32874

To

Librarian Andrew J. McLemore

A Morehouse man, attorney and editor, who turned the library at a small African American college into a major resource and research center.

Accomplishing this feat by using his skills, talents, and dedication with limited resources and a great staff, he succeeded in shaping the world of scholarship.

Arkansas's Gift to the Republic

Larger
Than life
   With
Out-sized appetites
   He
moved Democrats
   And
The Black Vote
Center-Right
(Incredibly)
   Taking
all sides with
Evangelical delivery
   Easily
An American Original
   Whose
   Impact
Upon
Party, policy, principle . . .
   Challenges
Wisdom conventional

—Nadra

Contents

Notes on a Native Son

A Foreword by Frederick C. Harris

I accidentally stumbled upon Professor Hanes Walton over a decade ago. In the west wing of the University of Georgia's main library, some stories above the Richard B. Russell Library for Political Research and Studies, a research library named in honor of Georgia's former segregationist senator, I came across a series of books that would open my eyes to new possibilities. My discovery was prompted by a term paper assignment for a rigorous course on southern politics which was being taught by Professor Charles S. Bullock III, a leading scholar in the field. V. O. Key's seminal work, *Southern Politics*, which I read for the course, was the only text I read as an undergraduate that highlighted the politics of race and the political life of southern African Americans. Key's book inspired me to know more.

Lined up on a library shelf stood a group of books that fed my curiosity—*Black Politics: A Theoretical and Structural Analysis*, *The Study and Analysis of Black Politics: A Bibliography*, *Black Republicans: the Politics of Black and Tan*, *The Political Philosophy of Martin Luther King Jr.*, *The Negro in Third Party Politics*, and the then recently published *Invisible Politics: Black Political Behavior*. They all bore the name of Professor Hanes Walton Jr., then the Callaway Professor of Political Science at Savannah State College, a historically black institution in southeast Georgia. Consuming the ideas in these books revealed to me what was not entirely clear from the texts I had read for my course on southern politics: though African Americans had long been "objects" in the politics of the South they were now, and had always been, "agents" of political change and resistance in the region.

Indeed, Professor Walton's scholarship makes what is often invisible in the study of American politics visible. While the discipline marches toward formalistic models of politics, the work of Professor Walton reminds us, as the work of Harold Gosnell and V. O. Key did a generation ago, that context matters in the science of politics. Contextualizing southern politics has been a contribution that Professor Walton has made throughout his career as a political scientist, and *Reelection: William J. Clinton as a Native-Son Presidential Candidate* is a welcome continuation of Professor Walton's work.

Reelection explores an often overlooked factor in American electoral behavior. It illustrates that localism and regionalism are significant factors in the formation of voter preferences. Through the analysis of Clinton's elections in Arkansas, this book demonstrates how candidates receive a greater level of support from voters who share that candidate's geographical origins than voters who do not. Geographical distinctions in voter behavior—whether they are drawn within states or across regions—have nearly disappeared from research on electoral behavior. The absence of localism as an explanatory factor in voting studies is relatively new in the study of electoral politics. As Professor Walton points out, post–World War II era behaviorists such as Harold Gosnell and V. O. Key were sensitive to geographical distinctions in their studies of American electoral behavior.

Reelection revives that tradition in voting research by chronicling Clinton's electoral performance as a candidate for Congress, state attorney general, governor, and president in his native state of Arkansas. The research shows that native-son candidates who receive support from voters who share their geographical locale are just as important to the formation of voter preferences as issues and party affiliation, factors traditionally viewed as determinants of voter choice.

Reelection is Professor Walton's second contribution to research on the native-son factor in electoral politics. In *The Native Son Presidential Candidate: The Carter Vote in Georgia*, Professor Walton unearthed the level of electoral support from Carter's home region in central Georgia and from "Black Belt counties" throughout the state. Black Belt counties, a phrase coined by Key in *Southern Politics*, are rural counties in the South where blacks are a numerical majority. During the Jim Crow era Black Belt counties were centers of white resistance to racial equality. As with Clinton's support in his native state, Carter gathered strong support from his home county of Sumter and from Georgia's Black Belt counties in the 1976 and 1980 presidential elections. The comparable results from the Carter and Clinton presidential contests demonstrate the continuing significance of the native-son factor in presidential elections.

The appeal of native-son Democrats to black southerners is further confirmed in *Reelection*. In the presidential elections of 1992 and 1996 Clinton received his strongest support in his home state and from Black Belt counties throughout the region. For instance, as Carter had a decade before, Clinton assumed the native-son mantle as the preferred candidate of black voters in Georgia. In Hancock country, a rural Black Belt county in southeast Georgia, Clinton fared better than left-of-center candidates Tom Harkin and Edmund "Jerry" Brown Jr., both of whom criticized Clinton for being too conservative for the Democratic party during the 1992 Democratic primary contests. In the Georgia primary Clinton received 69 percent of the vote in Hancock county while Harkin and Brown both received less than 10 percent of the vote. Black support for Clinton in the 1992 general election made the difference in his slim margin of victory in the state. Clinton defeated George Bush by less than 14,000 votes. In Hancock country, which cast nearly 2,500 votes, three-quarters of those votes went to Clinton. That level of support in Black Belt counties such as Hancock helped Clinton capture the state's 13 electoral votes, and contributed to the president's thin victory (43%) over Bush (42%) in Georgia.

These voting patterns raise questions about the force of the native-son factor in electoral politics. Do native-son candidacies always trump the influence of political ideology or partisan loyalty? If so, in what ways? Why do black southerners prefer native-son candidates more than do white southerners? Does the weight of the "native-son" factor in elections vary between male and female candidates? And what are the foundations of the cultural affinities that make the native-son factor a viable force in contemporary southern politics?

These are questions for researchers to ponder in future work on the native-son factor in the electoral politics of the South. However, I would like to offer some speculations on the cultural aspects of the native-son factor, especially in the context of black support for Democratic presidential candidates.

Friends and Neighbors in Black and White

In *Southern Politics*, V. O. Key discussed how candidates in the one-party South built voter loyalty through a "friends and neighbors" approach to voter appeal. Candidates portrayed themselves as personal friends of voters and voters responded to candidates who best approached the "fellow next door." In modern southern politics norms of neighborliness may have diminished somewhat since the segregationist politics of the past, yet these norms do linger in the region. Among the black southern electorate the perception that white Democratic candidates are friendly to black interests undergirds black support for native-son candidates. But how do white Democrats communicate their interest in black voters? More to the point, how do white Democrats become "native sons" of the black electorate?

In the introduction to Professor Walton's *The Native Son Presidential Vote*, Professor Tobe Johnson wrote that "whatever its value as an explanatory variable, the regional loyalty concept is a provocative one because it assumes a cultural kinship between the two races in the region." He noted further that the "affinity between blacks and whites in the South, Walton seems to feel, may be greater than that between white southerners and northerners—which would explain in part the support given Jimmy Carter by southern black leaders over more liberal Democratic presidential contestants in 1976 and 1980."

Part of the explanation for a cultural kinship between southern blacks and whites lies in the tradition of southern Protestantism. Religion, however, is not the only point of cultural contact between blacks and whites in the South; they also share similar dialects, foods, and musical traditions. Both groups practice norms of "civility" that are common to the region. Yet the South is the nation's most religious region and the legacy of the Christian fundamentalism which swept the South more than three centuries ago in the First and Second "Great Awakenings" has left an imprint on its cultural life. It is not surprising then that native son candidates have often employed religion as a way to convey that they are "friends and neighbors" to black voters.

Jimmy Carter relied on his religious roots to mobilize black support for his presidential candidacies. In the foreword to Professor Walton's Carter study Roosevelt Green recognizes the religious foundations of black support for native-son candidates. He notes that "certain commonalities" exist between southern blacks and whites: "African-American culture had its origins in the South where black churches. . . originated. . . . Blacks were exposed to the same type of religious fundamentalism that Carter was taught." In 1976 Carter circumvented the influence of black elected officials by consolidating his black support through southern black clergy and Atlanta's civil rights elite.

If Carter perfected religious commonality for political gain, Clinton developed it into an art. In 1992 and 1996 Clinton held his inauguration's religious services at the Metropolitan AME church, the national church of the African Methodist Episcopal Church, a black Protestant denomination that dates back to the late 18th century. And not only has Clinton built an army of black ministers as campaign and policy supporters but, unlike Carter, Clinton has incorporated the preaching style of southern Protestantism into many of his political speeches. This folksy oratorical style, used by political actors as diverse as Jesse Jackson and Pat Robertson, helped to create the native son image among black voters. As a reporter for the *New York Times* notes: "Many blacks have felt a spiritual kinship with Mr. Clinton, a son of the South with an abiding sensitivity toward racial matters."[1]

What is remarkable about Clinton's native-son image among blacks is that it has stuck despite Clinton's conservative past as chairman of the Democratic Leadership Council (DLC) and despite his policy decisions during his presidency that many perceive as antithetical to black political interests.

Consider Clinton's sermonic oratory on black criminality in the wake of his signing the Crime Bill, a measure that brought about the explosion of minority youth being jailed for nonviolent offenses. Delivered before the annual meeting of the Church of God in Christ, a predominately black Pentecostal denomination, Clinton sidestepped the issue of jailing nonviolent offenders and preached a message of self-help through spirituality:

> That is not freedom—the freedom to die before you're a teenager is not what Martin Luther King lived and died for. If you had told anybody who was here in this church—where Martin Luther King gave his last speech before he was assassinated—that we would have abused our freedom this way, they would have found it hard to believe. And I tell you it is our moral duty to turn this around. Sometimes, there are no answers from the outside in. Sometimes, the answers have to come from the values and the stirrings and the voices that speak to us from within. . . . The Scripture says, "You are the salt of the earth and the light of the world," that "if your light shines before men, they will give glory to the Father in Heaven." That is what we must do. And I will work with you.

> *Speech delivered November 13, 1993 at the Annual Convocation of the Church of God in Christ, Memphis, Tennessee*

Native Sons and the Politics of Redemption

Clinton's native-son credentials have helped him maintain and strengthen his black support, despite—or because of—the push for his impeachment over the Monica Lewinsky affair. The Lewinsky affair has transformed Clinton into a Bigger Thomas–like figure: the character in Richard Wright's novel, *Native Son*, who digs himself into a deep hole by trying to cover a misdeed. Blacks are supportive of Clinton for many reasons, among them the number of black appointees in his cabinet and the president's interest in African affairs; however, Clinton's treatment by White-water prosecutor Kenneth Starr may symbolize, for many blacks, the unfairness inherent in the nation's criminal justice system. Novelist Toni Morrison captures these feelings of unfairness best in her implicit observation of Clinton's native-son status in black politics and society:

> African-American men seem to understand it right away. Years ago, in the middle of the Whitewater investigation, one heard the first murmurs: skin notwithstanding, this is our first black president. Blacker than any actual black person who could ever be elected in our children's life time. After all, Clinton displays almost every trope of blackness: single-parent household, born poor, working class, saxophone-playing, McDonald's-and-junk-food-loving boy from Arkansas.[2]

In a national poll conducted in mid-August, little less than three months before the 1998 midterm elections, blacks expressed more support for Clinton than did whites.[3] The enormous gap between black and white opinion on Clinton further reflects Clinton's native-son status among blacks. In the poll, blacks were more likely than whites to think that Clinton was doing a good job as president (94% compared to 60% of whites); were about twice as likely to think of Clinton in favorable terms (82% compared to 42% of whites); and were three times more likely to think that Clinton is more honest than most politicians (60% compared to 21% of whites). Moreover, on questions regarding Clinton's morality and credibility, blacks were far more understanding, and presumably more forgiving, than whites. Twice as many blacks (86%) than whites (46%) trusted Clinton to keep his word as president and more than twice as many blacks (71%) than whites (29%) thought that Clinton "shares the moral values most Americans try to live by." Furthermore, twice as many blacks (63%) than whites (36%) blamed Clinton's political enemies for creating the scandal rather than blaming Clinton himself.

What explains these differences in opinion? As I have already mentioned, religion is a site of connectedness between southern blacks and whites, but among black Christians the belief in redemption is a central theme of their religious tradition.[4] The idea of redemption, the belief that one can be redeemed from one's mistakes if one confesses his or her sins and asks for God's forgiveness, has been employed by politicians of all stripes who find themselves in a fix. For instance, in her analysis of Marion Barry's political comeback, Jonetta Rose Barras observed how Barry used religion to win over black voters in Washington D.C.: "Barry, honing his redemption theme each day, frequently referred to God as if he were his personal friend, and to his own political resurrection as if he had been nailed to the cross and personally deserved the same adulation as Jesus Christ."[5]

Like Barry, a native son whose cultural roots lie in a sharecropping community in Mississippi, Clinton employed the theme of religious redemption as the scandal became public. And like evangelist Jimmy Swaggart, a native son of Louisiana who was also involved in a sexual scandal, Clinton confessed "I have sinned." Speaking before a group of black supporters on Martha's Vineyard who were gathered to celebrate the 35th anniversary of the 1963 March on Washington, Harvard Law Professor Charles Ogletree spoke of his support for Clinton on the grounds of reciprocity and the power of redemption: "All these times it was very easy for us to be with you because you were with us, and now in difficult times, I want you to know that the people here understand and feel your pain, believe in redemption, and are here because of you, and are here with you through thick and thin."[6] Anita Hill, who accused Justice Clarence Thomas of sexual harassment during his confirmation hearings, also echoed Clinton, saying that she too believes in the power of forgiveness and redemption.

The political uses of religious redemption are not confined to the secular sphere of African American life. While black political elites on Martha's Vineyard were calling for Americans to forgive Clinton's transgressions, the predominately working class members of the all-black National Baptist Convention were deliberating the fate of their president, Dr. Henry Lyons. Lyons, who was served with state and federal indictments for racketeering, theft, and fraud, and who was also involved in a sex scandal, confessed—with the phrase that Clinton used weeks before—that he had been involved in an "inappropriate relationship" with a denominational official. The rhetoric of forgiveness and redemption prevented Lyons from being ousted from his church and from the presidency of the Baptist convention until his Federal conviction.

A deacon from Lyon's church in Florida embraced the theme of redemption, reasoning that since his pastor apologized to the public and to his church there was no reason for Lyons to give up the pulpit: "We follow what the Bible says. . . . We have to forgive. . . . Everybody makes mistakes."[7] Reverend E.V. Hill, chairman of the Baptist convention's ethics committee, and ally of conservative political activist Reverend Jerry Farewell, also excused Lyons on the grounds of Christian forgiveness: "We don't have a ministry of condemnation. We have a ministry of reconciliation. White people don't understand that in their institutions, so they pull down their [Jim] Bakkers and [Jimmy] Swaggarts."[8] Reverend Roscoe Cooper, the convention's general secretary, defended Lyons as well, arguing that people who "screw up" in American society are given "no possibility of Redemption."[9]

As an institution central to black civil society, black churches, with their traditions steeped in southern Protestantism, provide sacredly ordained justification for a politician's need to redeem himself. As one Brooklyn minister said of Clinton: "I believe it's important for him to make a clean slate now and move on. Anyone can do that if they go through Christ. . . . He seems to be a churchgoing person; I've always thought that. I think he can get through this."[10]

Clinton's native-son status among blacks proved helpful during the 1998 midterm elections. Days before the election the beleaguered president directly appealed to black voters, mobilizing them against congressional Republicans who were driving the impeachment movement. He spoke at a black church in Baltimore, chatted on the "Tom Joyner Show," a nationally syndicated black radio program, and was interviewed on a Black Entertainment Television (BET) news program. Black turnout increased remarkably from the 1994 midterm elections and helped to halt Republican gains in the House and Senate. Black voters were a solid share of the coalitions that defeated Republican incumbents Alfonse D'Amato of New York and Lauch Faircloth of North Carolina, two of the most vocal senators driving the impeachment movement. Indeed, the Republicans' lackluster performance in the midterm election forced Newt Gingrich, the Speaker of the House and Clinton's political nemesis, to resign. The irony here is that Clinton, who as a candidate in the 1992 primaries and general election distanced himself from black voters and their issues, would now, as a means to save his presidency, surround himself with black supporters and directly appeal to black voters.

The pages ahead offer us a history of Clinton's electoral support. They reveal the curious relationship between Clinton and black voters in Arkansas, as well as between Clinton and the "hometown folks." One hopes that *Reelection* will be followed with a similar analysis of Lyndon Johnson's electoral history in Texas, to complete the trilogy of southerners elected to the White House in the post–World War II era. Until then, *Reelection* and Professor Walton's work on Carter fill the void in electoral studies on the native-son factor in presidential politics.

Introduction by Robert A. Brown

As this millennium comes to an end and a new one begins, William Jefferson Clinton will end his second term as the nation's seventh Democratic president during the 20th century. It will have been a century during which Republican candidates for the office often regarded as the most powerful in the world were more successful than their Democratic opponents in winning the presidency. While each party has had five presidents since World War II, there has been a pivotal and significant pattern on the Democratic side. The last three successful candidates—Lyndon Johnson, Jimmy Carter, and Bill Clinton—have all been from the South. It is this phenomenon and its relationship to Clinton's two-term success that professor Hanes Walton adeptly explores in *Reelection: William J. Clinton As A Native-Son Presidential Candidate*.

As President, Bill Clinton has been a figure of almost Shakespearian complexity and ironies. Arguably the consummate politician of the 1990s, Clinton has been one of the rare Americans who did not let go of the childhood dream of becoming president, devoting his entire life to attaining such a difficult goal. The first baby-boomer to become president, he is the 1960s antiwar protester and McGovern campaign worker with seeming leftist sympathies who became the first Democratic president to proclaim that the era of big government had ended. And while he has proclaimed himself to be a "New Democrat" seeking a so-called third path between Democratic liberalism and Republican conservatism, becoming a political chameleon of sorts, Clinton has not completely abandoned the Democratic legacy of Social Security and Medicare, masterfully using these issues to control Republican challenges.

Though it is too early to tell, his historical legacy will be one of dramatic successes, humiliating failures, and unfortunate moral frailty. The successes during his administration would make any past president envious: the transformation of the nation's greatest budget deficit to a surplus, single-digit inflation rates, the lowest levels of unemployment and poverty over the past twenty-five years, and staggering growth in the nation's stockmarkets. Yet Clinton has presided during a time in which the Republicans regained control of both houses of Congress for the first time in over forty years. Finally, his own administration, from the very beginning, has been mired in and tainted by legal battles as he, his wife, and members of his cabinet have been the subjects of constant and indeed withering scrutiny under a host of independent prosecutors. Despite this adversity, Bill Clinton has clearly reshaped the Democratic party and has altered the national electoral environment in such fundamental ways as to make future Democratic candidates highly competitive in the next century's presidential contests.

Building upon a line of research initiated in his book *The Native Son Presidential Candidate: The Carter Vote in Georgia*, Hanes Walton has produced a work that makes a strong and persuasive argument for the influence of the native-son variable on presidential electoral politics and the character of the nation's political parties. Walton traces the evolution of the variable, situating it in the works of Harold Gosnell, V. O. Key Jr., Michael Lewis-Beck and Tom Rice, and Steven Rosenstone. However, he is not content merely describing the variable, its intellectual development, and the notable insights and findings regarding its influence in presidential electoral politics; he has a far greater ambition and goal. In building the case for his argument and analysis, Walton offers sound and constructive criticism of the approaches scholars have used in attempting to understand American elections and the voting behavior associated with them. He categorizes the approaches into three perspectives: the mandate perspective, the individual attributes perspective, and the realignment perspective. Scholars employing a mandate perspective focus on a single election as it occurs, while those with the individual attributes perspective search for the single most important voter characteristic that explains how voters generally voted. And those using the realignment perspective limit their attention to answering whether partisan realignment continues or ends. Although he acknowledges that these approaches have contributed some interesting insights and findings to our understanding of American electoral behavior, Walton argues that their utility and their search for meaning have been seriously compromised by the scholars' tendency to regard elections and voters solely through the analytical binoculars of their chosen approach. Limiting their gaze primarily to what they see, these scholars neglect many of the things occurring outside of those lenses—in his view, the all too important relevance of time, context, and history. One of the book's hallmarks is its deep commitment to the influence of history and context on political parties and the role of a pivotal political figure in changing the character of the Democratic party as he seeks the presidency. Much of the research in contemporary political science, in Walton's opinion, often and unfortunately makes the grave mistake of failing to consider the power of history in shaping the political phenomena we examine and seek to understand. This book challenges political observers of all types—scholars, journalists, pundits, and citizens—to look back to the past in order to understand fully the current political environment.

Walton seeks to rectify the shortcomings of these approaches. His call for a return to history is offered within what he terms a "political party perspective," an approach largely absent in recent scholarship. He attributes the lack of a perspective concentrating upon the political parties to the current vogue of believing that they no longer exist, that they have been replaced by candidate-centered politics. However, Walton uses the political party perspective to situate his historical analysis of Clinton and his electoral ascent within the parties' continuing dance with the enduring American dilemma of race. If we are to determine any significant meaning in the nation's recent presidential elections, Walton proposes that an outlook examining how the parties have defined themselves using race will greatly advance our understanding of the parties and their ongoing attempts to define and redefine themselves for electoral success. This perspective is one that effectively combines empirical analysis with a diligent and nuanced historical analysis. And it is with this perspective that Walton seeks to contextualize and develop the southern native-son presidential candidate variable.

In developing the southern native-son variable, Walton begins with a depiction of the state of Arkansas and the history of its politics and voting behavior. It is a state with an old tradition of electoral support for the Democratic party, and Walton provides a detailed and comprehensive examination of Arkansas voting behavior from the Reconstruction era to 1996 by political party support in all presidential, congressional, and gubernatorial elections. His analysis reveals the state context in which

Clinton grew up, was influenced by, had to campaign in, and in which he ultimately won and lost elections as he moved up the ladder from attorney general to governor to president. Yet Walton does not limit himself to a state-level exploration of Arkansas. He goes beneath this level of analysis to examine the historical experience of African American voters in Arkansas. And it in his investigation of Arkansas's Black voters that Walton explains that he was forced to perform "political archaeology." Although other southern states also failed to maintain precise, consistent electoral records, Arkansas is unfortunately notorious for never having had a formal statewide registration system and for, as Walton explains, depending on poll tax lists rather than registration lists to identify voters. Nonetheless, Walton's diligence here results in a rich analysis of the electoral evolution of Arkansas Black voters, one that uses empirical analysis to understand the history of "invisible" voters who become very visible in the modern electoral contests in the state.

The next stage of Walton's investigation documents the electoral rise of Clinton from his defeat in his initial foray into politics, running for Congress; his subsequent success in being elected state attorney general; his successes and recovery from defeat in being elected governor; and in finally being elected president. It is here that Walton truly details the process by which Clinton became a native son candidate, showing the electoral coalitions that were pivotal for his success at each step of his political quest. As the empirical analyses of these chapters so convincingly reveal, Clinton's electoral coalition shifts from a modestly more rural base to a more urban one as he is reelected governor. Walton's demographic analyses also examine the voting behavior of the counties in which Clinton grew up (his home counties), finding that these counties have tended to support Clinton at some of the highest percentages of all Arkansas counties in his gubernatorial and presidential elections. Yet the African American voters of Arkansas have been the one group which consistently has been a major part of his electoral base throughout his entire political experience. Indeed, the Black Belt counties of Arkansas voted for Clinton at percentages significantly higher than his own home counties throughout all of his gubernatorial elections and in both presidential elections. Clearly, a southern native son candidate is based fundamentally on the support of African American voters.

Yet the modern power of the southern native-son presidential strategy necessarily combines African American support with the support of whites attracted by the subtle conservatism and racially moderate views of southern native son candidates. Clinton has definitely mastered this strategy, as this book so impressively proves. Clinton, the self-proclaimed New Democrat, has emerged as a consciously moderate president who has sought to balance the liberal wing of the Democratic party with the larger, conservative, zeitgeist of the American public. Clinton's political mastery in the presidential elections was even effective in the most politically hostile areas of the country. In Atlanta, often regarded as the capital of the New South, Clinton increased his share of the vote in two staunchly Republican counties, the land of Newt Gingrich: in Gwinnett county, Clinton received just under 30 percent in 1992 and over 33 percent in 1996, while in Cobb county, he received just under 33 percent in 1992 and just under 37 percent in 1996. His strategy is one that has largely paid off for the Democratic party and one that it will seemingly return to for the 2000 elections, with the potential nomination of the current Vice President, Al Gore. However, the southern native-son strategy has not gone unnoticed by the Republican party, as Texas Governor George Bush Jr. becomes a looming figure, one who is increasingly regarded as the Republican frontrunner and the most viable challenger to the recent Democratic control of the presidency. Professor Walton's work provides us with a perspective and a variable of great insight and theoretical power in our efforts to understand the contemporary terrain of political party and presidential politics, having an uncanny prescience as we consider these prospects at this century's end.

Presidential Politics and the Native-Son Contextual Variable

A Prologue by Vincent C. Hutchings

An exploration of the native-son contextual variable provides an important opportunity to enrich our understanding of presidential election outcomes. Building on previous research, Professor Walton's analysis of election return data makes a compelling case that the Democrats' ability to remain competitive in the South, and therefore nationally, in the post–Civil Rights era owes much to the strategy of selecting southerners to lead the party. An analysis of survey data largely supports Walton's thesis.

As Walton and others have also indicated, just as the Democrats were developing an effective way to counter the Republicans' southern strategy at the presidential level, the GOP was making significant gains in southern state houses and in a number of congressional races. Yet the recent midterm elections apparently proved again that the Republicans have not yet developed a consistent lock on the South.

In spite of losing some ground in the 1998 midterm elections, Republican support in the states of the Old Confederacy is not likely to fade anytime soon. Future presidential contests are likely to prove interesting since Republicans may well begin fielding their own (southern) native son candidates. Whether or not this strategy will result in any additional gains for the Republicans awaits future elections. All that can be confidently said at this point is that such an eventuality will continue to make the native-son contextual variable important to both scholars and party strategists for some time to come.

The Native Son Variable and Individual Level Data

In providing a comprehensive analysis of the electoral history of Bill Clinton, Walton examines Arkansas election return data at the county and state levels. Additionally, he examines similar data to show how well Democratic nominees have performed in the South since the passage of landmark civil rights legislation in the mid-1960s. A useful complement to Walton's work involves the use of individual level or survey data. Although there are some drawbacks to this approach (e.g., the inability to validate who respondents actually voted for) it does provide a benefit typically lacking in aggregate level data—that is, survey analysis allows one to identify more precisely the stated voting preferences of specific voters. With this technique, we can identify more confidently how white southerners and others responded to the presidential campaigns of native-son and non–native-son presidential candidates.

Does such an analysis provide additional support for Walton's thesis? An analysis of National Election Study (NES) survey data from 1976 through 1996 allows us to answer this question. Focusing only on the percentage of the two-party vote that each major candidate received from white respondents reveals a number of interesting points. First, as Walton argues, successful native-son Democratic presidential candidates in the post–Civil Rights era have succeeded largely because they have been able to disrupt the Republicans' southern strategy. An analysis of the NES data shows that in each of the Democrats' successful presidential drives (1976, 1992, and 1996) they have been competitive among whites in the South and border states. In 1976, for example, Carter gained 46 percent of the two-party vote among whites in this region. In 1992, Clinton gained the vote of a majority (55%) of whites in the South and border states[1]. In 1996, against Kansan Robert Dole, he still held on to 49 percent. As Walton has indicated, in only one of the Democrats' successful post–civil rights era efforts have they won a majority of the South's electoral votes. And this one example, Carter's victory in 1976, is due in part to the decidedly unusual circumstances following the Watergate scandal. Clinton has shown that as long as Democrats can limit Republican successes in the region they can still win the White House.

We also learn from the NES data that neither Mondale nor Dukakis (nor Carter in 1980) did well among southern whites. The two non-native son candidates trailed their Republican opponents by an average of 27 percentage points. Such losses in the South by these non-southern Democratic candidates would not have been so devastating if they had made offsetting gains in their home regions (the midwest for Mondale and the northeast for Dukakis). However, this was not the case. Mondale did about as badly in his home region as he did in the South and border states, trailing Reagan by some 32 percentage points in the north-central states. Dukakis did somewhat better in his region than he did in the South but, among whites, he still trailed Bush by about 16 points in the northeast (he trailed by 22 points in the South and border states).

Ironically, southern native son candidates are also more successful than their more liberal counterparts because they run so well in the northeast. Carter in 1976, and Clinton in both 1992 and 1996, gained their greatest support among white voters in the northeast, the onetime stronghold of the Republican party. According to the NES data, the northeast was the only region Carter won among white voters outright in 1976. Clinton beat Bush by 26 points here in 1992, and he defeated Dole by 24 points in 1996. Clinton's level of support was much smaller among whites in the other regions of the country.

Recent Republican Gains at Local, State, and Congressional Levels

Prior to the Clinton victories of 1992 and 1996, the Republicans had all but a lock on the South at the presidential level in the post–civil rights era. As Walton argues, this is in part because of their successful adoption of the Wallace southern strategy. However, until recently this did not translate into Republican success at the state and congressional levels. Things began to change during the Reagan-Bush years. More and more southerners began to identify with the Republican party and in 1992, for the first time, the Republicans gained more support among congressional voters in the South than outside the south[2].

This was just a prelude to the even greater changes that took place in the 1994 midterm election. Republicans picked up 52 seats in the House and defeated 35 Democratic incumbents. A disproportionate number of these gains came in the South, where Republicans won a majority of southern congressional seats for the first time in history[3]. Predictably, with the Republicans now in charge of the House of Representatives for the first time in forty years, many conservative southern Democrats switched to the Republican party.

All of this should have signaled a solidification of Republican success in the region in the 1998 elections, but surprisingly this did not happen. Republicans lost bids for the governor's office in Georgia, South Carolina, and Alabama, as well as in the border state of Maryland. Moreover, incumbent Republican Lauch Faircloth lost his Senate race in North Carolina. These losses can be attributed in part to the efforts of a native-son president and vice president to mobilize the black vote. The President, Vice President, and First Lady appeared at several black churches and on a number of high-profile African American media outlets in the days leading up to the election, encouraging blacks to vote. Exit polls show that, nationally, turnout among African Americans was about as high in 1998 as it was in the last midterm election. However, in the deep South and some border states, black turnout was indeed up. For example, the Joint Center for Political and Economic Studies found that blacks constituted 19 percent of the voters in the deep South in 1994, but they made up 29 percent in 1998. Although many Democratic gains in the 1998 elections were due to support from African Americans (especially in Georgia, North Carolina, and Maryland) these moderate southern Democrats are likely to continue the Democratic Leadership Council's policy of not appearing to be too cozy with black voters.

Native-Son Candidates and Republican Counterstrategies

Despite the setbacks for the Republicans nationally and in the South, there was a bright spot or two for Republicans in the 1998 midterm elections. Although anticipated for some months, the election of Jeb Bush in the Florida governor's race and the reelection of his older brother George W. Bush as Texas governor may well provide an indication of the Republicans' own native-son strategy.

Now that the Republican party has found a home in the South it is inevitable that they too would someday select a native-son candidate for the highest office in the land. At the time of this writing it seems likely that the next Republican nominee will be Texas Governor George Bush. According to conventional wisdom, this could pose problems for the Democrats because Bush has demonstrated some ability to appeal to minority voters.

Still, the attractiveness of a potential Bush candidacy may be overstated. Having not yet gone through the rigors of the Republican primary process, Bush is still able to appear to be all things to all people. Also, upon closer inspection his ability to appeal to black voters was hardly overwhelming. According to exit polls, Bush garnered about 27 percent of the African American vote and 49 percent of the Hispanic vote[5]. Thus even with a relatively weak Democratic challenger, Bush failed to appeal to about three quarters of blacks, although he almost broke even among Hispanics. Bush cannot realistically expect to face such a weak candidate in the 2000 campaign, especially if his opponent is Vice President Al Gore.

Finally, even in a potential Bush-Gore contest, the Democrats would only have to hold about one-third of the southern states in order to fashion a winning strategy. Whether or not they can accomplish this remains to be seen, but if such a matchup does evolve it should provide an additional opportunity to explore an important contextual variable.

This is the first systematic, comprehensive analysis of William J. Clinton as a native-son presidential candidate. Using county level election returns from Arkansas and the South, and election returns from the nation, an empirical theoretical portrait is developed of this native-son variable and its influence and impact on American voting behavior. This study is a refinement of an earlier pioneering work on the native son presidential candidate in general and the southern native son variant in particular.[1] The only times that the Democratic party has captured the White House since the passage of the 1964 Civil Rights Bill have been with three natives of the South—Lyndon Johnson, Jimmy Carter, and Bill Clinton. As southern native-son presidential candidates have become a significant phenomenon in the last half of the twentieth century, they deserve analysis. In addition to these three winning Democratic standardbearers, the South has also provided others, such as Strom Thurmond and George Wallace.

The roots of this study lie in part in my childhood years in Athens, Georgia. Growing up I became quite aware of southern native-son leaders. The first was Dixie demagogue and four-time governor Eugene Talmadge. His last campaign in 1948 was like the three before it in its race-baiting and the racial violence that it unleashed against the African American community[2] while the white political leadership in Athens stood by and did nothing. For it was in Athens that the Ku Klux Klan had been reborn in the 1920s. Of this city and the pivotal role that it played in the revival of the KKK, historian Nancy MacLean writes:

> Athens is the county seat—home of the University of Georgia . . . and, in the 1920s, of Athens Klan number 5. Once described by W. E. B. DuBois as the "invisible Empire State," Georgia was the birthplace and the national headquarters of the second Klan.[3]

Both the political leaders of the city and the state were in some degree or other integrally involved with this organization of suppression and repression. As I grew to college age, here was the out-front southern native political leadership. Supposedly, somewhere in the shadows, was a more benevolent one. It hardly surfaced in the 1950s and early 1960s. My understanding of native-son leaders initially came from the experiences which the tightly segregated African American community endured, as well as from the crusade waged against that community by the KKK.

At Morehouse College, at the start of the sit-in movement, my political science professors, Robert Brisbane, Tobe Johnson, and Arthur Banks, examined political leadership and its southern variant with keen insight. They gave their students an academic and theoretical context into which to fit their practical experiences. College President Benjamin Elijah Mays, in his weekly Tuesday lecture at Chapel,[4] further widened our intellectual vision with his thoughts and reflections on southern political leaders. He, like Brisbane, Johnson, and Bush, was captivating on the topic.

And these academic insights were coming to life as southern political leaders reacted to the student sit-ins. What I had seen in statewide political campaigns as a child and high school student now became a daily occurrence, as state leaders such as Griffin, Harris, Vandiver, and Herman Talmadge, the son of Eugene, took to the airwaves, the print media, and television to revive white supremacy.[5] Among these were men with both state and national aspirations. The African American community was told repeatedly that these native son leaders had fought off challenges to segregation and their own power before, and both they and segregation had survived. They would do so again.[6] They had nothing to fear from college students.

So the analyses of Brisbane, Johnson, and Banks were anything but sterile college lectures. They were taking place in the middle of a social revolution. The opponents and power holders were real. The battles were real. Textbooks might describe and assess distant revolutions, French,

English, and Russian. These were all far away and in the distant past; they did not involve African Americans. But what was happening outside was real. The political science lectures were therefore profound.

At Atlanta University, Samuel DuBois Cook turned his scholarly focus on the question of political leadership and the southern variant. Using V. O. Key Jr.'s *Southern Politics*, the works of his classmate Martin Luther King Jr.,[7] and the best academic literature on leadership, both American and international, he stripped the southern politicians of their pretensions, revealed their glib rationalizations, and laid bare their philosophy of white supremacy in their final moment of defiance as crusaders for the lost cause of inequality. Cook sorted out the strengths, weaknesses, and limitations of their leadership and assessed it on a moral level. He created a multidimensional portrait of southern native-son leaders at the regional, national, and international levels. At a time when southern political leaders were strongly supporting George Wallace, Cook gave his students an invaluable grasp of the fundamentals of political leadership and the context in which we could fix our past and present experiences.

Harold Gosnell at Howard University brought to bear on the question of political leadership not only the influence of history, philosophy, institutions, and ideology, but of behavior as well. He dealt with the empirical rendering of leadership motives, motivations, and personal psychology. Bernard Fall, N. P. Tillman Jr., and Emmett Dorsey added to Gosnell's insights the rich textual analysis of the best scholarship of their day.

Collectively these scholars demonstrated how southern political leadership had influenced the American political process. And at the very moment that these men were sharing their wisdom, a native son, Lyndon B. Johnson, was walking into the White House as president. Few knew what to expect.

I remember, as a first-year graduate student, waiting to hear what the new southern native-son president was going to say on civil rights. Great hopes had been placed on the liberal Democrat from Massachusetts. As President Johnson continued to speak without mentioning civil rights, we expected the worst. Surely a southern native-son president would halt, or at best slow, civil rights. It seemed as if he would not mention it at all.

Then, just as he was about to end his speech, President Johnson announced that he would strongly support the Civil Rights Act. It was, he said, the American thing to do. No one was perhaps more surprised than this southerner, who had all his life seen the worst of southern leaders, only hearing about the best ones, who were restricted to the back room. President Johnson on that day made visible, at least for me, a new and different type of southern political leader. His was, in the era of George Wallace, a welcome, very welcome, new voice. And it was now out in the open. In fact, he risked his own presidency with such a bold statement.

Yet he did not hesitate. And when he won election on his own in the fall of 1964, he helped to make possible the other southern native-son presidents of this century, Carter and Clinton.

In undertaking this book, I received help from several quarters. The Arkansas Secretary of State, Sharon Priest, and her election division assistant, Annette Leach, quickly answered all my requests and sent me records of available state elections data. The director of the Arkansas History Commission, John L. Ferguson, sent me the microfilm data on poll tax payments in the state from 1920 through 1967.[8]

In preparing this work, the noted sociologist Roosevelt Green Jr. at Lockhaven University, Pennsylvania, and a native of Athens, Georgia, brought Nancy MacLean's book to my attention. It was an eye-opener. It shed clear light on the supportive environment, not only in our calm community with it treelined streets and pleasant social manners but hidden and vicious behavior, but in the state's context as well. Professor Green is a sage for those who toil to understand the American and southern political terrain.

Telephone calls from friends and colleagues during the time of this work brought both joy and pain. As I was putting the finishing touches on the manuscript, my high school and college friend Samuel Richard Davenport called to say that my college roommate's son Titus Washington, a freshmen at Morehouse College, had died in a car accident. It was an arresting and trying moment. I called his father, Dr. Elijah Washington, and we talked about our time at Morehouse. We all shall miss the native son leadership of Titus over the years to come. Then came the call from my brother, Thomas Nathanial Walton, that my cousin, Mrs. Eleanor Guest Perry, had passed. Along with her daughter Tanya and ever-wonderful mother, Margaret Guest Poole, she had kept my spirits together during my graduate work with the vigorous scholar, Samuel DuBois Cook, at Atlanta University. The word about Eleanor was crushing. It was a moment that I shall never forget. We all had worried under the governance of southern native-son leaders.

Alice, Brandon, and Brent Walton helped me put Arkansas's raw election data on spreadsheets. They helped to check the data for errors. Once cleaned and recorded, the data was coded into demographic categories. Alice worked long hours to reorganize the basic, alphabetically arranged, data into the demographic scheme and checked it over and over to ensure its accuracy. It was a tiring and boring task, yet she did it all with a smile.

The task of making graphic and tabular presentations of the data fell to my very imaginative and innovative computer expert and former colleague, Greta Blake. Mrs. Blake had just received her master's degree, had a new job, and had to work in my many requests in a new work environment. Clearly she succeeded.

Analysis and interpretation of this electoral data fell upon the author, but the typing of the manuscript was done by Margaret Mitchell-Ilugbo. She continually amazed me with her ability to decipher my handwritten drafts. She is able to do so even when I cannot. Following Margaret's work, Lester Spence, a doctoral candidate here in the Department of Political Science, who is one of my graduate student instructors and a research assistant, read the manuscript and offered numerous helpful suggestions. I am fortunate to have such a talented young scholar working with me.

Also, I would like to thank my sage college classmate, Dr. Thomas J. Washington III, for the long telephone conversation we had about President Clinton while I was writing this book. As always, he was well-informed and well-read. It was a very insightful talk. Good friends are always helpful. Beyond the aid of Dr. Washington, I want to thank three colleagues, professors Frederick Harris, Vincent Hutchings, and Robert Brown, who took the time from their busy schedules to write the rich and reflective foreword, prologue, and introduction. Each of these is an original contribution to this book. Next a word of thanks goes to law professor J. Clay Smith Jr. for tracking down the Justice department consent decree for the final lawsuit against Governor Clinton. Both Clay and his wife Patti have been a great source of clippings and conversations. I appreciate their continuing support.

As always, let me offer my gratitude to Thomas and Gean Walton, Albert and Theresa Williams, Gene, Rose, and Patrick Williams, Gilbert, Terry, and Brittany Williams, James and Arie Williams, Dennie and Flossie Riley, Calvin and Minnie Riley, Laynette, Corey, and Collin Reedy, Trann and Ida Brown, Mrs. Margaret Guest Poole, Eleanor Guest, and Tanya Smith.

Collectively, these workers of miracles made this manuscript possible. And because of their fine commitment to duty and voluntary participation, I take full responsibility for any and all errors.

Hanes Walton Jr.
Ann Arbor, Michigan

Reelection

CHAPTER ONE

Elections

Bill Clinton was reelected president on November 5, 1996. With this victory, President Clinton became the first Democrat since Franklin D. Roosevelt to win two consecutive terms. Harry Truman and Lyndon B. Johnson did not seek, for a variety of reasons, a second term. John Kennedy did not survive his first term. And Jimmy Carter was unsuccessful in his reelection bid. Clinton's initial election, which unseated a incumbent Republican president, and his reelection, were historic.

Election results carry significant meaning and consequences for the political order in this democracy, as V. O. Key Jr. writes:

> Elections perform certain functions in the system as a whole. The electorate responds in some way or another to great events, to competing candidates, or to the conditions of the times, and moves toward a decision which has both meaning and consequences in the context of the political system.[1]

Key's remark came in reference to *The American Voter*, with its innovative techniques and procedures for analyzing, assessing, and ascribing meaning to American elections.[2] With this book, analysts and the public no longer needed to probe for telltale patterns and trends in election return data but could focus on individual attitudes and attributes. Yet this was only part of the change involved in understanding American elections. *The American Voter* demonstrated that with the sophisticated use of preelection surveys and polls, the predispositions and the voting intentions of individual voters could be assessed and their vote choice predicted. Like meteorologists, skilled academics could now forecast elections, and demonstrate in a new way the meaning and significance of elections for the political order.

Immediately after its publication in 1960, *The American Voter* ushered in a virtual cottage industry of single presidential election analyses.[3] Each presidential election from 1964 to the present has undergone intense scrutiny and detailed analysis. Although sociologists, political scientists, and journalists had produced a small smattering of such analyses before *The American Voter*, today the sheer number of single election analyses is unprecedented.[4] Yet such efforts carry hidden costs and limitations.

This cross-sectional analysis of every presidential election requires that the meaning and significance of presidential elections for American's democratic political order had to be generated from a single moment in time. Longitudinal studies of elections add the critical component of a time dimension. "Many of the great and really significant political action-units of political behavior take place over comparatively long periods of time." Therefore, "by the observation of a greater variety of types of situations it may be possible to tie the study of electoral behavior more directly to the workings of the state."[5] Key again: "Explicit attention to the time dimension of electoral decision would probably bring to light a variety of characteristics not readily perceptible by the observation of a single case."[6]

Single studies try to determine meaning from the essence of the single event, the momentary, the current, and the contemporary. The past and history are set aside for the present. But this, despite its immense epistemological problems, is inherent to survey and polling methodologies which take things out of the political context in which they reside. Here is how a leader in this survey and polling movement put it:

> Contextual factors are often treated in an informal and qualitative fashion, especially when contrasted with the great specificity attached to properties of the individual voter. Despite occasional substantive and methodological outcomes, it is only in recent years that systematic effort has been devoted to contextual effects.[7]

Thus with these innovative instruments (surveys and polls) unable to provide a time-based contextual dimension to assess electoral meaning, analysts nevertheless did the one thing that was possible: they sought to discover how and why individual voters gave the newly elected president a mandate. And what message did the voters send?

Electoral Meaning as a Political Mandate

In the first book published on the 1996 election, here is how the mandate is described: "On the cusp of a new millennium—the ultimate change in the calendar—America's voters rejected change and chose to preserve the status quo by re-electing the Democratic president and the Republican Congress."[8]

The first of the single-election studies which ascribed meaning in terms of a mandate was that of the 1976 election. "Obviously in 1976 candidates and voters alike considered that 'private' moral beliefs had become public issues. Part of this, undoubtedly, was due to Watergate."[9] And when "Carter made arguments in favor of a reorganized and simplified government that citizens can understand as part of the Jefferson tradition," he was elected over a sitting incumbent president.

> In 1976, Americans were worried about the most basic aspects of political identity: they were concerned with the social and moral foundations of community, and they felt the need for ties with each other as much as or more than they felt the need of ties to Washington.[10]

The election meant a resolution of this social issue which was of concern to people.

In the 1980 elections, the message of the meaning was stated in this way: "By throwing out incumbent Democrats across the board, the voters were sending out a clear message: It was time for a change."[11] The analyst continues:

> The election results raised many questions about the nature of the Republicans' "mandate," whether the voters had chosen Reagan because of his strongly conservative issue positions or in spite of them. The notion presented here of the election as a referendum on Carter seems to suggest the latter.[12]

President Reagan's reelection in 1984 led to this description: "A new political era is coming to birth, but not necessarily an attractive or a happy one."[13] The observer adds: "Ronald Reagan has presided over the demolition of the old politics in the years after 1984, it will be necessary for Americans to see if they can build anew."[14] Thus the meaning of the 1984 election was that it created a "morning in America," a new political beginning.

Although President Reagan's Vice President, George Bush, won in 1988, the meaning ascribed to this election was not quite clear. "Neither Ronald Reagan nor George Bush has been willing to ask Americans to sacrifice and where their policies have imposed burdens, they have almost universally fallen on the less fortunate."[15] Thus the best meaning that could be teased out of the 1988 election was that it offered an opportunity for public renewal and civility.[16]

President Bush's reelection bid in 1992 resulted in the election of a Democrat, Bill Clinton, and of that election it has been asserted that "in 1992, confidence did not point Americans to the future, it drew them to the past; and the election, a vote for change, was also a hope for renewal."[17] "Clinton's skillful race still fell far short of a national majority, and his victory can be explained by third-candidate defectors more than any increase in Democratic strength."[18] In short, there was no mandate for Clinton or the Democratic party. Some scholars made the point that "a final difficulty of Clinton's electoral situation is connected to his only mandate, which was to not be George Bush."[19] The meaning of this election, if one existed, was quite unclear.

A retrospective on the Bush presidency stated that "in terms of initial voter volatility and with loud expressions of disgust and anger easily picked up by pollsters, 1992 was an election year without modern parallel."[20] There was no distinct Bush legacy, since "he had very feeble interest in any aspect of American domestic politics" and "displayed a striking mixture of rigidity and policy zig zag, all in the context of profound indifference."[21]

With the election of November 5, 1996, the search for meaning in single elections continued. "As with all elections, the last one of the century told us much about the nation and its people. [Voters] wanted government to work, and they did not want either party's extreme to have undue influence."[22]

> Clinton's legacy would be more than the man who vetoed the budget . . . . By governing in the middle, borrowing ideas from both sides, and eschewing polarization . . . he made interdisciplinary politics a winner again, after years in which the two parties were moving further away from it.[23]

Thus the meaning of the 1996 election was a call for moderation and centrism. This was a vague and indeterminate mandate because less than half of all voters—49.2 percent—supported the president for reelection.

Other views of the election varied:

> In the shallows and silences of 1996, it is possible to made out signs of a political redefinition waiting for its season. Half postponement and half prelude, the election of 1996 let Americans off the hook for a while longer; and they were happy to be spared.[24]

And:

> The electoral verdict of 1996, however, conveys no clear message. The voters were not called on to decide between clear alternatives of philosophy or policy. Dole and Clinton sought the moderate center and gave little attention to their ideological purists, the Republican religious right or the Democratic liberal left.[25]

While many of these assertions of meaning offer intriguing comments about each presidential election, they do not advance our knowledge and understanding very far. Single moments in time, no matter how well analyzed, can only yield so much. Revealing electoral meaning from the perspective of the mandate of a single election is not possible.

Electoral Meaning as a Change in Individual Attributes

Not everyone was engaged in distilling a meaning out of presidential elections from the standpoint of the mandate perspective. Some pursued another path.

Born with *The American Voter* and reasserted in *Elections and the Political Order* was the idea that the essence of elections in America lies in the role which individual psychological, sociological, and economic attributes play in determining the outcome of elections.

The initial voting studies of the 1940s and 1950s declared that social attributes and characteristics (income, social class, and education) determine voting behavior and election outcomes.[26] Later studies declared that psychological attributes and characteristics (party identification, candidate preferences, and issue preferences) determined vote choice and shaped the outcome of elections.[27] As a result of the work of a team of Michigan scholars—Campbell, Converse, Miller, and Stokes—these psychological attributes took center stage in describing and explaining elections, after which it become fashionable to use these attributes to capture the meaning of elections.

In *Elections and the Political Order*, the role and function of individual attributes—sociological, psychological, and other—in giving meaning to elections and the political order was made quite clear.

> One must assume that most changes in the collective behavior of the public reflect some change in the underlying motivations of the individual members of the public . . . and their behavior expressed the character of their motives. The problem is to identify what this motivation is.[28]

Having established psychological attributes as the key factor in the search for meaning in elections, the authors discussed how the psychological attributes inherent in shaping voting behavior and vote choice could explicate meaning. Their book profiled the intrapsychic factors inherent in the "flow of the vote itself." A change in these attributes leads to an understanding of the meaning of elections. They used the 1960 election—another single election focus—as a test case.[29]

The authors then looked at how changes in the vote shaped the party system: understanding the central attributes at work in determining voting behavior could lead to a grasp of the dynamism or lack thereof in the party system.

Part 3 of the book sought to remove any doubt that the approach to the nature and consequence of meaning in elections was culturally bound. Reliance on individual level attributes could be just as insightful in other countries as in the United States. In short, the attributes approach was crossculturally viable.

The book closed with an essay positing that individual level attributes could provide insight beyond the electoral and party processes into political institutions. Attributes could reveal the meaning of elections in institutions such as Congress.

However, the book lacked a summary or concluding chapter. Therefore it was suggestive rather than confirmatory. Individual level attributes could give meaning, but exactly how was left up to the imagination of the reader.

At best *Elections and the Political Order* pointed to a direction but did not offer a set of specifications about how meaning was to be derived from the study of individual level attributes. But that did not stop the efforts of academics, pundits, and researchers.

Studies in which a single attribute or a combination of attributes were seen to determine the outcome of every presidential election from 1960 until the present poured forth. First there was the matter of the role of religion in 1960. By 1964, the attribute under analysis was ideology. With the help of V. O. Key Jr.'s book *The Responsible Electorate*, the search in 1968 and beyond was the issue attribute. Later economics was pressed into service to provide meaning to the nation's elections. With the election of Reagan and Bush, the attribute was conservative ideology. Gender was also seen as a factor in these elections. In President Clinton's initial election, the economic attribute played a major role, while in his reelection, economics was joined by gender, as expressed in the "Soccer Moms" vote. Gender had reemerged as a major attribute.

The search in every election for the single most significant attribute led to disputes about which attribute determined the election and gave meaning to it. The Michigan team and many of its disciples argued that psychological attributes such as party identification were central to the true meaning of every election. Others vociferously objected. Eventually one of the original founders of the party identification attribute urged the discipline to return to the basics.[30]

After analyzing the variable in ten presidential elections, Warren Miller concluded: "There is no indication from any recent election that party identification is less relevant to the vote decision in the 1980s than it was three decades earlier." In fact, Miller's analyses reveal that in presidential elections from 1952 through 1988, there were only two atypical elections—1964 and 1972—where party identification did not affect the electorate's presidential choice.[31] Miller's insights notwithstanding, the dispute continued, since many analysts were not willing to see each election explained by "assigning a main explanatory/causal role for party identification in the context of presidential election" or any other single attribute.[32] One or some combination of attributes could not extrapolate the collective behavior of Americans in national elections.

If the mandate perspective provided an uncertain grasp of the meaning of elections, so did the attributes approach. But these two perspectives do not exhaust all possibilities.

Electoral Meaning as a Political Realignment

The concept of realignment was born as a tool for plumbing the meaning of elections. Emerging from the man who told the discipline that elections have meaning and consequences for the democratic political order, Key's conceptual device of realignment typed elections based on the degree and magnitude of change in each. Here is how Key explained the need for and functionality of such a typology.

> Among democratic orders elections . . . differ enormously in their nature, their meaning, and their consequences. Even within a single nation the reality of election differs greatly from time to time. A systematic comparative approach, with a focus on variations in the nature of elections, could doubtless be fruitful in advancing understanding of the democratic governing process. . . . The foregoing remarks provide an orientation for an attempt to formulate a concept of one type of election . . . which might be built into a more general theory of elections.[33]

In the article, Key developed the idea of critical realignment. This type of electoral realignment occurs in a single election where party loyalists make a sharp, dramatic, and durable shift to the other political party.[34] In one election, people drop their habitual partisan attachment and alliances and acquire another. Nationally, the New Deal election of FDR was such a critical election.

The second type is a secular realignment, which occurs when there is a shift to another party, but this realignment takes place over several presidential elections instead of one.[35] These changes are also durable.

One realignment is instantaneous, the other gradual. And they have different meanings and consequences for the political order. Elections of the former type produce abrupt changes in the political order, while the latter mean "steady expansions or contractions, as well as time for slow adjustment." In fact, this "long term partisan reorientation reduces political friction, which reduces the cumulative effect of great social changes."[36]

Several analyses of recent presidential elections have sought to find meaning from the standpoint of party realignment. A vigorous search has been undertaken in these election analyses to discern if a "critical" partisan shift has occurred.

The weight of the vast realignment literature posits that 1964 was a turning point election. The chorus of voices designating 1964 as such reads like a Who's Who of the discipline. The journalistic voices followed the academics and the pundits have followed both. Now the voices are a deafening roar.

Listen as Edward Carmines and James Stimson mark the moment:

It was already clear . . . that the 1964 presidential election had set into motion political forces that would transform the nature of American politics. . . . The 1964 presidential election thus marked the decisive turning point in the political evolution of racial issues.[37]

Robert Huckfeldt and Carol Kohfeld write:

Before 1964 the electorate saw little difference between the two parties in terms of race. After 1964, however, the electorate developed a clear perception of the Democratic party as more favorable to black interests. . . . In short, the events of 1964 served to restructure permanently the relationship between the parties on issues of race.[38]

Amid the sea of voices are those of African Americans. Katherine Tate wrote:

It was not until the 1964 presidential election that the overwhelming majority of Blacks began to identify themselves as Democrats. . . . The 1964 presidential election was a pivotal election; by the time of this election, a full 80 percent of Blacks identified with the Democratic party.[39]

Michael Dawson says: "Indeed, the black Democratic vote would not solidify until 1964, when it became clear to the nation that the Democrats would support black interests and civil rights more than the Republican party."[40] Lucius Barker and Mark Jones note that "Black support for the Democrats was, of course, enhanced by the strong anti-civil rights politics and conservatism of the 1964 Goldwater campaign."[41]

All these voices argue that a racial realignment between parties took place in 1964. African Americans switched to the Democrats and whites, particularly southern whites, shifted to the Goldwater-led Republicans. Race was the cleavage or wedge issue realigning the parties. The meaning, as these observers noted, was that whites were angry, and this anger was focused and channeled against the Democratic party. "The Democratic party had lost touch with the mainstream of the American electorate which was white, middle-aged, and middle class."[42]

Some, looking at the supposed turning point, read and interpreted the data not as a *racial* realignment but as a *southern* realignment.

Beginning with the passage of the Civil Rights Act of 1964, White southern voters increasingly supported Republican presidential candidates. . . . Although Democrats continued to control state and local offices, their base steadily eroded throughout the 1980s as increasing numbers of white middle-class (and many low-income white) voters abandoned the Democratic party and voted for GOP candidates at all levels.[43]

Republican candidate Goldwater carried the five Deep South states in his 1964 presidential bid and regional native son George Wallace carried four of them in his third-party presidential bid via the American Independent party in 1968.[44] Nixon in 1972, Reagan in 1980 and 1984, and Bush in 1988, further swept the South into the Republican coalition at the presidential level. "Republican victories, particularly at the presidential level, were the death of the solidly Democratic South and suggest fundamental realignment." These southern observers saw it as natural that the transformation of southern party politics would generate a considerable body of scholarship on the realignment of the South toward the Republican party.[45]

Yet there was dissent in this considerable body of scholarship. Other voices demonstrated that "no southern realignment has occurred, Democratic dominance continued."[46] Others suggested only dealignment in the region. Given the growing debate, southern political scientists tried to resolve the matter by devoting a book to the subject—*The South's New Politics: Realignment and Dealignment*—suggesting that a "creeping realignment" had occurred in the South.[47] Despite the controversy about whether the South had or had not realigned, these studies agreed that "southern [and national] Democrats have been more supportive of civil rights, redistributive, and social welfare stands than have southern [and national] Republicans." Such stances have both mobilized and converted the southern electorate to the Republican party.

However, not everyone has been content with the concept of realignment, whether it be race- or region-based. A third perspective, that of dealignment, has emerged. This concept has been defined as that moment when "a growing proportion of the electorate no longer identifies with either major party . . . where voters abandon their old party ties but fail to develop a psychological attachment to another party or where party identification becomes less central to political decision making."[48] From this perspective, the number of independent voters is rising and the party that they support in any given election would win the national electoral contest. In the context of Republican presidential victories, the Democratic party was out-of-step with the American electorate.

James Sundquist states that "American presidential elections are now decided by the independents attached firmly to neither party and by the partisan whose attachments are weak. They make up a majority of the electorate."[49] Dealignment is the step between alignment and realignment. The meaning of elections from a dealignment perspective is that the new Republican majority may be transitory given the mobility of the independent voters.

The different interpretations and the meanings generated from the realignment and dealignment perspectives are open to debate. Like the mandate and attribute perspectives they provide only part of the complete portrait. Clearly more is needed for a rounded picture.[50]

Electoral Meaning: The Missing Political Party Perspective

What happens to political parties in an election captures a part of the meaning of that election, yet both academics and journalists insist that the party era had passed, and that we are in something of a post-alignment era,[51] an anti-party age[52] in which parties are in decline and candidate-centered politics has replaced parties. As a result, the political party perspective has been missing from the vast majority of electoral analyses.

The respected political columnist David Broder has emphatically told the public that the party was over.[53] Then came a wave of academic studies: American political parties, we were told, were beginning to decay. Others said that parties had started to fail in the United States.[54]

One academic took the matter further. It was not simply a matter of failure, but of "the decline of American political parties."[55] The second edition advanced the argument into the 1990s. American political parties were on their deathbed. By 1997, one text asserted: The heyday of the political party . . . has passed. In the twentieth century, many social, political, technological, and governmental changes have contributed to party decline.[56]

> Politically, many other trends have contributed to the parties' decline . . . . Both television and consultants have replaced the party as the intermediary between candidate and voter.[57]

Thus the American political process is seeing candidate-centered politics instead of party-centered politics.

According to Steven Rosenstone, Roy Behr, and Edward Lazarus:

The old campaign managers were experienced politicians who knew how to win votes. Expertise could be found only within the existing parties. [Today] technological innovations have permitted candidates to be increasingly free of political parties. . . . Little more than a computer, telephones, a postage meter, and a consultant are needed.[58]

With a fax to launch a political candidacy, political parties can now be bypassed.

With enterprising and politically ambitious candidates as the captains of their fate, parties became unimportant and obsolete, yielding few insights to journalists, academics, or pundits. Their day had passed. The political party perspective never really emerged in the intellectual equation as an analytic perspective from which to understand the meaning of elections. The action lay elsewhere.

Yet the alternative perspectives of mandate, attribute, and alignment are not only incomplete analytical frameworks, but they evolved at the very moment when the major American political parties were redefining themselves and their images.

Political parties in the United States are always defining and redefining themselves. Domestic and international upheavals and societal transformations mean that parties must adjust and revive their images if they want to continue to exist.

On this point, Key is emphatic:

For almost a hundred years catastrophe has fixed the grand outlines of the partisan division among American voters. . . . A catastrophe, the war of Rebellion, . . . burned into the American electorate a pattern of partisan faith that persisted in its main outlines until 1932.[59]

It remained for a second catastrophe, the Great Depression, to produce a major alteration in the pattern of partisan division within the voting population.[60]

Lorenzo Morris argues that party identity

feeds on the myth that these parties have no concrete historical character, and therefore no independent political identity of their own, except of course for the character they are thought to capriciously acquire from their ever flexible constituents.[61]

In addition, this embedded myth about partisan identity and identification ignores the ever present efforts at party definition and redefinition at every election. These external forces are obfuscated by the internal intrapsychic ones. Crises and catastrophes remake and reshape the historical character of political parties; otherwise, like the old Whig party, they pass from the political scene. In the twentieth century, FDR and his New Deal remade and transformed the modern Democratic party. A crisis, events, and a political personality changed party character and image. It realigned the American electorate. The Democratic party came out of the New Deal and World War II with a new character and image.

Prior to FDR and the New Deal, World War I and the economic setbacks of his age let Woodrow Wilson remold, reshape, and recast the Democratic party's image and character. President Wilson was able to transcend, in certain respects, the portrait of the party that William Jennings Bryan was painting in his role as head of the Democratic National Committee. Thus FDR, in his four terms in the White House, could continue and adjust the party's course, given the rise of new crises and events.

Parties change, yet in the very midst of their redefinition and transformation part of their historical character and image does not change. Nor is change itself always uniform, comprehensive, or systematic. The New Deal changed the economic character and politics of the party and the government's interventionist role and function in regard to this new economic outlook.

However, neither Roosevelt, nor Wilson before him, changed the Democratic party's historical character and image in regard to race.

After Reconstruction, Democratic party leaders, particularly the Dixie demagogues, reshaped the party's position, character, and image on race. Eventually the Democratic party was wedded to white supremacy and segregation became the party's policy on the matter of race. By the turn of the century, the southern Democratic party had a fixed character and image. The last disenfranchising state Constitution was in place by 1901.

The southern demagogues who etched this character and image launched an effort to extend it beyond its southern base and give it a national anchor. The tactics and techniques were twofold. First, southern demagogues became leaders in the Democratic party's national organization. They advanced men of similar persuasion and ideas, notables such as William Jennings Bryan and Woodrow Wilson.[62] Besides becoming institutionalized in the national organizational leadership, they also controlled the local and state governments in the South and sent delegates to each national convention who set the rules, drafted the platform, and provoked sympathy for their "race problem" and its solution—segregation. Although there was an African American alternate delegate to the 1924 Democratic National Convention, there were no African American delegates at any convention from 1860 until 1936.[63] The Democratic National Convention was lily-white until the New Deal. And, when an African America minister from Philadelphia gave a prayer at the 1936 convention, a leader of the South Carolina delegation walked out.[64]

In 1934 African Americans on the south side of Chicago elected the first African American Democratic Congressman, Arthur Mitchell. Upon arriving in Washington in 1935, he wrote the president.[65] African American Democrats had now arrived at the national level, as southern Democratic demagogues had done with the Wilson administration in 1913. African American voters were a part of Roosevelt's electoral coalition and he made a number of African American appointments to significant sub-cabinet posts. The racial image that southern Democratic demagogues had so carefully crafted was starting to come unglued. World War II both abated and stimulated matters. At the 1944 Democratic National Convention, southern delegates led by the governor of Georgia insisted that the racial politics of the Democratic party—segregation—remain unchanged.[66] While several southern political leaders sought the party's vice presidential spot, African Americans from South Carolina had formed a satellite Democratic party known as the South Carolina Progressive Democrats and sent two delegates to challenge the seating of the all-white delegates. Here was an initial effort to reshape and recast the party's historical character on race. Their effort could not offset the entrenched white southerners. Yet the plowing of the ground had started. Southern African Americans and whites were now inside the party and fighting over the party's image on race.

At the 1948 convention, southerners walked out and formed the Dixiecrat party, insisting that the national Democratic party would be punished unless the party's historical character and image on race remain the same. The national party led by Harry Truman went on to victory without them and the South responded with a growing independent unpledged electors movement. In some southern states, such as South Carolina in 1944, the Democratic party was not even listed on the ballot. But the independent unpledged electors movement was a regional tactic. The southern definition of the party had to become a national movement with a popular base. The fact that southerners held the majority of committee chairmanships in the House and Senate was not enough to fight off the rising insurgency in the party's national organization. Enter George Wallace.

To create a mass national base for the southern definition of the Democratic party, George Wallace developed an eclectic set of tactics and strategies. A native son of the region, a delegate to the 1948 National Democratic Convention, treasurer of the Dixiecrat party, an apologist for segregation "today, tomorrow, and forever," as well as a defender of the party's white supremacy position, and an elected official, Wallace found a way to protect the southern definition and image of the Democratic party.[67] He began in 1964 by entering the Democratic presidential primaries in 9 of the 16 states and the District of Columbia that held Democratic presidential primaries that year. Wallace received nearly 11 percent of the total votes cast in these states. And in Wisconsin, Maryland, Indiana, and Illinois, all non-southern states, Wallace demonstrated that there was a mass base for the southern image and character of the party.

> Wisconsin's Catholic hierarchy and the entire Protestant religious establishment, the state's Democratic party, and organized labor condemned Wallace as a bigot and an "apostle of discord." Three weeks before the election, Wisconsin's governor predicted the southerner would not receive 10 percent of the primary vote.

TABLE I.I   The Wallace Vote and Percentage in the 1964 Democratic Presidential Primaries

States in Which Wallace Was on the Ballot	Votes	Percentage
Wisconsin	266,136	33.8
Maryland	214,849	42.8
Indiana	172,646	29.8
Write-In Votes for Wallace		
Pennsylvania	12,104	4.8
Illinois	3,761	4.2
Oregon	1,365	1.0
Nebraska	1,067	1.7
Massachusetts	565	1.0
New Jersey	491	1.3
Total	672,984	10.8

Adapted from McGillivray and Scammon, *America at the Polls: A Handbook of American Presidential Election Statistics*, 909.

On election day, however, 34 percent of the voters chose Wallace. Three weeks later in Indiana, with two Ku Klux Klansmen coordinating the Wallace campaign out of the phone booth of a filling station, the Alabaman took 30 percent of the primary vote. In Maryland he claimed 43 percent and as he always darkly suggested afterward— "that was with them countin' the votes."[68]

Here is how one senatorial candidate assessed the 1964 foray:

Wallace's astonishing achievement decisively confirmed George Bush's conviction that most Americans—certainly most white Texans—would not support a candidate who backed the Civil Rights Act. On the day after Wallace's surprise finish in Wisconsin, Bush told a reporter for the Dallas *Morning News* that the Alabama governor's success at appealing to northern voters showed that there was a "general concern from many responsible people over the civil rights bill all over the nation."[69]

Few saw this repositioning effort as a drive to sustain the southern character and image of the Democratic party. President Lyndon B. Johnson pushed through and signed the 1964 Civil Rights Act, the Wallace political sideshow notwithstanding. And this single act of President Johnson's remade and redefined the Democratic party. It gave the party a new image, one that broke with the southern definition and its historical character as derived from that region. In response, Wallace turned to Republican Senator Barry Goldwater, who had voted against the 1964 Civil Right Bill.[70]

Just prior to the 1964 Republican National Convention and with the old image of the party slipping away from him and the South, Wallace dispatched a Republican representative to Goldwater with a request that he be made Goldwater's vice-presidential running mate. The man from Arizona refused on the grounds that Wallace was and had been a lifelong Democrat. This difference in partisanship, not philosophy and opposition to the Civil Rights Act, sealed Wallace's fate. Dan Carter, Wallace's biographer, writes of that meeting: "It just was not possible; Goldwater . . . already had the support of the South. Moreover, he added, George Wallace was still a Democrat and 'this *was* a Republican Convention.' "[71]

Goldwater's rebuff did not stop Wallace's effort to sustain the Democratic party's traditional position on race. To teach both major parties a lesson and push them towards a position of maintenance of the South's position on the race issue, Wallace formed his own independent third party.

Against all the odds . . . Wallace cobbled together the American Independent Party and fought his way onto the ballots of all fifty states. Flying in an obsolete turboprop airplane, and with almost no professional advance staff, the candidate careened around the nation [and] across the nation his support grew steadily through the spring and summer of 1968.[72]

Political scientists captured the moment:

George Wallace ran in 1968 because the major party nominees' stand left conservatives on racial and urban unrest issues unrepresented. Wallace seized the opportunity to capture the Conservative vote.[73]

Wallace seemed unconcerned with the charges of racism that followed him, believing racism to be the key to his success.[74]

When the dust cleared, he had won in the five deep South states that the Dixiecrats had carried in 1948, capturing 46 electoral votes and almost 10 million popular votes. The lesson was clear. There was a mass base for the southern definition of a political party in racial terms.

In 1972 and 1976, Wallace moved backed into the Democratic party. However in the 1972 Democratic primaries in Maryland an assassination attempt left him paralyzed below the waist. Thus the maintenance of the Democratic party's image had to be left incomplete. By the 1976 Democratic primaries, Wallace could not wage a strenuous campaign against another southerner and personal friend, former Georgia governor Jimmy Carter. Carter in Florida delivered the coup de grace to the fledging Wallace campaign, which failed to finish the primary season.[75] Yet Wallace's efforts bore significant fruit by transforming not the Democratic, but the Republican, party's character on the race issue. Wallace had sought to maintain the Democratic party's historical character and image on the race issue and in so doing he would transform the Republican party's.

What made the Republican party more responsive? Numerous studies question the status of the Republican party after World War II as no longer being the majority party.[76] Even with the Eisenhower victories of the 1950s the Republican party was essentially a minority party in the American political process.

To rebuild itself the party eliminated its liberal wing by 1964, embraced hardline conservatism, and added race to its mix of social issues. This proved successful.

The reluctance of neoconservatives to claim Wallace—with his gamy aura of racism—is understandable. But the fundamental differences between the public rhetoric of the Alabama governor and the new conservatism sometimes seem more a matter of style than substance. In Barry Goldwater's vote against the Civil Rights Bill of 1964, in Richard Nixon's subtle manipulation of the busing issue, in Ronald Reagan's genial demolition of affirmative action, in George Bush's use of the Willie Horton ads, and in Newt Gingrich's demonization of welfare mothers, the Wallace music played on. The new rhetoric— carefully tested and marketed by political consultants—may lack Wallace's visceral edge (and wit), but it reflects the same callous political exploitation of the raw wounds of racial division in our country.[77]

Thus Wallace helped to rebuild the character and image of the Republican party. Of the seven presidential elections since Wallace's 1968 third-party challenge, the Republicans have won four, and captured both houses of Congress in 1994. Such dramatic victories have shifted the Democrats to the center of the ideological spectrum, if not to the right of center. Wallace can be said to have affected both the Republican and the Democratic parties.

In 1985 Governor Bill Clinton, along with several other southern elected officials and Democrats from around the country, formed the Democratic Leadership Council (DLC) specifically to reshape the party character and image from liberal on race to conservative. Governor Clinton was one of the founding members of the DLC. The southern drive to restructure the party's character and meaning on race was continued and updated.

The DLC "since its inception . . . has seen its mission as developing new themes and ideas for the Democratic party, in order to dilute the influence of the new left ideology—referred to by the DLC as 'Liberal fundamentalism' in the Democratic party."[78] "The DLC served as a forum and a rallying point for moderate-to-conservative Democrats in an era when they appeared to have been marginalized within the national party."[79] With Clinton's victory in 1992, "the South recaptured the Democratic party and the White House. . . . His success revived the southern wing of the Democratic party and brought the DLC and its PPI (Progressive Policy Institute) think tank into major positions of power and authority in Washington, DC."[80] However the same observer forecast that "the reemergence of the southern wing of the Democratic party needs to be confirmed by a successful Clinton presidency followed by reelection in 1996."[81]

Another observer remarked that

this in-house formal organization to recapture and redefine the Democratic party got a huge boost when its founding leader, William J. Clinton, became president in 1992 and won reelection in 1996. . . . The DLC has not always been popular with the national party leadership, which has sometimes viewed it as a potential rival, but it nurtured and strongly backed Bill Clinton's candidacy in 1992 and 1996.[82]

The DLC is composed of more than one hundred current and former Democratic officeholders such as Senator Sam Nunn of Georgia and House Minority leader Richard Gephardt of Missouri; several DLC leaders were appointed to positions in the Clinton administration and to the top leadership positions of the Democratic National Committee.[83] Once in power, President Clinton and the DLC have continued their recapture and redefinition of the Democratic party—a process which is still underway.

The tactics of George Wallace to create a mass electoral base for the southern view and definition of the Democratic party contrast sharply with those of President Clinton and the DLC, which are more formal and structured by party elites now in power. We know something of the success of the former, while we are currently watching the latter process play itself out. Both examples, while at different ends of the definition-making process, reveal something of the strength and weaknesses of both forces in the Democratic party. In addition, they tell us much about the ways in which American political parties in general, and the Democratic party in particular, can be transformed and reinvented from election to election. A political party perspective is essential to grasp the meaning and consequences of elections. And the party perspective encompasses a time dimension, not just a single election focus.

Yet there is more. Not all efforts at recapture and redefinition use informal and formal mechanisms with voters and elites. President Jimmy Carter did not use a formal mechanism like the DLC or an openly verbal and rhetorical strategy like George Wallace's to gain a mass base.

Jimmy Carter . . . showed little interest in his national party. Elected as an outsider in 1976, Carter and his top aides at first viewed the party as another extension of the Washington establishment they had pledged to ignore. Carter and his DNC [party] chairman failed to develop the Democratic Party organizationally and financially in order to keep it competitive during a critical period, while the Republicans were undergoing a dramatic revitalization stimulated by their desire to recover from the Watergate scandal.[84]

Because of the nature of the times and the relationship between the party and the presidential candidate, the victorious Carter could distance himself from the party and the process of recapture and redefinition that had been put into place.

> During the Carter presidency, DNC Chairman Kenneth Curtis and his successor John White were creatures of the White House; they acted as cheerleaders for their chief executive but did little to keep the Democratic party competitive with the then-strengthening GOP organization.[85]

In point of fact, "during his unsuccessful 1980 reelection campaign, Carter was properly criticized for diverting Democratic National Committee personnel and resources to his presidential needs, such as travel and Christmas cards, rather than permitting them to pursue essential partywide electoral tasks."[86] And how did he deal with the party's relationship to the race issue?

> Jimmy Carter turned to religious imagery to lift himself out of the liberal quagmire. Aided by the Richard Nixon—Gerald Ford travesty of established political ethics, he could present the comforting electoral alternative. Given his centrist views on economic issues, he had room to be liberal on race. However, like McGovern, he refused to recognize the substance of racial issues. Instead he denied that racial-ideological concerns existed by using black supporters and numerous black appointments to substitute for issues.[87]

The conclusion is simple: "In effect, Carter simply said blacks are essential to the party, and nothing can be done about it."[88] But that was just the opposite of what Wallace had shown. Something could be done about it. Enter Ronald Reagan.

Carter left the party's new definition and image as set into place by Lyndon Johnson and the African American civil rights movement, but limited the African American–Democratic alliance from one of public policies like civil rights, voting rights, and the rights of people in poverty, to one of political appointments. Carter made a subcoalitional redefinition to maintain the party and enhance and enlarge its African American base. This was a partial, pragmatic, redefinition.

In the civil rights and post–civil rights eras, elite and mass-based efforts to remake the Democratic party used informal and formal techniques that were both overt and covert. There were various efforts to redefine the linkage between the party and one of its constituent groups. Each effort helped to redefine the party. And no sooner were the party image and character on race restructured than they came under attack by competitors—the Republican party, as well as the DLC.

The crisis of the World War II era and the events of the 1960s have led to major intraparty efforts to recapture and redesign the Democratic party, as well as efforts by the Republican party to take an opposing position on the race issue. The missing political party perspective suggests that part of the meaning inherent in recent elections is based in a particular view of race. Party success and failure in these elections emerged because they advanced certain images, beliefs, and values about race. Due to the parties' stance on race the electorate aligned and dealigned, and electoral coalitions were transformed and remade. The success which a party achieves because of its racial stance will affect its position and stance in future elections. Thus each election has consequences for the future of the democratic order.

A political party perspective involves a focus on a nongovernmental political entity, an organization that legally seeks to capture and transfer power in the political system. Secondly, this perspective reveals that the degree and type of power which this organization comes to control is determined in part by how the party is defined and defines itself in terms of the crises and events of its day. Parties, this perspective asserts, are adaptable because they define and redefine issues in ways that will make them victorious. Even when catastrophes and crises have redefined parties and the party system, they do not do so in a permanent fashion. The New Deal did not fully and completely define the Democratic party, as the 1940s, 1950s, and 1960s demonstrated. Even after these redefining decades had passed, the process of definition continues—particularly if it involves such a powerful issue as race.

Ultimately, the political party perspective indicates that in recent elections, party electoral coalitions with different definitions of racial citizenship vigorously clash with each other and these clashes can determine and influence the outcome of the elections. Meaning in elections can be derived in part from the electorate's values and beliefs about race and the manner in which it associates one party or another with these racial values. It is through this perspective that we view the role and impact of the native-son presidential candidate, and in the case of Bill Clinton, the southern native-son candidate.

There is more: All of the other perspectives use a variety of variables to measure and quantify their concepts and offer empirical support and estimations for their findings. The southern native-son concept when deployed as a variable permits an empirical rendering of the political party perspective, provides a means to contextualize the party identification attribute, provides a longitudinal time dimension to the analysis, and builds into the portrait the electoral behavior of the southern electorate in local, state, and national elections. With the southern native son as a variable, it is possible to see, at least on a collective voting basis, how the electorate responded to different regional presidential candidates who articulated different definitions of the party's character and image on race.

To gain a comprehensive view of elections a fourfold perspective is necessary. The mandate perspective tell us only about public policies which the electorate wishes to be passed or reversed.

A perspective generated from individual level attributes tells us about what determined the voter's psychological predisposition and thereby his or her voting intentions and choices. This perspective reveals much about the role of party identification. Yet the defining role of crises, events, and personalities gets lost.

The realignment perspective is a macrolevel view of a single election. The singleminded search for a new cleavage in the electorate and therefore a new partisanship pattern is far too narrow, as is its focus upon a single election. The realignment perspective is far too confining. It assumes that one and only one thing matters—a permanent change in the electorate. This belies the different types and categories of realigning elections. This perspective overemphasizes one factor to the detriment of all others.

The political party perspective is an organizational vision of the election which, when coupled with the mandate, attribute, and realignment perspectives, does justice to all the facets of a presidential election. Here one can see how candidates, party leaders, and elites respond to an enduring issue in light of the civil rights movement which defined in law an image commensurate with the Constitution, but to which a region and its supporters nationwide objects. The mandate covers the winning presidential candidate, the attribute covers the individual vote, the realignment covers collective voting behavior, while the political party perspective covers the organizations that mobilize the citizens, provide the candidates, and structure the issues and platforms. Together, all components of an election are covered. And it is to this last perspective, the underexplained and unexamined one, that we can now turn for help in grasping the meaning and consequences of elections to the political order.

Part One

Epistemology and the Native-Son Candidate

Political scientists study presidential elections and individual voting behavior by analyzing a host of demographic, economic, social, psychological, and political variables. After the publication of the innovative *The People's Choice* in 1944 and *The American Voter* in 1960, they were also used to explain individual vote choice, intentions, and voting predisposition. In fact, preoccupation with individual voting behavior has led inevitably to the dominance of psychological variables in the discipline.[1] Variables are the key to our epistemology of elections and voting. Yet they are not all known or fully explored.

One of the underexamined variables is that of the native-son presidential candidate. Although the variable has been identified and some of its characteristics described, there has been no effort to fashion a theory about the variable. The scattered, diverse, and fragmentary facts about this variable have not been organized and structured into a theoretical foundation. There is a lack of knowledge about this variable. Due to this lack of knowledge, the discipline has circumscribed and limited insights that it can offer in regard to presidential elections and individual voting behavior in these elections. Moreover, this also limits the knowledge that the discipline can generate about the linkage between individual voters and presidential elections.

Why? Part of the answer lies not only in the discipline's preoccupation with psychological variables and the individual voter, but also in how the discipline responds to unique factors and features that only appear in certain presidential elections. In addition, awareness of the variables which make for this uniqueness has to be coupled with how this important and crucial variable is interpreted. The 1960 presidential election is a case in point.

Democratic candidate John F. Kennedy's Catholicism made the religious variable a major issue and a relatively unique feature of the 1960 election. Political scientists rushed to examine the role of this "new" variable. V. O. Key Jr. found that "of the appeals peculiar to the campaign, the religious issue [variable] evidently by far outweighed all others. For some people it reinforced the pull of partisanship; for others, it ran counter to the tug of party loyalty."[2] While significant, it was not uniformly influential. "It is obvious that a goodly number of Democrats could not bring themselves to vote for a Catholic for President. . . . Probably the best guess is that Kennedy won in spite of rather than because of the fact that he was a Catholic."[3] Key's was a macrolevel analysis of election return data. But at the moment he was writing, the discipline was shifting to survey exploration of individual voting behavior and the uniqueness of the religious variable in 1960 set into motion microlevel analyses of this phenomenon.

Of the influence of the religious variable at the individual level, Philip Converse says:

> It has become clear that religion played a powerful role in shaping voting behavior in the 1960 election. This force generated differences quite beyond the customary, longstanding ones between the major religious groups in the United States.[4]
>
> Provisionally we locate the Kennedy candidacy [and religious variable] as a short-term force since it is still too soon to tell in any reliable way if these vote shifts have affected party loyalty.[5]

Another survey analysis of the 1960 vote stated:

> Kennedy won a vote bonus from Catholics amounting to about 4 percent of the national two-party popular vote [and] within the 1960 non-Southern electorate, Kennedy's net gain from the Catholic increment amounted to better than 5 percent of the two-party vote. The same rate of gain represented less than 1 percent of the Southern popular vote.[6]

Thus from both a macro- and microlevel analysis, the religious variable helped make the 1960 presidential election special. Key felt that the impact of the religious variable was basically ambiguous. As he saw it, the variable worked both ways. The Michigan scholars saw the variable as a short-term force relevant to this one election. Both interpretations marginalized the variable. From these analyses, this variable's further importance beyond this one election was indeed questionable.

While the 1960 findings set into motion a retrospective analysis of the religious variable in the 1928 presidential election,[7] no theory of the variable evolved. Only after the presidential elections of 1984 and 1988 and the presence of religious candidates such as Reverend Jesse Jackson and Pat Robertson did theory about the variable start to take shape.[8]

When new or unique variables surface, they may be identified and measured, but because of the manner in which they are finally interpreted, findings about them do not necessarily lead to any organized and structured theory. Such variables may not add to any knowledge which the discipline can use to advance further crucial insights.

Therefore, to advance and expand our knowledge of presidential elections and individual voting behavior, in chapter 2 we collect and analyze the scattered insights and findings of the initial thinkers on the native-son presidential candidate variable. And once data on the variable is organized and structured, in chapter 3 we collect and analyze the methodological techniques used by the thinkers and theorists to acquire an empirical rendering of this unique variable.

Collectively these two chapters provide background on the origins and evolution of the variable and the ways in which its impact has been measured. With such information, we can marshal some understanding of the strengths and weaknesses of the current literature and then design new analytical procedures and techniques with the objective of building a theoretical foundation for this variable.

CHAPTER TWO

Theory

The 1928 presidential election was the first in which the Democratic party responded to a Republican strategy to break up the solid South, by nominating a southern native-son vice-presidential candidate. At their national convention in Houston, Texas, the very first in the South since 1860, the Democrats nominated as their vice presidential candidate, on the first ballot, Arkansas Senator Joseph T. Robinson. He was the first southerner to be nominated for national office by either major party since the Civil War.[1]

One observer writes: "The 1928 Democratic National Convention was an Al Smith rally, with southern overtones. Smith's votes on the national committee put the convention in Houston, Texas. There was no mention of the two-thirds rule."[2] Balancing the ticket by selecting Senator Robinson of Arkansas as his running mate was Smith's "southern strategy." With such a strategy—a southern convention site and a southern native-son vice-presidential candidate—the Democratic ticket carried Arkansas plus five other states (Louisiana, Mississippi, Alabama, Georgia, and South Carolina). The Republican party carried the other five states of the old Confederacy. Here was born a tactic to block the Republican sweep of the region.

However, in 1928 the Republicans tried to capture the solid South by use of other major social and cultural issues—religion and Prohibition.[3]

With these deeply ingrained regional, cultural, and social issues the Republican party was partially successful and penetrated the region.

By 1964 they had another social and cultural issue—race. Again they began the process of penetration. Lyndon Johnson, a regional native son (as Senator Robinson had been) held them at bay, but did not stand for reelection. Another native son, President Carter, held them at bay in one election and was overwhelmed in the next. Now the next native-son presidential candidate, President Clinton, has beaten the Republican candidate in both of his presidential elections.

However, the use of this strategy was not recognized by academic political science until Professor Harold Gosnell's pioneering 1942 work, *Grass-roots Politics*. And the power and influence of the southern variant went unrecognized until Steven Rosenstone's work in 1983. Few academic studies have taken this variable into account. Although the discipline of political science has marched on without much concern for the variable, the Democratic party has used it to help hold the solid South in the Democratic column in the four presidential elections that the Democrats have won in the post–civil rights era. While practical politicians understand the value of the variable, academics have been slow to grasp it, due to the constant search for individual-level voting attributes. The most recent southern native-son presidential candidate provides another opportunity to develop an empirical rendering of this variable.

An Introduction

Of the three southern Democratic native-son presidents of the post–civil rights era, Bill Clinton has been the only one to win reelection. President Clinton's reelection offers a window to fashion judicious insights into why the Democratic party since 1956 has been more successful with native-son southerners as party nominees—Johnson, Carter, and Clinton—than with nonsouthern candidates—Stevenson, Humphrey, Mondale, and Dukakis.

The 1996 reelection marked the first time that a southern native-son president would have two terms to redefine and remake the Democratic party's image of itself, beyond the New Deal and Cold War images. If the Democratic party is to have a new image for the new century, it just might take shape in the aftermath of the 1996 reelection. Elections do provide the moment of reconvergence and redefinition. If President Johnson started the process of party redefinition, it is now possible for President Clinton to finish the process one way or another.

V. O. Key Jr., in his seminal article "The Future of the Democratic

Party," wrote: "The shortest route to fruitful speculation about the future of the Democratic party may be by way of a side excursion through a theory of the relation of disaster and party alignment."[4] For Key, disasters, catastrophes, and crises like the Civil War, the Great Depression, the civil rights movement, and the Cold War led to the redefinition of political parties in general and the Democratic party in particular. This study views this redefinition process via a southern native-son presidential candidate.

The Evolution of the Native-Son Variable

Harold Gosnell in his pioneering 1942 work on state voting behavior in presidential elections was the first to identity the role of the native-son variable. He wrote: "A state which has a native-son candidate invariably gives him a larger vote than would be 'normally' expected unless, of course, both major party candidates are natives of the same state."[5] Gosnell brought to the attention of the discipline a variable that could impact the outcome of elections and potentially cause a shift in the partisan balance. But this is where Gosnell left the matter—at the level of identification. This new variable was left unexplored, underdefined, and underanalyzed. When the discipline moved on in 1944, 1948, and 1960 to study voters, the study of elections fell into the background and with it the concept of the native-son variable.

However, Gosnell's famous student V. O. Key Jr. resurrected the concept in a different form. In his analysis of the internal unity of the politics of the South, Key discovered that one of the recurring empirical realities was the "friends and neighbors" vote for local candidates. "A local potentate or a leading citizen of a county who takes a notion that he wants to be governor polls an extremely heavy vote in his own bailiwick." This friends and neighbors phenomenon Key dubbed "localism":

> A powerful localism provides an important ingredient of [one party] factionalism. Candidates for state office tend to poll overwhelming majorities in their home counties and to draw heavy support in adjacent counties. . . . In this extreme form localism justifies . . . a susceptibility to control by their relevant appeal to support the home-town boy.[6]

With scattergrams and cartographic data, Key showed the extent of this phenomenon in Alabama, Florida, Georgia, Mississippi, North Carolina, South Carolina, Texas, and in the overall party system. Key took his teacher's concept, discovered its variant form in southern politics, and dubbed it localism. The native-son concept was now a state as well as a county or multicounty variable.

Gosnell first remarked on the variable in 1942; Key's insights came in 1949. Key's version of the concept was pressed into service to analyze the politics of Alabama in 1973 and Mississippi in 1975.[7] Others would remark on the concept and measure the impact of the variable, but it would not be revisited in a major way until 1983, when the state-level version of the variable was reborn.

In the article "Localism in Presidential Elections: The Home State Advantage," Michael Lewis-Beck and Tom Rice wrote:

> The forces of localism are believed to operate in presidential races as well as in state ones. Indeed, every national contest brings forth numerous claims of home state advantages for presidential candidates. . . . While the hypothesis of a home state advantage in presidential races is attractive, it is yet to be tested. . . . The first purpose of this brief study, then, was to assess the magnitude of the home state advantage in presidential elections. Second, we wanted to establish whether there had been any trend over time, such as a declining home state advantage, in response to the nationalization of political forces. Third, we wanted to discover factors that help predict a presidential contender's potential home state advantage.[8]

With this article, the native-son concept was given a rebirth in Gosnell's original form. But its roots were traced by the authors not to Gosnell but to V. O. Key Jr. "In the research literature on state and local politics, this proposition is most fully developed by V. O. Key Jr., in his *Southern Politics*."[9] Thus Key, not Gosnell, became the originator of the native-son concept. Part of the reason for this is that in Key's book, he refers to the book in which Gosnell made his assertion about the "native-son candidate" variable and links it to his discussion of "friends and neighbors" voting, yet he does not link it to his remade variant of localism.[10] While it is quite true that Key's localism was more fully developed than was Gosnell's native-son concept, the connection was never established.

The authors found that (1) "on average, a presidential candidate can count on an increase of about four percentage points in his home state vote share beyond what he would otherwise expect," (2) "interestingly, the strength of this local support has remained undiluted since the turn of the century, despite the forces of nationalization that seem to be overtaking other aspects of the electoral process," and (3) "among the several explanatory variables that seem important, state population size stands out. The smaller the home state the larger the margin of the candidate's advantage."[11] With this pioneering article, Lewis-Beck and Rice firmly established the empirical impact of this variable in presidential elections.

The second work in 1983 to address this variable was Steven Rosenstone's *Forecasting Presidential Elections*.[12] In his chapter titled "A Theory of Elections," Rosenstone devotes an entire section to the home-state and regional effects on the outcome of elections. "To explain elections requires a theory that accounts for changes over time in the electorate's behavior." And one of the factors that can account for the change, notes Rosenstone, is the home state variable: "In an election the candidates' home states and regions also vary, which also may effect who wins."[13] Rosenstone placed this variable into his election forecasting model and found that:

> Jimmy Carter's southerness brought in few votes. Although Carter
> won 10 of the 11 former Confederate states, only a small proportion of
> his vote total in the South—2.7 points—can be attributed to a
> friends-and-neighbors effect. (This small vote advantage, however,
> was sufficient to bring victory in at least two states.)[14]

Rosenstone's landmark work established the empirical impact of the influence of "friends and neighbors and home state." Second, he revealed that in the 1976 election, this variable had a regional influence as well. Unlike the Lewis-Beck and Rice article, the book arrived at its conclusions after a multivariate analysis. Their article was a univariate analysis. Most important, Rosenstone's work was concerned with crafting a forecasting theory—not a general theory of elections per se. Rosenstone used the state as his unit of analysis. Nevertheless, this was a clearcut advance for the concept.

Overall these two works established the empirical foundations of this variable. The article provided a precise measurement—a 4 percent average increase—for the native son inside the candidate's home state. The book provided a precise measurement—a 2.7 point increase—for a southern native son inside the region. Here are empirical findings of both state and regional influences. Rosenstone offered a qualification by noting that "a regional friends-and-neighbors effect exists only when a presidential candidate is from the South."

Strom Thurmond and George Wallace drew an additional 2.7 percent of the southern vote in 1948 and 1968 because they were southerners. . . . That a friends-and-neighbors effect holds only in the South should not be surprising—given the region's unique historical experience. Moreover, the small effect indicates that the lion's share of Strom Thurmond's and George Wallace's support in the South resulted from their issue stances, particularly on race, rather than their southern background.[15]

What Rosenstone's finding and assertion missed is that their southern background is significantly defined by their racism and the historical influence of race in the culture. One cannot substitute race for southern regional influence or vice versa because these two things are highly correlated in southern political behavior. There is a southern regional influence, because of race.

Despite the differences in findings between the article and the book, both works use the state as a unit of analysis (as did Gosnell) and they both agree that the variable is a significant independent factor in shaping the outcome of presidential elections because it has the potential of altering the partisan balance in elections.

This variable has been seen in various ways. Gosnell identified it as a state level variable, Key modified it to a county or multicounty variable, and Lewis-Beck and Rice restored it to the state level, with influence in presidential elections. Rosenstone continued this but extended its reach by showing that in presidential elections it can also have regional influence in the South. Gosnell's concept had now travelled full circle and beyond.

Carter as a Southern Native-Son Candidate: Theory in the Making

President Carter's reelection bid in 1980 provided an opportunity not only to revisit the concept in its own right, but a chance to begin to develop some of the theoretical foundations of a theory about elections and the Democratic political order. President Carter was the second southern native-son Democratic presidential candidate in the post–World War II period and his candidacy came during a moment in political time when the Republican party was contending for this regional bloc of electoral votes. In both of his presidential elections, President Carter's native-son status had significant impact both inside his home state and in the region as well. As Professor Rosenstone had found, southern native-son candidates have a measurable and discernible regional influence.

Carter's native-son characteristic went beyond his two presidential elections. In 1984, President Carter's former Vice President, Walter Mondale, ran for the Democratic party nomination with President Carter's backing. In the Georgia primary on March 13, Mondale, with the backing of Bert Lance, Hamilton Jordan, Carter and several black leaders, narrowly won.[16] Carter's native-son status permits scholars to see for the first time that this attribute is not individually confined and static. It is, under certain circumstances, a dynamic factor.

From an analysis of the 1976, 1980, and 1984 elections, new theoretical insights have been developed about the role of the native-son variable in presidential elections.

> Analysis of the Carter vote in Georgia, at least in presidential elections, suggest that a native-son candidate might (1) heighten the turnout in his state, (2) reverse partisan loyalties in the state, (3) reverse partisan loyalties at least in the southern region, (4) maintain his party in a winning mode in the area when all other states in the region are shifting back to old partisan loyalties, and (5) under certain conditions, transfer some of his/her influence to other presidential candidates.[17]

These findings from the Carter analysis significantly enhanced and enriched what the discipline knows about this variable and led to the development of testable propositions about the (1) home state presidential primary, (2) the native-son candidate, (3) the home state electorate, (4) the home state African American electorate, (5) the southern regional electorate, (6) southern regionalism, and (7) future presidential candidates. But the evolution of theory about this variable and its role and function in the political order did not stop with the Carter years.

The election of Clinton and Gore, two southern native sons, in 1992 provided the opportunity to revisit the variable and further advance our knowledge of this factor. A limited analysis emerged and revealed that in Georgia:

> both in 1984 and 1988, the Republican pluralities in the state stood at 20 percentage points. But in 1992, a native son candidate from the region gave the Democrats a 1 percentage point plurality. Clearly, Clinton significantly reversed the surging Republicanism in the state as Carter had done in 1976 and 1980.[18]

Al Gore had a similar impact on his home state. In 1980, the Republican plurality in Tennessee stood at 1 percentage point. By 1984, it was 16 points. In 1988, it was 16 points again. In 1992, Tennessee, in a presidential year, shifted back to the Democratic column, giving the party a 5 point plurality. Again, a native son reversed party fortunes in his own state.[19]

The 1992 analysis also demonstrated that a trend was taking shape in which the southern native-son Democratic candidate could electorally exploit a weakness inherent in the Republican southern strategy.

> Southern Republicanism at the presidential level has at least one major flaw: It can be significantly reduced by a native son presidential candidate. Both the Carter and Clinton candidacies provide evidence that this flaw exists. . . . The black vote plays a major role in the electoral victories of these southern native son candidates that halts and limits this recent surging southern Republicanism at the presidential level.[20]

Together these two southern native sons carried 4 of the 11 southern states in the 1992 election.

One more testable proposition emerged from this 1992 analysis. With two candidates from the South on the same ticket, voter turnout, both African American and white, increased.

Beginning with Gosnell's identification of this variable in 1942, the gradual development of the theory and the elections of 1976, 1980, 1984, and 1992, have provided occasions to expand upon this underdeveloped factor in presidential elections. These four elections have made it possible to map out this decisive factor in the partisan competition of the post–Cold War era. Since President Clinton's Vice President, Al Gore, may follow in the footsteps of Carter's vice president and run for president in the year 2000, this variable may give us some insights into the initial presidential election of the twenty-first century. Gore is a southern native-son candidate who speaks not only to the problem of the Republican party's southern strategy but to the nature of the New Democrat designed to replace the New Deal Democrat.

The Native-Son Theory and the Political Party Perspective

President Clinton's reelection provides an opportunity to use the theory in an exploration of the political party perspective. President Clinton's recapture of the White House gives him a temporal moment that neither

Presidents Johnson nor Carter had. President Johnson's election in 1964 gave him the unique moment to add to the New Deal's definition of the Democratic party. FDR had redefined the party in economic terms. President Truman had begin the process of adding to that definition with racial liberalism. But his single term did not allow him to complete the process. But Truman's successor as the party's presidential candidate, Adlai Stevenson, did not continue Truman's initiatives. Stevenson reversed the process by capitulating to the image of the party that the Dixiecrats had set into motion in 1948. In both the 1952 and 1956 presidential campaigns, Stevenson advocated a return to the status quo. Thus the Truman definition nearly disappeared.

However "the Truman administration left a mixed civil rights legacy, but its actions suggested the likely direction of civil rights policies in the 1950s. . . . Truman was unable to secure his civil rights legislative program in the face of southern and partisan opposition."[21]

When the 1946 elections produced a Republican Congress, southern Democrats developed a conservative alliance between Republicans and themselves to further strength their hand in recapturing the party and maintaining its stance on race.[22] When Truman won in 1948, they were positioned to halt Truman's efforts at redefinition. And when Truman refused to run for reelection, the southern Democrats used their delegate power and electoral promises at the national convention to maintain their party's image. "Northern Democrats and their candidate, Adlai E. Stevenson, sought reconciliation with the white South and suspended extensive debate on civil rights."[23] On the major civil rights issue of the campaign— a permanent Fair Employment Practices Commission (FEPC)—Democratic presidential nominee Stevenson was hesitant; when he spoke he was vague and low key. "Advocates of federal enforcement of fair hiring had found little to encourage them in the 1952 presidential campaign, for Democrat Stevenson's support of FEPC was lukewarm at best and Eisenhower advocated only state responsibility."[24]

To ensure that the southern party image maintained itself in that election, South Carolina Governor James Byrnes and Virginia Senator Harry Byrd endorsed Eisenhower.[25] And Eisenhower helped matters with an "open courtship of southern white voters" by touring the South, where he joined in the singing of Dixie.[26] In the end, with no alternative, African American voters stayed with the Democratic party. The southern definition of race marched on. The Dixiecrats' strategy had not derailed Truman's efforts, but it influenced his successor, as Stevenson began to reverse the image of the party that Truman had tried to put into place. If the 1952 Democratic presidential campaign started the reversal of the image that Truman set into motion with his strong civil rights plank in the party's platform, Stevenson's 1956 campaign would complete the reversal process.

In 1954 the Supreme Court issued its decision in *Brown v Board of Education*, which sent shockwaves throughout the South. And the South counterattacked. The Dixiecrats' presidential candidate, Strom Thurmond, led the charge.

> In the nation's capital over ninety percent of the region's congressmen and Senators signed a 'Southern Manifesto' drafted by die-hard Dixiecrat Senator Strom Thurmond of South Carolina. Branding the high court's decision in the *Brown* case a substitution of naked power for established law, the declaration called upon whites to unite in an unbroken phalanx of opposition to any changes in the South's racial system.[27]

The Democratic party, regionally and nationally, was not immune.

At the 1956 Democratic National Convention the southern delegates tried to ensure that the presidential nominee would accept and advance southern opposition to any changes in its racial system. George Wallace delivered a seconding speech to the nomination of South Carolina's Governor George Bell Timmerman. When this insurgent southern strategy failed, Wallace endorsed former governor of Illinois Adlai Stevenson and his running mate from Tennessee, Estes Kefauver, "as the best the South could hope to get at this time."[28]

Prior to the convention, Stevenson had responded to the southern manifesto by dispatching "one of his southern advisers, Harry Ashmore, in an effort to minimize the political fallout, because he had staked his renomination for the presidency on the support of southern moderates."[29] With the manifesto, the hardliners extracted from Stevenson a commitment to their party image. This became evident during the campaign when Stevenson fully endorsed and advocated their position.

NAACP leader Roy Wilkins, seeing that Stevenson had so embraced the southern image of the party, "sharply criticized his desire to keep the civil rights issue out of the campaign." Stevenson replied to Wilkins by saying: "we must recognize that it is reason alone that will determine our rate of progress." Faced with such a grudging acceptance of the issue of civil rights and a possible remaking of the party's historical image on race, Wilkins "proceeded to denounce the candidate's blithe vagueness in such blistering language that Stevenson's friend Eleanor Roosevelt threatened to resign from the board of the NAACP."[30]

Wilkins understood that Truman's remaking of the party's image was slipping away and his tactic of public criticism was all that the organization had to try and keep its hard-won gains in party politics.

If Wilkins and the NAACP were pressured into an acceptance of the Stevenson reversal, other voices in the African American community were not so easily silenced. African American Democratic Congressman from Harlem Adam Clayton Powell Jr. accepted an invitation to the White House from President Eisenhower. After their private meeting on October 11, Powell emerged to endorse Eisenhower for reelection, saying that he would do more for civil rights than Stevenson.[31] Congressman Powell justified his call for a Republican presidential vote as a repudiation of Senator James Eastland, a Dixie demagogue from Mississippi who was in the forefront of the southern Democratic movement to maintain the party's policies of segregation. In Congressman Powell's view, Democratic presidential nominee Stevenson had come to support the stance of Senator Eastland.

Stevenson reflected on his 1952 and 1956 presidential campaigns: "If the only way I can get elected is by pandering to people's fears and hatreds, I want no part of it."[32] The truth of the matter is that under his leadership, the Truman image of the party was superseded by that of the Dixiecrats, George Wallace, and the Dixie demagogues such as Senator Eastland. Stevenson's legacy was the reversal of the emerging party image of racial liberalism.

Courtship of the southern Democrats continued into the Kennedy campaign and presidency. Although Robert Kennedy had placed a call to Martin Luther King Jr.'s wife while King was jailed, as a way to help recapture the African American vote that had gone to President Eisenhower in 1956, for the first two-and-a-half years of his administration, President Kennedy refused to sponsor civil rights legislation or to actively commit the Democratic party, except in minor ways, to the Truman image and the cause of civil rights. It took the marches and demonstrations of Martin Luther King and the Birmingham protest demonstration of 1963 to force the President's hand.[33] After Kennedy's assassination, it took a native son of the South, Lyndon Johnson, to reverse the image left by Stevenson and to complete the initiative launched by President Truman and continued by President Kennedy. With a bold legislative program that included the 1964 Civil Rights Act, the 1965 Voting Rights Act, and the 1968 Open Housing Act, President Johnson remade the historic character of the Democratic party on race. In the face of stiff and continuing opposition from his native South, President Johnson persisted. By the end of his one full term, Johnson had combined the New Deal image of the party—economic liberalism—with racial liberalism. The union was made and the issues joined. By 1968 the Democratic party image was one of both economic and racial liberalism.

No sooner than this image was born that it came under renewed fire and incessant attack and criticism. And the central figure who mobilized the South and elements from the rest of the nation in attacking this new party image was Alabama Governor George Wallace. In his two presidential campaign efforts, Wallace created a mass electoral base of opposition to this new image.

Born in and raised to political maturity amid a variety of southern strategies such as the unpledged electors movement, states rights third parties attempts to capture the Democratic party nomination in 1972 and 1976 presidential primaries, the instant conversion of Democratic party leaders and individual voters to the Republican party, delegates' revolts, Wallace had, by the Johnson era, risen to governor of Alabama. He now had a political base from which to operate, and a political party image to contest. And contest he did.

Although he was not physically present at the 1968 Democratic National Convention, Wallace was a force and an influence. The party's presidential nominee, Vice President Hubert Humphrey, wavered and waffled. His stance was to moderate the party's new image of racial liberalism. For Humphrey, racial liberalism would become racial moderation. With Humphrey's unsuccessful 1968 presidential campaign against Richard Nixon, the party image began to move to the right of center.

In 1972 the Democratic presidential candidate, George McGovern, enlarged the liberalism of the party. Whereas economic and racial liberalism had defined the party's image, McGovern embraced cultural and social liberalism and enhanced the limited liberalism of the Humphrey campaign. Race was incorporated into the larger mix. This expanded liberal image which now included economic, racial, and social liberalism did not attract enough voters to prevent President Nixon's reelection. But in defeat McGovern redefined the Democratic party. The Nixon White House overreached, set Watergate into motion, and thereby led to the resignation of President Nixon. After Watergate and the installation of Gerald Ford as President, a native-son southerner, Jimmy Carter, captured first the Democratic party and then the White House, yet had no new thrust for the racial liberalism of the Democratic party outside of his own reelection. That reelection effort failed. Enter Carter's Vice President, Walter Mondale.

In 1984 Walter Mondale was faced with an African American rival for the nomination, Jesse Jackson. He finessed the matter of race in the primaries, but in the campaign against President Ronald Reagan, Mondale developed a strategy of benign neglect. The candidate did nothing to promote, enhance, or embrace racial liberalism. Mondale simply accepted the party image concerning racial commitment as a historical given. Congressman Charles Rangel, the African American Democrat from Harlem, seconded his top aide, George Dalley, to the Mondale camp during his campaign. Congressman Rangel continued to pay Dalley's salary when he was assigned to Mondale's national campaign headquarters in Washington, D.C. Dalley was given a small desk near the wall, out of the main traffic flow, and told he would be contacted. Yet during the entire campaign he was never asked to a strategy session, was never asked for any advice, and he was never given any duty to perform. He played no role in the campaign; not even a minor one.

Reflecting on his experience of systematic isolation, Dalley indicated that the atmosphere was that African American voters had no other place to go and therefore the Mondale campaign did not have to do a thing to get their vote. Thus there was no role for Dalley to play.[34] Such a new party stance so infuriated Andrew Young that he publicly criticized the Mondale campaign (as Roy Wilkins had previously criticized Stevenson) by saying that "this election was too important for these smart ass white boys to lose."[35] Mondale was defeated by a Reagan landslide.

Coming out of the Mondale presidential defeat was a refined party image, with racial liberalism as something that the party had been about in years past. The 1988 Democratic presidential nominee, Michael Dukakis, vacillated but embraced his party's redefined image. Faced with Jesse Jackson as a rival for the Democratic party nomination as well as a challenge from President Reagan's Vice President, George Bush, Dukakis would not even embrace the word liberalism. Only near the end of the campaign did he finally admit to being a liberal. But he moderated that by selecting not Jackson as running mate, but Senator Lloyd Bentsen of Texas, following the tradition of the Kennedy-Johnson ticket of 1960.

Late in the campaign, Jesse Jackson and a group of African American leaders had a two-hour meeting with Dukakis in his home in Massachusetts in which they discussed how important it was for him to have the Democratic party maintain the image given it by Truman, Kennedy, and Johnson. Afterwards, Dukakis left the meeting and proceeded to go out alone to speak to the media waiting outside. Jackson and the other leaders stopped him and noted that it was this type of insensitivity that was straining the African American alliance with the party. With all of these African American leaders present, Dukakis was not willing to bring one outside with him nor to be seen in their presence. Yet he was presumably going to speak for them.[36] Such action was a flagrant slap in the face. Only with more discussion and lobbying did the Democratic presidential candidate relent. But his one joint photo and media session did not alter the larger and broader pattern taking shape. The Democratic party's newly acquired image of racial liberalism was to be marketed as a thing of the past. George Bush defeated Dukakis. The party image continued.

During the 1992 presidential campaign, the DLC leader and Democratic candidate, Bill Clinton, never mentioned the issue of race. "In 1992, however, race was a dog that did not bark, noteworthy for its relative absence as an issue in the campaign. . . . The silence was more evident because the occasions of racial conflict were so thunderous"—namely the rioting in Los Angeles that followed the verdict in the trial of the police officers who had arrested and beaten Rodney King and which "set off a rash of riots in urban centers around the nation."[37] Yet both presidential candidates ignored the issue.

The main point of this analysis is twofold. First, to break out of the "presidential synthesis" which historians in 1948 had rejected as the only explanation of American political history and elections. Such a synthesis focused solely upon the president in office, not on other individuals and events. Presidential candidates can and do attempt to reshape and remold political parties just as incumbent presidents do. The classic example in the Democratic party is William Jennings Bryan.[38] Although defeated for the presidency three times, Bryan became chairman of the Democratic National Committee and remade the Democratic party in his image.[39] In their turn, Humphrey, McGovern, Mondale, and Dukakis all tried as candidates to manage and reshape the Democratic party image and character of racial liberalism handed to them by Truman and Johnson.

This bring us to the second point—the question of continuity and discontinuity. Presidential hopefuls as well as presidents themselves can continue within the party's image. They can maintain the historical character of the past. Or they can began a process of adjustment and reformation. Stevenson, Humphrey, McGovern, Mondale, and Dukakis all sought to some degree to reshift the Democratic party's image. Party image and character are both fixed and fluid. Crucial to the discussion here is that southern Democrats both fixed and tried to altered the party's portrait.

The Unpledged Electors Movement

Segregationist third parties, insurgent leaders like George Wallace, and instant regional conversion to the Republican party did not exhaust all the options and efforts that southern leaders used to recapture and maintain the Democratic party's historical character and image on the question of race. There was also the unpledged electors movement.

The leading scholar of this movement, Samuel DuBois Cook, describes how

> Echoing the Dixiecratic strategy of trying to deadlock the Electoral College and force election of the president by the House of Representatives, certain states' righters, prior to every presidential contest, engaged in what the *Atlanta Journal* called a "battered old crutch" and the "slickest confidence game going." The electoral game is called independent or "free" electors. This movement is based on a theory of the balance of power and electoral juggling.[40]

This tactic was employed in several states by various party leaders. Such a tactic held out the possibility that these leaders could show white voters that they were indeed struggling to save white supremacy. Why was it constantly used? Cook again:

> The assumption is that the South, in order to force a stalemate in the Electoral College and thereby compel House selection of the president, should withhold its electoral votes from both Democratic and Republican nominees. The hope is that, through some kind of political chemistry, the South will be able to secure a states' rights sympathizer, if not a states' rights president, in the White House. This fantasy expressed itself in Mississippi as early as 1944.[41]

Although the first southern Democratic unpledged elector appeared in 1932, the Mississippi effort in 1944 spearheaded the fledgling effort.[42] The unpledged electors movement based itself on the format begun by the division of the Republican party in the South into two factors in 1889—the Black and Tans and the Lily-Whites.[43] Both of these factions usually put up separate tickets at elections and were still doing this at the very moment of the creation of the Democratic unpledged electors movement.

In 1944 Texas and South Carolina joined Mississippi in this movement. Arkansas remained uncommitted in that year. By 1948 the budding unpledged electors movement merged into the Dixiecrat party. This time Arkansas gave significant electoral support to the party of states rights: when the party failed to reemerge in 1952, the movement continued in the American First party lead by Senator Harry F. Byrd of Virginia. The Byrd-driven effort quickly fizzled.

In the 1956 presidential election the unpledged electors movement was reborn in Alabama, Louisiana, Mississippi, and South Carolina. One of the 11 Democratic electors chosen in Alabama cast his Electoral College vote for Walter B. Jones and Senator Herman Talmadge. Besides this elector, the movement also had a popular base, as "196,318 votes were cast in Alabama, Louisiana, Mississippi, and South Carolina for Independent electors or for States Rights election tickets not officially pledged to any candidate."[44]

In 1960 Mississippi cast its 8 electoral votes, and Alabama cast 6 of its 11 votes, for Senator Byrd; Alabama and Mississippi electors also cast 14 votes for Senator Strom Thurmond for vice president. At the popular level, "169,572 votes were cast in Louisiana for Independent electors and 115,248 in Mississippi for an unpledged Democratic electors ticket."[45] Although Arkansas Governor Faubus declined the nomination of the National States Rights party, the party polled 28,952 votes in Arkansas, by far the best showing among all states where the party was able to get on the ballot.[46] This was 7 percent of the state's 1960 presidential vote.

In 1964 only in Alabama did 210,732 votes appear for an unpledged Democratic elector ticket. In 1968, as it had done in the past, the movement merged with another party, George Wallace's American Independent party. And in 1968 Arkansas gave all 6 of its electoral college votes to the Wallace party. This despite the fact that, unlike several other southern states, Arkansas had not passed a state law or resolution requiring an unpledged elector ballot. In 1968 the Arkansas electorate shifted their Democratic partisanship and partisan identification, even if only temporarily, to the American Independent party. And this became one of the legacies and traditions of the Democratic party in the state. It was part and parcel of the political context that existed as Clinton evolved as a native son.

The unpledged electors movement was predated by homegrown efforts led by Arkansas party elites. First to help map the party's image was Senator James K. Jones, national party chairman of the Democratic party from 1896 to 1904. A William Jennings Bryan man, he shared with him a low and demeaning view of African Americans, and a penchant for white supremacy.

Another Senator, Jeff Davis, held similar views. His biographer notes that he "carefully read everything that he could get his hands on that Bryan ever wrote, . . . never failed to attend a Bryan lecture or speech. . . . His admiration for Bryan was genuine and unbounded, and he believed that everything Bryan said or did was right."[47] And in his years as chairman of the state Democratic party and delegate to the National Democratic Convention, he promoted Bryanism and its negrophobia.

In 1928 Senator Joseph T. Robinson, a major party activist, became the vice presidential candidate on the Al Smith ticket. This "Senate Minority leader . . . had little opposition for the vice presidency and was nominated on the first ballot with 914 votes. Senator Albert W. Barkley of Kentucky finished a distant second with 77 votes. After a vote switch, Robinson had 1,035 votes."[48] Although the Democrats lost the 1928 election, Senator Robinson remained active and was named chairman of the 1936 Democratic National Convention.[49] Like the Senators before him, he carried the white supremacy image of the Democratic party forward.

After Senator Robinson's death, the state's promotion of white supremacy in national party circles declined but was again taken up by Governor Orval Faubus in 1957. It continued, in limited voting for states rights candidates and parties, and culminated in the Wallace presidential bid of 1968.

The point is that Arkansas native sons have been actively engaged in individual efforts to redefine and maintain the image and character of the Democratic party. Although they have been less visible in regionwide efforts, Arkansas Democratic party leaders and activists, beginning in the late 1800s, left a legacy and a tradition of working to keep the party's image in line with the customs and mores of the region. This is part of what the Arkansas political context offers in the development of any theory about the native-son presidential candidate. Senator Robinson's 1928 vice presidential candidacy is symbolic of these realities as well as having been the initial step in the rise of southern native-son presidential candidates such as Johnson, Carter, and Clinton.

Theorizing About the Native-Son and Political Party Perspectives

Theory in this study simply means an empirically informed discussion about the relationship between two or more variables. The central variables here are William J. Clinton as a southern native-son candidate and the Democratic party's prevailing character and image. The preceding discussion was to identify and clarify some of the major factors (i.e., independent variables) in this relationship and some of the forces that have shaped and set these factors in motion.

The pioneering study on President Carter as a native son began the crafting of a theoretical model for thinking about the southern native-son presidential candidate variable.[50] President Carter's tenure in the White House and President Clinton's election are separated by a period of nearly twenty years—a full generation. A simple replication study using the Carter model would miss the political changes and realignments that have taken place since the last southerner held the White House. An uncritical adaptation of the Carter model would be static and inflexible. Currently so much of political science analysis rests on the continued static application of theoretical models, rendering quite a few findings and interpretations inadequate. It is essential to acknowledge the changes in both the long-term and short-term factors that may be shaping the political process and the Democratic party.

Carter's election to the presidency in 1976 marked the end of George Wallace's efforts to create a mass base in the national electorate for the South's image of the Democratic party. At the same time as Wallace's political insurgency was ending, the Republican party's southern strategy was just beginning.

> By the election of 1972, the turn of the wheel was complete. The President who had promised to "bring us together" unleashed a political campaign that emphasized his commitment to containing Welfare costs, his opposition to busing, quotas, and affirmative action (including the repudiation of many of the programs begun by his own administration), and a continued hammering away at the theme that the Democratic party was out of touch with mainstream values in American society.[51]
>
> George Wallace was finished [but] Richard Nixon had understood Wallace's political role [and] the 1972 campaign marked a critical realignment in American politics. . . . The growing Republican dominance in the South was the single most important outcome of the elections of 1972.[52]

The 1972 realignment became real in 1980 as President Carter was swept from office. It continued in 1984 and 1988, stalled in 1992, and culminated in the midterm congressional election of 1994. But the story is not just in the continued realignment process. The story is in the rise of Patrick Buchanan in the 1992, 1996, and 2000 Republican presidential primaries. With Patrick Buchanan, George Wallace's influence was reborn.[53]

In 1964, 1968, 1972, and 1976, George Wallace had driven southern whites out of the Democratic party over the party's character and image portrait on race. These were the Reagan and Bush Democrats of the 1980s. Another major change since President Carter's term in office is the renewed political rhetoric of anger, resentment, and fear in the Republican party, announced in harsh, vivid, and dramatic terms by Patrick Buchanan and David Duke of Louisiana. Wallace is back.

Good theorizing must also recognize the rise of the DLC and its close connection to Bill Clinton. While Carter was president, no formal organization existed with the sole purpose of reshaping and remaking the Democratic party's character and image. With the DLC, President Clinton's redefinition of the party was already underway before his election as president.

As this century comes to a close, there are long-term factors in the Democratic party seeking to redefine its character and image. The strategy has remained the same but the tactics have changed. Southern native-son presidents and organizations like the DLC are now dominant. Opposite the long-term Democratic efforts are the emergence and evolution of southern Republicans. Southern Republicanism is a countervailing force. It is also an electorally competitive factor in the region.

Among the short term factors are political insurgents like Patrick Buchanan and David Duke, African American presidential contenders like Jesse Jackson, racial events, and civil rights crises. All these forces influence this redefinition of the Democratic party by southern native-son presidents. The question at this point is: Can we capture in an empirical manner some of these long- and short-term forces? Can we measure some of these independent variables? If we can, then our theorizing will be built on hard and measurable evidence and the underanalyzed native-son variable will provide the discipline with a greater purchase in understanding elections. This is what the missing political party perspective can add to this study.

Theorists and Their Perspectives: An Overview

The insights that the political party perspective can bring to a theory of the native-son presidential candidate variable must be put into an overall theoretical perspective.

Figure 2.1 provides an overview of the initial ideas and thoughts on this variable, as well as a synthesis of those ideas so that new points of departure can be made.

The figure lists the theorists involved to date in developing and describing insights into the variable. These five have tried to map out the specifics of the variable. There have been both direct lines of influence as well as indirect ones.

Column two indicates what these theorists noted about the variable. Gosnell identified it. Key reconfigured that identify. Rosenstone and Michael Lewis-Beck and Tom Rice were chiefly concerned with the measurement of the influence of the variable. And Walton would attempt to develop a formal theoretical statement about the variable as well as a foundation.

The different theorists focused on different levels. Gosnell saw the variable as a state level force and factor in national elections. Key saw the variable as a county (local) level force and factor in southern elections. Lewis-Beck and Rice continued Gosnell's original theory by showing that it was and is a state level variable influencing the outcome of national elections. Rosenstone's research showed that it was not only a state-level variable, but one that was even more powerful as a southern regional variable. His work moved the variable beyond its initial state and local level encapsulation. Walton sees the variable as a county, state, and regional one that is influential in national elections. And his research, which includes the missing political party perspective, helps to demonstrate the regional impact of the southern native-son presidents as exemplified by Johnson, Carter, and Clinton.

Figure 2.1, which summarizes this chapter, tells us who the theorists are and what they were saying in regard to this variable. The figure gives us the (1) theorist, (2) their characteristic features of the variable, and (3) the levels of the political system from which they made their reflections. First in modern behavioral political science there is the identification of the variable. Second there are attempts to measure the influence of the variable once it has been identified. But this is not enough. Identification and measurement leave the variable bereft of any systematic theory. Missing from the identification and measurement efforts is the formal crafting of theory about the variable from what is already known about it and what can be ascertained when critical omitted perspectives are restored to the equation. Finally there are the insights that can be generated from new studies of the variable itself.

Theory building in this study will begin by collecting and organizing those insights already available in the scattered data on the variable as generated by the pioneers in the field. Next the missing political party perspective will provide the opportunity to explore ways in which the variable

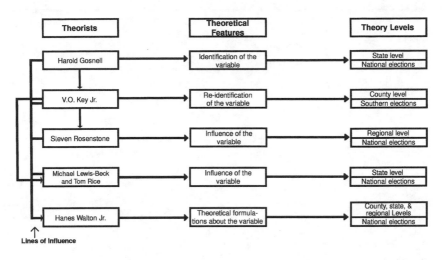

FIGURE 2.1 The Theorists and Their Perspectives on the Native-Son
Presidential Candidate Variable

is influential beyond the county and state levels, and to structure a new
study to include this missing but very germane perspective. The theory
building effort will delineate testable propositions from the analysis of the
election and reelection efforts of President Clinton. This study will permit
the refinement and enhancement of features found about the variable in
the study of Carter, as well as some of the factors and features that have
arisen since Carter's tenure in the White House. At the heart of this work
is an intellectual effort to develop testable propositions about the native-
son variable in presidential elections.

CHAPTER THREE

Methodology

Southern native-son presidents and presidential candidates were there at the inception to shape the national character and image of the forerunners of the Democratic party. How? Historian Richard McCormick tells us that:

> For roughly half a century, embracing fourteen presidential elections, the rules of the presidential game were quite unstable and even discontinuous. That is, the rules did not "evolve" in an orderly or sequential fashion. Rather there were four successive types of game, each with its own characteristic features.[1]
>
> From the inauguration of Jefferson to the reelection of Monroe in 1820, presidential politics were so dominated by Virginians that they can be described most aptly as "the Virginia game."[2]

McCormick again: "Not only did Virginians hold the presidential office for twenty-four unbroken years, they also reshaped the rules of the presidential game to ensure their pre-eminence and to reflect their conceptions of politics," and that of the Jeffersonian Republican party, a forerunner of the modern Democratic party.[3]

These Virginia men—Jefferson, Madison, and Monroe—anchored in place the historical character and image of the Democratic party as being pro-slavery and anti-black suffrage, with a philosophy of both white supremacy and states rights. Here was the beginning of the Democratic party's racial illiberalism. It was there at the beginning and Clinton is one in a long line of southern native sons who had and have a role in defining their political party.

Historian Nicol Rae states that:

> Looking to Clinton to overhaul the Democratic party organizationally and change its ideological orientation may also be misguided. Contemporary American political parties are not highly structured and disciplined organizations but rather are elusive and amorphous entities, incapable of being turned around by even a powerful incumbent President.[4]

This belies the fact that President Clinton helped to create and then lead the DLC while labeling himself a New Democrat and describing his public policies as such. To overlook or discount these purposeful activities is more than shortsighted for it displaces and renders unimportant the role and function that southern native-son presidents have played in addressing the character and image of the Democratic party in the post–civil rights era; it also overlooks the efforts of the early Virginians down through Arkansas's own Senators Jones, Davis, and Robinson in trying to reshape the party.

To be sure, events, crises, and catastrophes might make it impossible for President Clinton to carry out his stated aim for the Democratic party, but to dismiss it out of hand denies the party's past, the South's role in it, and the current Republican response to the new Democratic party image. Such an academic stance is either illusory or wishful thinking. Racial liberalism is *now* a central factor in Democratic party politics.

Rae's assertion is impressionistic. This study is based on empirical and quantitative data as much as possible. Theoretical models "attempt to identify important phenomena, provide the categories for organizing information, and suggest questions and relationships between political and other phenomena."[5]

Measuring the Native-Son Variable: The Pioneers and Beyond

In 1937, Swedish political scientist Herbert Tingsten used election return data from voting precincts in Stockholm to show how the context in which individuals live helps determine their voting and party behavior.[6]

Harold Gosnell, studying voting behavior with election return data in four typical states, identified the native-son variable.[7] Gosnell's student V. O. Key Jr. analyzed the eleven states of the old Confederacy using election return data at the county level to identity localism in voting patterns. Localism gives the hometown boy a significant electoral advantage over his out-of-town rivals. Key extended the insights of Tingsten and Gosnell to southern politics, using maps, tables, and scattergrams.[8]

Michael Lewis-Beck and Tom Rice, and Steven Rosenstone in 1983, measured the precise influence of this factor in state and presidential elections. Rosenstone showed that this variable was more important in the South than in other areas of the nation.

In a pioneering study of Jimmy Carter's elections, the county was the unit of analysis. Therefore one could follow how the native son emerged in the state electorate and his influence on the state and regional party systems. The study also followed the postpresidential influence of the native son by reviewing how President Carter influenced the electorate of his state on behalf of his former vice president, Walter Mondale.

In the Carter study, the model established the necessity of analyzing both the initial election and the reelection bid of the southern native-son presidential candidate. The model borrowed from Key and isolated the president's home county to find trends and patterns of localism, i.e., the votes of friends and neighbors. It also isolated the African American electorate's role in supporting the native son in local as well as presidential elections. The present work is the second stage in developing a theoretical model about southern native-son presidential candidates.

Clinton's Native-Son Elections

The data source for this study is shown in table 3.1. It is the 21 elections that Clinton has contested: 10 primary races, 2 runoff contests, and 9 general election races. Clinton won 19 of 21 of his elections.

Clinton ran for Congress once, which eventuated three races. He lost. Then he was elected state attorney general. Six attempts at the gubernatorial office meant 13 different elections. Finally are the two primaries and two general elections for the presidency. He lost once for Congress and once for governor in 7 national and 14 state contests spanning some 22 years in American politics.

These 21 electoral contests yield county level election return data on Clinton, the native-son candidate, as well as data on Democratic and Republican party politics in the historically one-party state of Arkansas.

TABLE 3.1 The Categories and Types of Elections Contested by Native Son
Bill Clinton, 1974–1996

Office and Year	Primary Election	Runoff Election	General Election	Total	Results
Congress					
1974	X	X	X	3	Lost
Attorney General					
1976	X		*	1	Won
Governor					
1978	X		X	2	Won
1980	X		X	2	Lost
1982	X	X	X	3	Won
1984	X		X	2	Won
1986**	X		X	2	Won
1990	X		X	2	Won
President					
1992	X		X	2	Won
1996	X		X	2	Won
Total	10	2	9	21	19 Wins, 2 Losses

Adapted from the election results published by the Arkansas Secretary of State.
*Arkansas election rules at this time did not provide for tallies in unopposed elections.
**Beginning with this election, the Arkansas gubernatorial term became four years.

This county level election return data illuminates some of the transforming events wrought in American political parties by such personalities as southern native-son Presidents Johnson and Carter, Republican Presidents Reagan and Bush, and presidential hopefuls Wallace and Buchanan on the right, and Jesse Jackson on the left.

The data help to capture recent and contemporary party politics in Arkansas and provide some perspective on the party. For instance, one of the central southern figures who sought to preserve the Democratic party's historical character and image on race was Orval Faubus. It was to Arkansas that President Eisenhower sent the 101st Airborne Division to force Governor Faubus, a strong segregationist, to obey the law of the land. Although his era was in the 1950s and 1960s, Faubus reemerged to run against incumbent Governor Clinton in the 1986 Democratic primary. The past was played out once again in the future.

The Clinton election return data are both rich and varied. The data offer insights into the southern native-son variable as well as into both the Democratic and Republican parties.

Clinton's Election Data: A Demographic Approach

To view the rise of Arkansas's first native-son President and to learn something about the nature and meaning of elections as well as the redefinition of the Democratic party's character and image, it is essential to structure and organize the county level election return data so as to demonstrate in empirical terms the patterns and trends in this historically one-party state as well as the manner in which this native-son President over his 21 elections fashioned his winning and losing political coalitions. To achieve this, the county level election return data have been categorized demographically.

This established methodological approach was used in Key's classic *Southern Politics*. Using county level election returns data, Key established the characteristics of historically one-party states in his insights about uni-, bi-, and multiparty factionalism in southern politics. His demographic characterizations advanced the discipline's understanding of one-party systems in a democratic political order. And his demographic organization of county level election data revealed the tendencies of the electorate in southern politics as well as its unique party politics.[9]

Following Key's pioneering use of county level election return data, J. Morgan Kousser employed similar data to describe the foundations of the South's one-party system.[10] With these data Kousser explains how the Democratic party came to dominate southern politics and eliminate its rival, the Republican party, as an electoral force in the region's state and presidential politics.

Using the same methodology, Gerald Gaither analyzed an important event that shaped political party history, character, and image—the populist revolt in the South. This work showed in empirical terms how the electorate in a historically one-party region can be drawn by economic and agrarian concerns into new party alliances.[11] Gaither's book showed that southern Democratic partisans could be dealigned and realigned with a new political entity, the Populist party. Such activity was an attempt to redefine and remake the Democratic party's image. It failed.

The Key, Kousser, and Gaither books cover the entire South. A recent prizewinning book by Raymond Arsenault uses historic county level election return data from Arkansas to explain the transformation of Democratic party politics in the state at the turn of the 20th century. Of the importance of demographic categorization, Arsenault notes:

> The cultural split between town and country was the primary basis for Democratic factionalism in early twentieth-century Arkansas. This is not surprising, since the urban-rural cleavage was the deepest division in white Arkansas society. . . . To some degree, Arkansas's farmers and town dwellers, despite their economic interdependence, had always lived in separate worlds.[12]

In the Arsenault book, county level election return data on the South in general, and Arkansas in particular, indicated a political conflict based on "geocultural rather than ethnocultural" forces. In the main, electoral politics in the South and Arkansas was "a politics of cultural resistance embedded in the demographic realities of its population."[13] Arsenault's work makes a compelling case for the demographic rendering of Arkansas's 75 counties. Besides this study, there are others on the state of Arkansas that make the same case.[14] There is a rich intellectual tradition at both the state and regional levels for using a demographic ordering of the state's 75 counties.

My initial work on a southern native-son president analyzed the demographics of Georgia's 159 counties and yielded a rich set of insights, established empirically based testable propositions, and generated a number of interesting hypotheses about this variable. A replication of such demographic ordering not only ensures comparability with the earlier study, but also offers an opportunity for further refinement and additional analyses.

Insights synthesized from two case studies built on a similar analytic structure and set of demographic topologies will provide a much stronger collection of insights than those based on facts from two distinct case studies.

Table 3.2 provides the quantitative pattern that emerges when Arkansas counties are characterized demographically. Seventy of the 75 counties are placed into three demographic categories: (1) rural—counties with populations of 5,500 to 10,700, (2) town—counties with populations of 10,701 to 29,999, and (3) urban—counties with populations of 30,000 to 350,000. The remaining 5 counties are put into special categories. Hempstead and Garland are President Clinton's home counties.[15] By isolating the President's home counties (Carter had only one) it is possible to see how "friends and neighbors" supported Clinton over his 21 elections. The other counties in the special category are the three African American

TABLE 3.2 The Number and Percentage of Arkansas Counties in the
Demographic Categories by Decades

DEMOGRAPHIC CATEGORIES	1970s		1980s		1990s	
Rural	21	(28%)	14	(19%)	15	(20%)
Town	34	(45%)	36	(48%)	35	(47%)
Urban	15	(20%)	20	(27%)	20	(27%)
SPECIAL CATEGORIES						
Clinton Home Counties*	2	(3%)	2	(3%)	2	(3%)
Black Belt Counties**	3	(4%)	3	(4%)	3	(4%)
Total	75	(100%)	75	(101%)	75	(101%)

*President Clinton was born in Hempstead county and lived there until his family moved to Hot
  Springs, which is in Garland county.
**Black Belt counties are those in which African Americans make up more than 51% of the population.

counties. In each of these three counties—Chicot, Lee, and Phillips—
African Americans made up more than 51 percent of the population and
have done so since the Civil War. These counties remained African American majority counties over the three decades of Clinton's 21 elections.

Election data are carefully gathered, collected, and stored according to
political parties, making the second major demographic group, the blacks,
the most difficult group in the state's electorate to follow. But because this
group is one of the key forces in Arkansas politics and because it is important to reveal the role that they played in Clinton's elections, these counties have been separated out for analysis.[16]

While African Americans have been the majority in these counties,
they have not served as elected officials in these counties until very recently. In Lee and Phillips counties the African American electorate had to
bring legal suits to become elected officials. Even though they have not
been a part of the governing coalition in these counties, they have been a
very active electorate and quite supportive of the Democratic party. In
addition, several African American urban precincts have been analyzed,
to further explore and explain the voting behavior of this segment of the
state electorate. Of the importance of this segment of the electorate,
Arkansas political scientist Diane Blair asserts: "It is assumed that Clinton received over 95 percent of the black vote in 1982; clearly, these 90,000
or so voters were a key part of his 78,000 vote margin."[17] By omitting this
segment of the state's electorate one might miss a major balance-of-power
force in state elections.

Thus Arkansas's 75 counties have been divided into demographic and special categories for analytical purposes, with further subdivisions to provide greater insight and interpretation.

Moving beyond the initial column in table 3.2, the next columns provide a decade by decade grouping of the changes in these analytical categories. It is crucial that our analytical construct reflect population shifts over three decades. If the state's population did not have any changes it would be necessary to have a static analytical construct—as in the case of Georgia.[18]

In Arkansas there were significant population changes at the county level between 1970 and 1980, with more stability in the decade 1980–1990. The population of rural counties declined and then steadied. A similar pattern prevailed for the town and urban counties.

The collection and analysis of the election return data took these shifts in population into account. There were no comparable shifts in the special counties.

Theorists and Their Methodological Techniques: A New Beginning

In the most comprehensive work on Arkansas politics to date, Professor Blair reminds us of the many ways in which demographically characterized county level election data can inform one's political analysis of the state, when she writes:

> Traditional Arkansas politics stemmed from ruralism and agrarianism, from economic dependency and physical isolation, from widespread poverty in material terms and severe malnutrition of mind and spirit. Above all, it stemmed from the encompassing supreme purpose of suppressing the black race. . . . County voting patterns . . . are very broadly descriptive [but] even with such caveats [they] offer important insight into strong and significant regional [demographic] tendencies in contemporary Arkansas politics.[19]

Arsenault, writing of the past in Arkansas, comes to a strikingly similar conclusion about a methodology rooted in the state's demography. He mentions that

> a cultural polarity between agrarian and new South subcultures fueled the fires of agrarian insurgency and encouraged bifactionalism; yet at the same time the almost inherent ambiguity of a cultural cleavage

based primarily on geography insured that this conflict could stop short of disrupting the one-party system or of effectively challenging the status quo.[20]

Arkansas was and is a one-party—Democratic—state, and its political rifts and clashes will be best discerned at the county level, past and present. However a recent observer remarked that

> In the 1990s . . . slow but steady Republican growth of the "top-down" variety is finally occurring in Arkansas. This growth is all the more impressive for its incremental pace, which proceeded unabated during 1992, 1994, and 1996, despite a set of in-state electoral disturbances.[21]
>
> In 1994, Clinton's troubled presidency dominated the public square in his home state, to the detriment of candidates competing for lesser offices. In 1996, the conviction of Clinton's 1990 running mate and successor, Governor Jim Guy Tucker, during the first Whitewater trial, headlined a parade of scandals that thinned the ranks of the state's Democratic establishment and seemed to open several windows of opportunity for Arkansas Republicans.[22]

As a result, "the Republicans not only captured the governorship by default but also held on to [Mike] Huckabee's vacated office [the lieutenant governorship] and gained David Pryor's Senate seat, as well." As of this writing, Republicans control 50 percent of the state's congressional delegation, as well as the offices of governor and lieutenant governor.[23] In the state legislature, Republicans advanced from 9 seats to 14 seats. The one-party nature of Arkansas politics is only slowly yielding. When Clinton entered state politics, it had been a certainty.

To learn how Clinton entered this party system, found a political floor, and built a coalition that essentially sustained him over 21 elections, it is crucial to adopt measurement techniques that are both sensitive to the peculiar historical one-party nature of the state as well as being linked to previous studies for purposes of continuity. Therefore the data that flow for this demographic structuring of the election return data have been analyzed based on measures of central tendency, measures of association, and measures of bivariate regression.[24]

Figure 3.1 provides an overview of the methodological techniques used. The first column provides the name of the theorist and the order in which

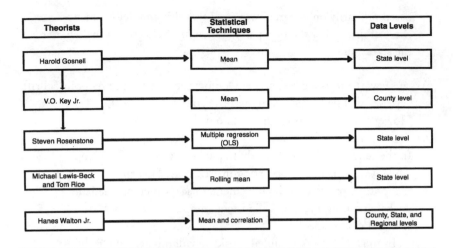

FIGURE 3.1 The Theorists and Their Methodological Techniques

Harold Gosnell, *Grass Roots Politics: National Voting Behavior of Typical States* (New York: Russell and Russell, 1970).

their work appeared. The second column lists the specific statistical methodology that the theorist used in providing an empirical basis for his or her interpretations and findings. Three of the researchers used the mean; one, multiple regression (OLS); and one, the mean combined with correlations. The mean statistical technique is the dominant methodology. The third column provides the level from which the election return data were taken and to which the methodology was applied. Although the state level dominates, recent studies have drawn from all three levels.

It can be concluded that there is essentially a dominant methodological technique in the literature and that the current methods used in this new study are not only linked to previous studies, but offer a chance for refinements with the correlation procedures. The aim in this new study is not only to have and establish continuity with the earlier literature in terms of one method, but where possible to used new methods that promise rich and more meaningful insights.

Thus this study of Bill Clinton as a native-son presidential candidate is not only grounded in empirical research but rooted in earlier studies of this variable.

Part Two

The Political Context of a
Native-Son Candidate

Native-son candidates such as Johnson, Wallace, Carter, and Clinton are politically made, not born. They come to political maturity and attain political age from a political landscape and terrain. They are made in the political dust and soil, political air and atmosphere, of their own native states, wherever they maybe. For Bill Clinton, it was Arkansas.

Political scientist professor Diane Blair, a friend and adviser to Bill Clinton, has been an astute observer of her native state and has recorded the vicissitudes of its political terrain and climate. Here is what she found about the political context that bought Bill Clinton to political birth and made him a native-son presidential candidate:

> The hallmarks of traditional Arkansas politics were a nonparticipat-ing public; a corrupted and unrepresentative electoral process; absolute domination by one political party; issueless campaigns; the deliberate subordination of the black race and the systematic exclu-sion of women; an unresponsive, often self-serving, and frequently ineffective governing elite; and a reactionary thrust to public policy.[1]

Central to the political environment of Arkansas are (1) a historically one-party system, (2) the white electorate, and (3) the African American elec-torate. And these central elements have all been tied or held together at different moments by race. While diminished in its unifying power, it still stalks the land. It was in this political context that Bill Clinton emerged and evolved.

Figure 2.1 reveals the strength of historic Democratic one-partyism in Arkansas in every presidential election from 1900 through 1996. The turn of the twentieth century was chosen as the point of departure for the analysis because, by the time of that election, the white electorate in Arkansas had disenfranchised the African American electorate and rebuilt and redesigned the Democratic party in the state to advance and promote the ideology and institutions of white supremacy. The figure shows not only the relationship of these 24 presidential elections to each other, but how party loyalty, in this instance, Democratic partisanship, in one election permits the prediction of subsequent elections in precise empirical terms.

Mean party loyalty for these 24 presidential elections in Arkansas stands at 55 percent. Voting behavior in Arkansas rested more on Democratic partisanship and party loyalty than on any other factor or variable. One-partyism truly had left a legacy on the political environment of the razorback state. Knowing how Democratic partisans voted in 1900 would enable an observer to predict exactly how 50 percent of them would vote in 1904, 52 percent in 1908, and 50 percent in 1912. Democratic partisanship as the key factor in shaping and structuring future party voting behavior peaked at 92 percent in the 1936–1940 presidential election cycle: knowing how Democrats voted in 1936 would permit one to forecast how 92 percent of them would vote in 1940. After the 92 percent high point, partisanship bottomed out in the 1948 presidential election. Only 2 percent of the Democratic vote could be forecast from the 1944 election. Things in the state truly changed by the 1948 presidential election. Democratic party loyalty after the 1948 election began to reemerge as the central factor in explaining presidential voting behavior. Between 1948 and 1956 party loyalty jumped from 12 percent to 79 percent. But the turbulent 1960s would bring it down again to 5 percent. The Republican era of Reagan and Bush, along with the Clinton presidential runs, restored Democratic party loyalty in Arkansas to new levels, almost near the peak set in the 1936–1940 presidential seasons.

Democratic party partisanship in a historically one-party state left some room for political issues and candidates as well as political events to determine how individuals would vote. Party loyalty and Democratic partisanship shaped over 50 percent of the state electorate's voting behavior in all but 7 of these elections.

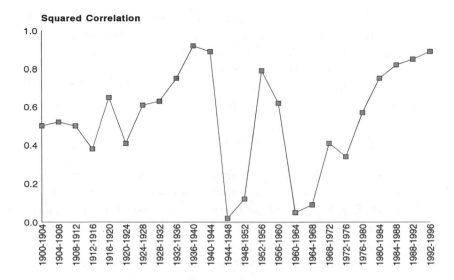

Squared Correlation

FIGURE PART 2.1 The Percentage of Arkansas's Presidential Election Vote
Determined by Democratic Partisanship: Squared Correlations of Paired Presidential Elections, 1900–1996

Adapted from McGillivray and Scammon, *America at the Polls, 1920–1956 and 1960–1992* (Washington, D.C.: Congressional Quarterly Press, 1994); Sharon Priest, "November 5, 1996 General Election Results" (Little Rock: Office of the Secretary of State, 1997), 1–2.

Democratic partisanship, while stable in this one-party state, does fluctuate in presidential elections. Outside forces exert an influence. In the 1912–1916 period there was the matter of progressivism. In the New Deal period, there was the matter of economic recovery and need. By 1944–1948, the states rights issue of the Dixiecrats and Truman's civil rights program came to the fore. In the 1960s, it was Faubus, and the African American freedom movement. Liberal Democratic standard-bearers like Humphrey and McGovern had an effect on partisanship, followed by southern native-son candidates Carter and Clinton.

The third element on the political terrain of Arkansas is the African American. Originally the context was that of slavery and oppression. "Under slavery, blacks lived where masters decided they needed them most. . . . Under slavery, paternalism and its myths forged slave mentality [and] masters dominated much of a slave's conceptions of the future."[2]

Therefore

Arkansas's 110,000 African Americans eagerly embraced freedom as
Northern armies conquered Confederates in Arkansas between 1862
and 1865. . . . Over five thousand Arkansas freedmen joined the
Union Army as it trekked across Arkansas from 1862 to 1865, to aid in
its quest for freedom. And when the war ended, The Freedmen's
Bureau entered the state to make freedom real.[3]

However by 1868 the Bureau was on its way out.

In 1868, many blacks and some whites feared for a future without the
bureau. . . . In contrast to freed persons, many whites rejoiced at the
prospect of the bureau's demise. Planters resented bureau interference
in contract disputes and longed for a return to antebellum days with
no outside intermediary for blacks.[4]

By the summer of 1869 the role of the Freedmen's Bureau in
Arkansas and in the South had, to use Langston Hughes's metaphor,
"dried up like a raisin in the sun."[5]

State Democrats moved nationally to ensure that no new outside interference would occur. Any rarely did until the 1950s. The Arkansas African
American community remained isolated and confined to the lower rungs
of society.

At last African Americans moved to shift their place in the political
context of Arkansas. They launched their counteroffensive in Little Rock
in September 1957. "The tragedy that placed Little Rock on the world
stage centered around Central High School, located in the heart of the
city. . . . The plans called for the entrance into Central High School of
nine Negro pupils when school opened on September 4, 1957."[6]

Georgia Governor Marvin Griffin and Georgia's state legislative
leader, Roy V. Harris, two of the South's most ardent segregationists,
rushed to comfort Governor Orval Faubus and Arkansas's concerned
white citizens. The crisis made Little Rock the center of the world.[7]

"Little Rock [became] the first desperate attempt by a State to maintain the old system by force of arms."[8] And in the struggle at Little Rock,
African Americans made a spectacular effort to alter their rigidly imposed
place on the state map. With the arrival of Bill Clinton onto the political
scene, African Americans continued the tradition launched at Little Rock.

While Clinton was governor, African Americans in Arkansas had to
once again invoke outside assistance, as they had done in Little Rock, to
shift positions on the political landscape. Beginning in 1988 the Legal

Defense Fund filed four suits, three naming the Democratic party, and one naming Governor Clinton, as defendants.[9] These efforts were led by Lani Guinier, a Yale University Law School classmate and friend of Governor Clinton, who sued the state and its Democratic party over its majority-vote primary runoff election laws under the Fourteenth and Fifteenth Amendments and the Voting Rights Act of 1965. Phillips county was cited as a demonstrable example because "no black candidate had ever been elect-ed to countywide or state legislative office from Phillips County and . . . race has frequently dominated over qualification and issues in elections."[10] In addition, "county officials have moved polling places ten times in as many elections, often without prior notice and sometimes to locations up to twelve to fifteen miles away, over dirt and gravel roads." And with 42 percent of blacks in the county with no car or truck and "30 percent of blacks [with] no telephone, . . . the election campaigns of black candidates must include a get-out-and-vote kind of funding effort that a poor black community simply cannot afford."[11] In this quest to attain equity in the political process, the court supported Governor Clinton. "The court . . . preferred to stick with this obviously unfair electoral scheme, reasoning that the majority should prevail even when the majority is the product of a completely artificial and racially exclusionary runoff system."[12]

Guinier wrote: "The Court failed to see that the unfairness wrought by a winner-take-all majority was inconsistent with democratic fair play in this county."[13] Nor did the five-term governor. Clinton did not try to work out the problems or settle out of court. He did not seek to get the contestants in Phillips county, which had so strongly supported him in his numerous electoral bids, to work out a comprise on their differences. Nor did he decide to help the larger African American community acquire political and electoral equity and fairness in his state.

Lani Guinier was later "nominated by President Clinton early in 1993 to be the administration's civil rights enforcement chief. Her nomination was withdrawn a few months later in the wake of an opposition campaign that evidently took a rookie White House staff by surprise."[14] President Clin-ton's eventual withdrawal of her nomination drew the African American community to her side. "For many blacks, my public ostracism was theirs, too. They identified in personal terms with what they saw as my repudia-tion."[15] The Democratic party lost control of the House of Representatives in 1994, when the African American voter turnout reached a new low.

While external forces tried to change the unfair electoral process which the African American electorate operated under, internal forces inside the state African American community also challenged other electoral procedures that disadvantaged them. On May 16, 1988, black registered voters in a dual-member Arkansas state legislative district filed an action challenging the multi-level structure of that district on statutory and constitutional grounds.[16] Once again Clinton defended the state's at-large legislative structure which diluted African American voting power. Once again there was no compromise worked out. But this time the courts supported the African American group.

There were other cases filed in the same period, such as *Perkins v. City of West Helena, Arkansas* (675 F. 2d 201 1982) and *Campbell et al. v. Lee County Election Committee* (No. H.C. 48–86), but they did not name the governor. Yet he did not come forth on their behalf nor did he seek to redress the situation with a political solution.

During his final gubernatorial term, a suit naming the governor arose dealing with judicial elections.

> [In 1988] the Rev. Marion Humphrey, a black lawyer, was elected municipal judge of Little Rock by a plurality. Little Rock . . . had not been subject to a majority-vote requirement. But after Judge Humphrey's election, the Legislature reacted quickly. It passed Act 905 of 1989, subjecting municipal offices in all cities and towns to a majority-vote requirement.[17]

Within a year African Americans sued Governor Clinton and the Arkansas Board of Apportionment, on which the governor serves as one of three members, for a judicial system of elections based on districts and plurality electoral outcomes. The Federal district court held for the plaintiffs. Governor Clinton and his secretary of state appealed the ruling, and the case followed the governor-turned-president in his initial White House years.[18] During this term in office, the Justice Department worked out a Consent Decree with the state, and several African Americans were elected judges. Afterwards a Republican group backed an Asian American in a suit against the state over these new district judges.

In the final analysis, a southern governor who saw himself as progressive, and whom many called a new progressive, acted much less than progressively on the matter of racial political participation in his state. He continued the tradition of the Democratic party's combativeness with the African American electorate.[19] Later, in an essay on African American voting rights, he would conveniently forget his less than progressive response and shift the focus to the issue of elected officials not being responsive to their constituencies. Barriers to the full exercise of the ballot were not the problem, unresponsive officials were. This was a clever way to sidestep his confrontational politics on behalf of the Democratic party.[20]

Embedded in the political context of Arkansas are both a cooperative and conflicted relationship among the state's historic one-partyism, the white electorate, and the African American electorate. A majority of the white electorate has struggled to define and use the hegemonic party to dominate its African American population. Likewise the African American population, out of necessity, has sought to use the same party to eliminate its oppression and raise its status in the state. Thus conflict has been more frequent than has cooperation.

When it has suited the white electorate, they have discounted their Democratic partisan leanings and loyalty and have supported the Dixiecrats, George Wallace, or the Republicans, with their overt and covert southern strategy.

In this combative and contentious political atmosphere, where cooperation was rare and limited, Bill Clinton evolved as a native-son presidential candidate.

> No President has yet come to office free of a past in which he himself did not benefit, at some stage, from the social power of white hostility. This should be no surprise. Innocence is a rare quality in political life. Such is the nature of the culture.[21]

Such is the nature of the political context of Arkansas.

The following chapter is devoted to the white Arkansas electorate and their relationship to the Democratic party, while chapter 5 covers the African American electorate.

CHAPTER FOUR

The Arkansas Electorate

In 1974 William Jefferson Clinton offered himself as a Democratic candidate in the 3rd Congressional district primary. At his entry into elective politics, the Arkansas political landscape and environment had a partisan character. Since the Civil War, partisan patterns and trends had been evolving and maturing. The state electorate had definite voting patterns, many of which had endured for nearly 110 years, from the era of the Civil War through to Bill Clinton's emergence as a political candidate.

Of the partisan parameters of Arkansas, V.O. Key wrote in 1948: "Most southern states exhibit in their politics some salient feature that gives each a distinctive character. . . . Perhaps in Arkansas we have the one-party system in its most undefiled and undiluted form."[1] Four decades later, after the civil rights revolution, when the South was realigning, Arkansas stood still. Two state observers noted: "Arkansas's presidential votes went more consistently and heavily Democratic than did those of any other state, and Democrats traditionally swept state and local offices as well, usually uncontested."[2]

However there was some partisan movement.

In 1968, Arkansas became the last southern state to deny its electoral votes to the Democratic presidential candidate . . . supporting Wallace over Nixon. . . . In 1972, it became the last southern state to actually vote Republican for president, supporting Nixon over McGovern.[3]

In 1980, 1984, and 1988, it backed Reagan and Bush. But in 1976, 1992, and 1996, southern native-son candidates brought the state back into the Democratic fold. Arkansas veered from its one-partyism in five presidential elections during the post–civil rights era.

All of these scholarly observers remark that since the Civil War, the Arkansas electorate has been essentially one-party in nature. With few exceptions the state's voters have been Democratic partisans at the presidential, congressional, and local levels. And this electorate was one-party in nature even before the Civil War.

Almost from the inception of parties in Arkansas, the electorate voted almost exclusively for the Democratic party and its antecedents. The electorate voted consistently Democratic from statehood in 1836 until 1968. "Arkansans have been in a standing decision to be Democrats."[4] The southern presidencies of Johnson, Carter, and Clinton have helped the state electorate continue its one-partyism. In the antebellum era, the electorate supported the local and state Democratic party much more than it did the national party. In the current era, only in the 1980 election did support for the national party nearly equal that for the state party. Despite upheavals, crises, and insurgent rebellions, voters has stayed with the Democratic party despite generational changes and the mobility of the electorate.

If events, crises, and the changing electorate did not alter the one-partyism of the state, neither did the endless parade of political candidates, elected officials, and political elites. The party's leadership has extended and prolonged the party's hold over the electorate and state political institutions. Under diverse leaders and over time, the Democratic party has thrived. Even while the South and most of the states inside the region have realigned or dealigned from the Democratic party, the Arkansas electorate has kept its substantial Democratic partisanship. In Arkansas, the "tradition of independence leads voters to cast ballots for attractive Republican candidates without abandoning their Democratic affiliation."[5]

The Democratic party's hegemony in the state has had one bedrock: the glue of race. Before the Civil War it was slavery, while after it was segregation. Before the civil rights era it was white supremacy, while after it has been limited desegregation.[6] Race has remained a source of continuity for the party. It has been the force for all seasons, and even as the seasons have changed, the racial subordination stance of the party has only slowly evolved.

When Bill Clinton arrived on the political landscape in Arkansas he was faced with two significant contextual realities: the state's electorate was and has been Democratic, and it had been and was Democratic because of its negative posture on the race issue. To establish himself, as a political neophyte, he did what Carter had done in Georgia, and Lyndon Johnson in Texas—he became a Democrat. He had to accommodate the question of race both within the party and within the electorate. The question of the politics of accommodation is a matter for a later chapter; here we describe and explain the empirical dimension of the one-partyism of the Arkansas electorate.

The Size and Turnout of the Arkansas Electorate

Since official voter registration and voting data on the Arkansas electorate have only been collected and published for the periods 1878 to 1924 and 1976 to 1996, the best way to see this electorate in a longitudinal manner is to look at the actual numbers of votes cast in presidential, congressional, and gubernatorial elections. Figure 4.1 provides an overview from 1868 to 1996. The vote for presidential candidates constantly rose over the years, the congressional vote fluctuated with off-year elections, as did the senatorial vote in odd and even years.

In presidential years, the numbers of congressional and senatorial votes are nearly identical. There was little roll-off of the vote in national contests. The Arkansas electorate voted nearly the same for all national candidates. This pattern was established before the Civil War,[7] and was maintained during Reconstruction and into the twentieth century. The electorate paid attention to national elections, particularly to local candidates who ran for national offices.

Although the disenfranchisement of the African American electorate reduced the vote count between 1888 and 1916, population growth permitted the voting electorate to grow before the turn of the century. The size of the electorate eventually caught up with pre-1900 figures in about two decades, when women entered the electorate.

Yet even with this reduced electorate, people in Arkansas who could, voted in a balanced fashion in presidential and congressional contests. This was not the pattern in Georgia. For example, congressional and senatorial voting did not match presidential voting there. In terms of votes cast in Georgia, there was a definite roll-off between the presidential ballot and other national contests. Unlike Arkansas, the Georgia electorate had a historical pattern of greater support for congressional candidates than presidential ones.

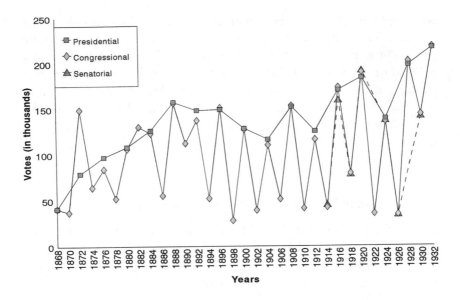

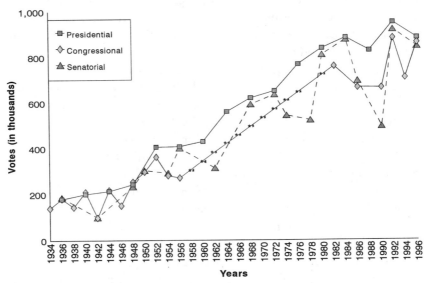

FIGURE 4.1 The Total Votes Cast in Arkansas's Presidential, Congressional, and Senatorial Elections, 1868–1996

*Adapted from Congressional Quarterly, *Guide to U.S. Elections* 3d ed. (Washington, D.C.: Congressional Quarterly Press, 1994).

*The votes were rounded off.

**Arkansas election law did not permit the recording of votes when only one candidate stands for election.

The Arkansas electorate had a significant voting coherence in national contests.

Party Voting in Presidential Elections in Arkansas

Beyond the size of the electorate is the question of the actual turnout of eligible voters in different elections. Given the gaps in the official collected state election data records, it is necessary to turn to federal election statistics collected by the Bureau of the Census, to provide a comprehensive longitudinal perspective on voter turnout in presidential elections. Figure 4.2 provides the percentages of the Arkansas electorate that actual voted in the 33 presidential elections between 1868 and 1996. Immediately noticeable is the significant and drastic drop-off in voter turnout after the 1888 presidential election and its steady decline until the 1964 presidential election. In these 19 elections—58 percent of the total—race was a major

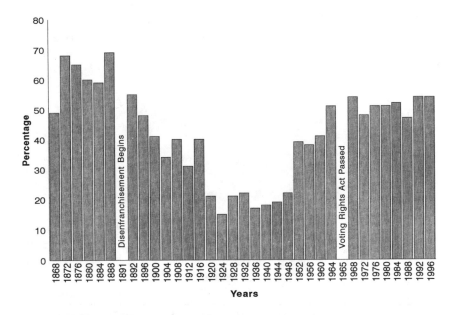

FIGURE 4.2 Voter Turnout in Arkansas for Presidential Elections, 1868–1996

Bureau of the Census, *Historical Statistics of the United States: Colonial Times to 1970* (Washington, D.C.: Government Printing Office, 1975) part 2, 1071–1072 for data through the 1968 election; Kimball Brace, ed., *The Election Data Book: A Statistical Portrait of Voting in America, 1992* (Lanham, Md.: Berman Press, 1993), 81 for data through the 1992 election; Priest, "November 5, 1996 General Election Results," 1–2.

factor. This turnout decline coincided with the disenfranchisement of African American voters (1891–1906) and the reenfranchisement of this vote in 1965 with the passage of the Voting Rights Act. The reappearance of the African American voter correlates with an abrupt resurgence of voter turnout in the state.

The second observable resurgence of voter turnout occurred in 1992 and 1996, the years in which the state's native son—Bill Clinton—was running for the presidency. Clinton, like native son Carter, mobilized the state electorate to go to the ballot box in near-record numbers. The only other time that the electorate responded in such record numbers was when another native son of the region was running— Alabama's George Wallace—in 1968, on a racial subordination agenda. Wallace proved that race still mattered to the state electorate. He won the state, beating both the Democratic and Republican presidential candidates.

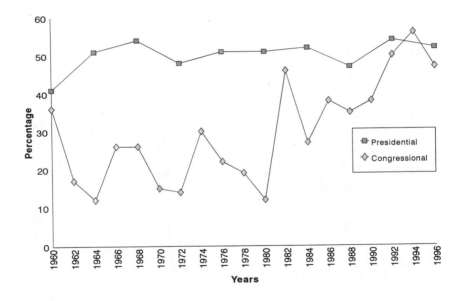

FIGURE 4.3 A Comparison of Voter Turnout in Arkansas's Presidential and Congressional Elections, 1960–1996

Bureau of the Census, "Projections of the Population of Voting Age for States: November 1976," CPS Series No. 626 (May 1976), 9; "Projections of the Voting Age Population for States: November 1988," CPS Series P-25; "Projections of the Voting Age Population for States: November 1990," CPS Series P-25 No. 1059 (April 1990), 14; "Projections of the Voting Age Population for States: November 1994," CPS Series P-25; and "Projections of the Voting Age Population for States: November 1996," CPS Series P-25.

The Republican party's initial presidential victory in the state, in 1972, marks a point of turnout decline, as does the Republican party's most recent victory in the state, in 1988.

In these 33 elections, the lowest turnout occurred in 1924, when 15 percent of the eligible voters went to the polls, while the highest turnout was in 1888, when 69 percent of voters went to the ballot box. The mean turnout is 42 percent.[8] Voter turnout in Arkansas in presidential elections is typical of states in the region.[9] And it was similar to the situation in Georgia when a native-son presidential candidate was running.

Knowing how many of the Arkansas electorate marched to the presidential ballot box leads directly to the question, for whom did they vote?

Except for seven presidential elections (1868, 1872, 1968, 1972, 1980, 1984, and 1988) the Democratic party has won the presidential vote in the state. Figure 4.4 shows that in 1968 a third party carried the state. Overall the Democrats have won 26 (79%) of the elections, Republicans have won 6 (18%), and a third party won once (3%).

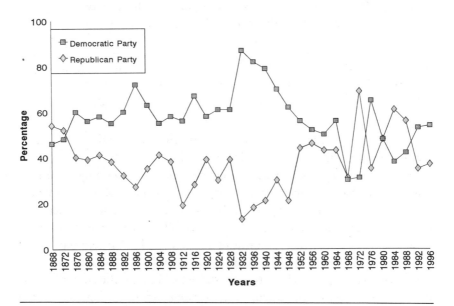

FIGURE 4.4 The Major Political Parties' Percentage of the Presidential Vote in Arkansas, 1868–1996

Bureau of the Census, *Historical Statistics of the United States: Colonial Times to 1970* part 2, 1077–1080 for data through the 1968 election; Scammon and McGillivray, eds., *America Votes 1994* (Washington, D.C.: Congressional Quarterly Press, 1995), 11–23 for data through the 1992 election; Priest, "November 5, 1996 General Election Results," 1–2.

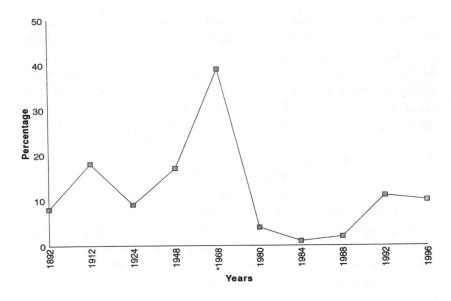

FIGURE 4.5 The Percentage of Votes for Significant Third Party
Presidential Candidates in Arkansas, 1892–1996

Bureau of the Census, *Historical Statistics of the United States: Colonial Times to 1970* part 2, 1077–1080
for data through the 1968 election; Scammon and McGillivray, eds., *America Votes 1994*, 11–23 for data
through the 1992 election; Priest, "November 5, 1996 General Election Results," 1–2. *In 1968, the
American Independent party, led by Alabama governor George Wallace, won all the state's electoral
college votes.

Figure 4.5 provides a comparative perspective on how this third-party
vote fits in over time, in an empirical rendering.

Figure 4.6 indicates that the Democratic party has won by large pluralities. The chart reveals that 1932 was the critical election year, in which
the Democratic party got 74 percent more of the vote than the Republicans. After that year the vote pluralities for the Democratic party declined
slowly, with some fluctuation, until 1972 when the Republican party captured the state with 38 percent more votes than the Democratic party. In
the preceding presidential election, Wallace had broken the state's Democratic hegemony and paved the way for the electorate to switch to the
Republican party. But in the very next election, another native son of the
region, Jimmy Carter, brought the state back into the Democratic party
with a 30 percent plurality.

Ronald Reagan recaptured the state with a mere 1 percent plurality in
1980, increasing to 23 percent in 1984. George Bush failed to mobilize as
many voters as Reagan, but still kept the state in the Republican column.

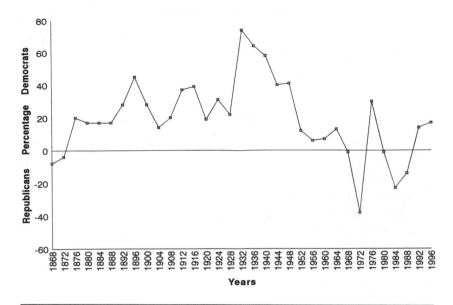

FIGURE 4.6 The Percentage of Party Pluralities in Presidential Elections in Arkansas, 1868–1996

Adapted from the data in figure 4.4 by subtracting the losing party's percentage from that of the winning party. In 1968, the American Independent party won the state with a 9% plurality over the Democrats and an 8% plurality over the Republicans.

However the inroads made by Reagan and Bush were lost when a native-son candidate carried the state in the 1992 and 1996 presidential elections by electoral pluralities of 14 and 17 points. As had Carter in Georgia, Clinton carried his southern state away from the Republican party back into the Democratic fold.

From 1968 to 1996, partisanship in Arkansas presidential elections shifted significantly, with almost complete reversals from one election to the next, moving from the Democratic party to George Wallace's American Independent party to the Republican party and finally back to the Democratic party. Partisanship volatility characterized the Arkansas vote in the last seven presidential elections of this period.

Before this, from 1876 to 1964, stability of Democratic party partisanship characterized the Arkansas vote in 23 elections. Key had it right in 1948. Historically, in presidential elections, Arkansas has been essentially a one-party state. And when this one-party partisanship has wavered, regional native sons—Johnson in 1964, Wallace in 1968, Carter in 1976—and their own native son, Bill Clinton, have won the state's votes and reattached the electorate to its historical partisan moorings.

Thus Bill Clinton came of age in a state with a strong Democratic past and partisanship in presidential elections. He was in lock-step with the Arkansas of his past and present. And he has carried the state into the political future by realigning it with its past.

Party Voting in Congressional Elections in Arkansas

Figure 4.1 indicates that voter turnout in presidential years has been basically steady. This was not true in off-year elections, which saw a substantial decrease in the total number of votes cast in congressional elections. Except for off-year elections, the Arkansas electorate casts nearly the same number of votes in presidential, congressional, and senatorial elections. This is unique since in most states there is a drop off of voting for offices below that of the presidency. Yet in Arkansas the level of turnout has meant a consistent or near consistent level of voter support for national candidates; in the main, for candidates of a single political party.

When the Seventeenth Amendment in 1913 decreed the popular election of United States Senators, the Arkansas electorate had already established its partisan habits: the party leaders had prevailed. In the initial popular election for a Senate seat, the electorate gave 75 percent of its vote to the Democratic candidate. Although this would change in the 1916 senatorial election when the Republican candidate got 31 percent of the vote, in the early years the highest vote for the Republican party came in 1920 (34%), the year that African American voters vigorously reasserted themselves in state politics.

The highest vote for the Republican party came in 1984 when it received 43 percent of the senatorial vote. Otherwise in Senate elections the Democratic party has reigned supreme. From 1914 until 1996 the Democratic party captured and held every Senate seat in the state. The Arkansas electorate has been content to send an unbroken string of Democrats to the United States Senate, including two women, Mrs. Hattie W. Caraway and Ms. Blanche Lambert Lincoln.[10] Senate elections in Arkansas have been, and are, Democratic affairs.

Although senatorial elections are statewide affairs, congressional elections are district-based. From the Civil War to the Goldwater election of 1964, Republican partisans were found in the northwest corner of the state, and in the Black Belt counties in the east when African Americans had the vote. After disenfranchisement, which began in the 1892 election, the axis of Republican partisan strength shifted to the northwestern counties, in which the Republican vote could reach more than 50 percent.

In the first academic assessment of the Republican party in Arkansas,

Alexander Heard writes: "The Ozarks of Arkansas, covering roughly the northwest triangle of that state, explain where Republican Arkansasers are found in greatest strength."[11] These were mountain Republicans. Yet this Republican bastion did not yield any congressmen. It was the Black Belt counties, with their African American voting majorities in 1868, 1870, and 1872, that gave the state its first Republicans in Congress—two in 1868, and one each in 1870 and 1872. Afterwards the Democratic party captured every congressional seat until 1966. The axis of the party had moved from the eastern part of the state to the urban centers of its northwest. From this urban and suburban base the Republican party would gain one congressional seat before 1992, and two of the state's four congressional seats after 1992.

When African American Republicans disappeared, so did Republican congressmen from the state. The mountain Republicans who remained were not able to sustain an elected official, or even a stable field of Republican candidates, to contest congressional seats. Figure 4.6 reveals the actual number of congressional seats at each election contested by the Republican party. From 1876 to 1974 the number of Republican candidates willing to contest congressional seats is wildly erratic. Either the party could not find candidates, or the candidates were not convinced that enough of a Republican base existed to give them a chance at victory. Only in the first four elections (1868–1874) and the most recently analyzed four (1986–1994) did the Republican party maintain some degree of consistency.[12] Alexander Heard, using a 5 percent cut-off, discovered that between 1920 and 1950, in a total of 112 races, the Republican party offered candidates for only 35 percent of House seats and for only 64 percent of the 14 senatorial races.[13] At the congressional level, Arkansas Republicans had either to back candidates of other parties or not vote. As with the Senate elections, the Democratic hegemony at the presidential level reproduced itself in House elections. This default voting had an impact on the mean percentage of the Republican congressional vote in the state.

With the disappearance of the African American vote, the mean percentage of the vote for the Republican party declined, and it has continued below the 50 percent mark until the present day. The wild fluctuations of the Republican vote indicated in figure 4.7 reveal that the party did not grow and evolve in any consistent or continuous fashion. The state's Republicanism in congressional elections changed from one election to the next. Only in 1980, with the Reagan-led national Republican tide, did party fortunes start to shift, but the Republican revolution was not able to sustain itself. Republican partisanship once again declined in the 1984, 1986, and 1990 elections. However in 1992 and 1996 another Republican surge started to appear. Whether it will sustain itself into the 21st century remains to be seen.

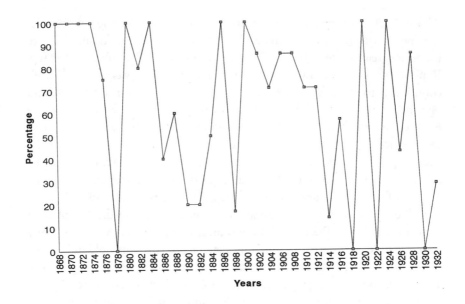

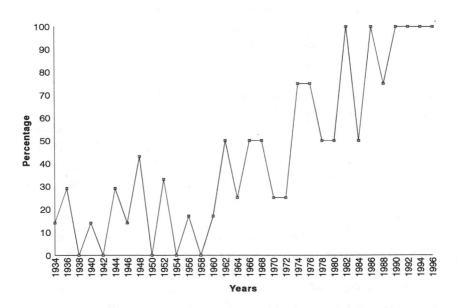

FIGURE 4.7 The Percentage of Congressional Seats Contested by the Republican Party in Arkansas, 1868–1996

Adapted from Congressional Quarterly, *Guide to U.S. Elections* 3d ed., 943–1321.

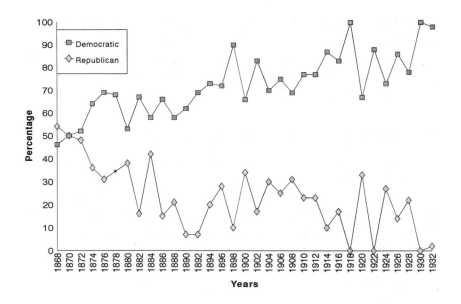

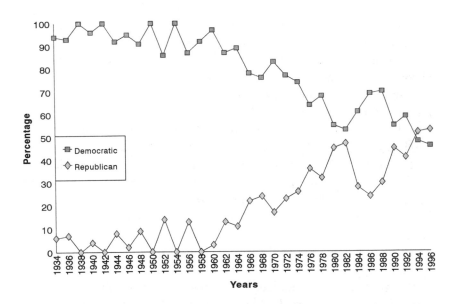

FIGURE 4.8 A Comparison of the Mean Percentage of Democratic and Republican Votes in Arkansas's Congressional Elections, 1868–1996

Adapted from Congressional Quarterly, *Guide to U.S. Elections* 3d ed., 943–1321. *In 1878, the Republican party merged with several third parties.

The clear and consistent trend is that Democratic partisanship has persisted through depressions, world wars, and Republican presidential dominance of both the White House and Congress. It has been enduring. At the presidential, senatorial, and congressional levels, in the words of V. O. Key Jr., Arkansas has historically been nearly an undiluted one-party state.

Party Voting in Gubernatorial Elections in Arkansas

Moving the analysis of the Arkansas electorate from national contests to a state office shows other features of this electorate, notably the turnout realities of primary and general elections. Numerous observers have noted that in the South more votes are cast in primary contests than in general elections. Since this is a one-party region, the real contests are the Democratic party primaries.

It has been noted that such is the case in Georgia. "Where actual votes are analyzed, a major factor about the electorate stands out: more Georgians vote in the Democratic primaries than in the general election."[14] How close does the Arkansas electorate come to matching its sister state's?

The data in figure 4.8 reveal a mixed pattern. From 1922 until 1950, turnout in Arkansas was greater in primaries than in general elections. Since 1952, except for 1962 and 1974, more people in Arkansas have turned out in general election contests than in primaries. For part of its electoral history, Arkansas has resembled the typical southern state, where primary elections were paramount. But more recently, Arkansas has reversed its traditional turnout pattern in gubernatorial elections and now turns out in record numbers in the general election. In a one-party state that has sent few Republicans to the state house, this is to say the least unusual.

For much of the state's history, gubernatorial contests were biennial. Of the 60 elections from 1872 to 1994, Democratic candidates have won 93 percent of the time, losing only in 1872, 1966, 1968, and 1980. The Democratic partisanship of the state electorate asserted itself at the gubernatorial level.

Unlike the congressional contests which also took place every two years, in only 6 of the 60 elections did the Republican party not put forth a gubernatorial candidate. Heard points out that in the 8 gubernatorial elections he analyzed within the period 1920 and 1950, Republican candidates for governor received more than 5 percent of the vote in 88 percent of those elections.[15] Republican voters had a chance in gubernatorial elections to express their party preference. But in contest after contest, the Arkansas electorate expressed a preference for the Democratic candidate.

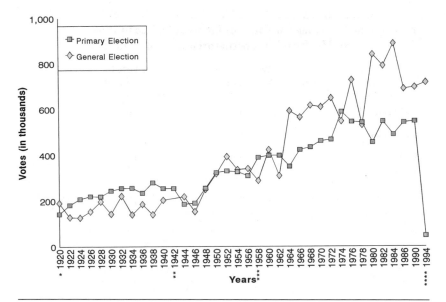

FIGURE 4.9   The Total Votes Cast in Arkansas's Gubernatorial Primaries
and General Elections, 1920–1994

Adapted from Heard and Strong, *Southern Primaries and Elections, 1920–1949* (Tuscaloosa: University
of Alabama Press, 1950), 21–36; *Guide to U.S. Elections* 3d ed.; and Priest, "November 5, 1996 General
Election Results."
*General election data for 1920 are incomplete.
**No data was reported for the 1942 general election.
***The votes in the Republican primary were combined with the votes in the Democratic primary.
****A Democratic primary was not held in 1994.

In 1970 George Wallace's American Independent party reconfigured
itself as the American party on the state level and ran Walter L. Carruth
for governor. He received 6 percent of the vote in that contest.

Table 4.1 demonstrates that Wallace was more of a force in energizing the state electorate around issues of race than was the gubernatorial
candidate. Wallace captured 38 percent of the vote to Carruth's 6 percent. In President Clinton's home counties, Wallace captured 39 percent
of the vote to Carruth's 8 percent. And in the Black Belt counties, Wallace got 39 percent to Carruth's 9 percent. At best, Carruth was a pale
imitation of his political mentor.[16] The simple correlation between the
Wallace vote and the Carruth vote is $r = .51$ while the $r^2 = .27$.

Even in 1970 there were still votes to be had in appealing to race and
racial cleavages. Although racism in the state had identified with and
evolved with the Democratic party, it also went beyond party in the
political culture.

TABLE 4.1 The Percentage of Votes for George Wallace in 1968 and for His Party's Gubernatorial Candidate in 1970

	% of Vote for Wallace in 1968	% of Vote for Carruth in 1970
Arkansas total	38	6
Home Counties		
Garland	34	11
Hempstead	43	4
Mean	39	8
Black Belt Counties		
Chicot	39	4
Lee	39	9
Phillips	37	14
Mean	39	9

Adapted from Scammon and McGillivray, *America Votes*, 25–26 and 34–35.

Support for the Democratic party in gubernatorial elections has been substantial. The Democrats have received nearly three out of every four votes cast from the era of disenfranchisement through the beginning of the 1960s. Only in the 1960s did the party support a homegrown Rockefeller over a well known segregationist, Orval Faubus. When first-term governor Bill Clinton faltered in 1980, the electorate sent a Republican, Frank White, to the State House. As in the Rockefeller victories, the Frank White victory had a particular contextual reality—in White's case, the Cuban refugees sent to the state by President Carter. Otherwise, gubernatorial Republicans have fared badly.

Arkansas voters have had a love affair with the Democratic party since the 1870s. Political leaders such as Jeff Davis have helped to forge solid Democratic partisanship in the state. Few political crises or economic changes have altered this partisan alignment. This alignment, and the partisan definition it created, allowed Clinton to rise to national power. Like President Carter, another native son, President Clinton has furthered the tradition and the foundations of this state partisanship. The question remains how well it can be projected into the future.

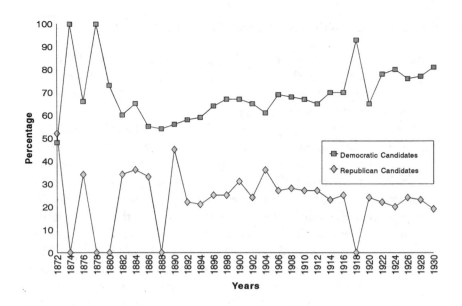

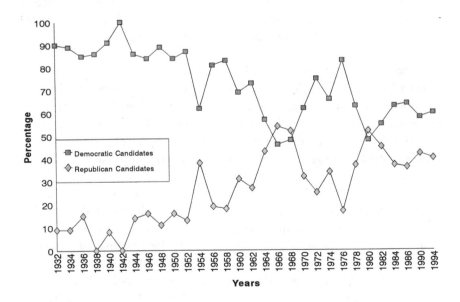

FIGURE 4.10   The Vote Percentage for Democratic and Republican
Gubernatorial Candidates, 1872–1994

Adapted from *Guide to U.S. Elections* 3d ed., 491–2. Data for the period 1988 to 1994 were taken from the
election results issued by the Arkansas Secretary of State.

Party Voting in the Presidential Home Counties

If partisanship is a contextual as well as a psychological matter, by analyzing the partisan vote in the county where the President was born as well as in the county where he grew up, we can get some sense of the partisan context of the President's political environment.

The mean party vote percentage for Garland and Hempstead counties appears in figure 4.11. Except for 8 of the 33 presidential elections—1868, 1872, 1904, 1952, 1956, 1972, 1984, and 1988—the mean vote in these counties has been Democratic. The President's home counties have carried the Democratic banner, as the total mean stands at 54 percent Democratic and 42 percent Republican. Like the state electorate, these two counties have marked Democratic allegiances. Besides the Republican years, only George Wallace's 1968 third-party effort displaced the Democrats. Wallace captured 43 percent of the Hempstead county vote and 34 percent of the Garland county vote. (Surprisingly, the Dixiecrat movement of 1948 did not fare quite as well as the Wallace movement. In 1948, the Dixiecrats got 15 percent in Garland county and 32 percent in Hempstead county, for a mean vote of 24 percent.) The Wallace candidacy got a mean vote of 39 percent. Race and racism had an electoral base in the President's home counties.

The future president evolved and was nurtured in counties with a strong Democratic partisanship. His friends and neighbors were Democratic voters. Local politics, or localism as V. O. Key Jr. calls it, was a Democratic affair. In his home counties Bill Clinton heard national politics discussed and electorally resolved in Democratic terms. With few exceptions, these counties backed Democratic presidential candidates.

At the state level this Democratic dominance held with few exceptions, as traditional support for the Democratic gubernatorial candidate endured. The percentages in figure 4.11 indicate that Democratic partisanship in gubernatorial elections is substantial in a longitudinal fashion. The electoral context nurtured Bill Clinton in a Democratic direction. The rising presidential contender had developed a state and national perspective about political issues, as well as social, political, and economic solutions framed in Democratic terms. Clinton's contextual environment nearly ensured that he would become, like Carter, a Democrat. Partisanship in this historically one-party state was rooted in the political soil of friends and neighbors.

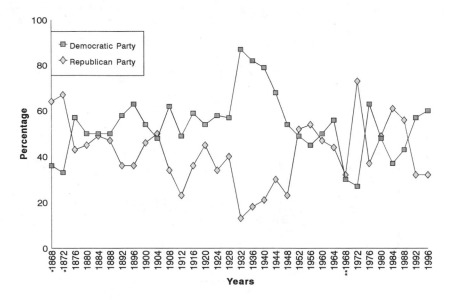

FIGURE 4.11 The Mean Vote Percentage in the President's Home Counties in Presidential Elections, 1868–1996. President Clinton's Home Counties Are Garland and Hempstead.

Adapted from Walter Dean Burnham, *Presidential Ballots: 1826–1892* (Baltimore: Johns Hopkins Press, 1955), 274–292; Edgar Robinson, *The Presidential Vote, 1896–1932* (Stanford: Stanford University Press, 1934); McGillivray and Scammon, *America at the Polls*; and Priest, "November 5, 1996 General Election Results," 59, 66.
*There were no data for Garland county for these years in Burnham.
**George Wallace's American Independent party won the state in 1968.

Southern native-son presidential candidates are reared, physically and politically, in an environment that was cultivated in a partisan fashion long before their arrival on the scene. In both Arkansas and Georgia, since the Civil War, political leaders have been nurturing the electorate toward Democratic allegiance. It was a cultural certainty over generations, with the enduring regularity of the rising of the sun and the shifting of the tides.

But becoming a Democrat is not just an end in itself. It can became a means to a political end. Carter and Clinton became, like many of their friends and neighbors, state Democratic leaders. And in the process, they become bearers of the very tradition that had given them political birth. In the final analysis, they further embedded the Democratic tradition in the soil, the climate, and the electorate of their respective states. Through

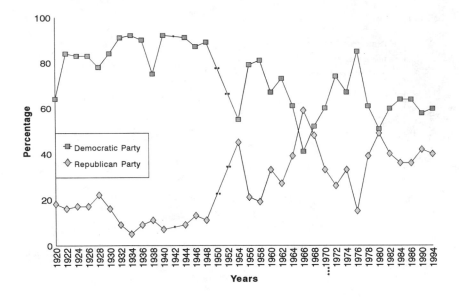

FIGURE 4.12 The Mean Vote Percentage by Party in the President's Home Counties in Gubernatorial Elections, 1920–1994

Adapted from Heard and Strong, *Southern Primaries and Elections, 1920–1949* and Scammon and McGillivray, *America Votes 1994.*
*There was no general election contest in 1942.
**Election results were unavailable for 1950 and 1952.
***A candidate from George Wallace's American Independent party ran for governor in 1970.

them, the tradition perpetuated itself. Through them, the Democratic bias moved into the present and advanced toward the future. Yet this was only at the state level.

Sowing the Democratic party seeds at the state level proved a staging ground for national partisan efforts. Both Carter and Clinton became regional leaders and then national movers of the Democratic party. In the South, with these men at the helm, the Democratic party could reassert itself. With the Republican party making inroads into the region via it message of racial cleavage, the Democratic party lost ground. Therefore, southern native-son presidential candidates had a chance to extend the influence of the party at both the regional and national levels. The Arkansas Democratic tradition was now exporting itself, as had the Georgia, Texas, and Alabama traditions before it.

With two terms, President Clinton has an opportunity that was not available to either Carter or Johnson to shape and reposition the

Democratic party for years to come. President Clinton's two terms provide the chance that these other native-son Presidents did not have. If President Clinton does shepherd the party into additional years in the White House and in control of Congress, then the contextual roots in Arkansas and their psychological manifestations will have a linked past, present, and future. And in a way, the state will have given the nation its partisan cast.

CHAPTER FIVE

The African American Electorate

The song is unmistakable and the refrain is continuous. African Americans are central to understanding southern politics. They are at the core of southern political behavior both in the past and in the present. On this point there is a near unanimous consensus among scholars, journalistic commentators, and outside observers. Yet this consensus was based on the population concentration of African Americans in the Black Belt counties and not upon their actual voting behavior and political participation. In time the concern with the nature of the southern African American voter became secondary if not tertiary. These individual men and women disappeared from the political compass. They both mattered and did not matter, all at the same time.

But they did exist. They had registered and they did vote. And where they could not, they instituted lawsuits to recapture their Fifteenth Amendment voting rights. Those African Americans who exercised the franchise were met with legal and extralegal measures and efforts to remove them from the voting populace. Yet they persisted. It is time to restore their visibility.

In Arkansas and other southern states this is made difficult by the nature of recordkeeping in the region. Arkansas never had a formal statewide registration system. The state depended on poll tax lists rather than registration lists for identifying voters at the polls.[1] Paying one's poll tax was tantamount to registering to vote. But even these records are incomplete. To find the African American electorate in Arkansas, it is essential to do some political archeology.

Political archeology, the scientific study of political behavior in ancient times, is a tool rarely used in political science. Contemporary political science sees itself as just that—a discipline concerned with current and future realities, a discipline concerned with prediction and forecasting. Searches of the past are left for historians and others who look back.

In this postbehavioral era, the argument has been advanced that the discipline has lost its focus and lacks "an agenda [on which] to focus its collective energies."[2] To offset the fragmentation, "drift and decline," and "proliferation of approaches," a recent work has called for a return to history and the study of the historical past. Inherent in this call is the understanding that "there is a growing body of postbehavioral literature that takes history both as subject and method, central to political science inquiry."[3] There is "a renewed historical sensibility in political science, of a curiosity about and critical engagement with the discipline's past, and of the turn to the history of the discipline to address our present and future prospects."[4] Political archaeology soon may be reborn. One major reason for this is a lack of historical political data on racial and ethnic groups, particularly concerning African Americans, in the discipline's knowledge banks.

Both the quality and availability of historical political data on African Americans is simply abysmal.[5] The sole exception is Louisiana, which had kept voter registration data since 1867. No area of African American politics stands in need of political archeology more than the area of voter registration and voting. For example, V. O. Key Jr. in *Southern Politics* used African American county populations as a surrogate for election data.

> So few have been Negro voters in the South that to estimate their numbers seems futile. . . . Estimation of the quantity of Negro voting is fraught with hazard. It must be mainly impressionistic. Estimates of supposedly informed persons on the extent of Negro voting in their own communities are highly unreliable.[6]

Of African American voters in Arkansas, Key stated:

> Arkansas, like most southern states, has no election or registration statistics worthy of the name, and one must rely for estimates of Negro voter participation on impressions. Estimates of voting in the

1946 Democratic primaries made by Negro leaders run from 3,000 to 7,000 out of more than a quarter of a million potential voters.[7]

Although Key provided the best impressionistic estimates of African American registration and voting in the South, his legacy to the discipline and the study of southern regional politics is the reliance on a surrogate measure, like sheer population concentration. Work after work on southern politics has followed blindly in the path that he blazed, with serious consequences. Chief among these is that no exploration or political archeology has been undertaken in this area prior to the *Smith v. Allwright* decision of 1944 which outlawed the white primaries in the region. Since that decision, the Southern Regional Council has sponsored numerous studies to gather data in a systematic fashion on African American registration and voting.[8] But the data collection efforts of the Southern Regional Council and its Voter Education Project notwithstanding, this aspect of Key's legacy has been perpetuated uncritically.

For instance, a recent book, *Quiet Revolution in the South*, designed to empirically assess the influence of the Voting Rights Act of 1965, contains single chapters on several southern states, as well as a collective chapter on African American voter registration in the region, yet all are devoid of a simple, single list of voting registration in these states.[9] Nor does the book provide much data on African American voter registration. Yet the book concludes that the Voting Rights Act has been a huge success, without ever once providing systematic and comprehensive voting registration data on African Americans in a single state. The book omitted Arkansas altogether despite the fact that the Legal Defense Fund had sued Governor Clinton for the failure of the state of Arkansas to abide by the Voting Rights Act.[10] As the suit indicated, the law had failed in the state, and Governor Clinton agreed.[11] Exactly why the editors of this volume left Arkansas out of the analysis is never made clear. Did they exclude it because it provided a poignant example of the failure of the Voting Rights Act and conflicted with their model and findings? Did they excluded it because they did not want to further embarrass President Clinton, who had withdrawn the nomination of Lani Guinier, who had originally filed the suit? The book is silent on these critical matters.

This book left the African American voter in the South and in Arkansas invisible. Here was a group of voters with no past. This book had simply dropped them from the political screen. Such flawed scholarship emerged from the Key legacy.[12] To avoid this type of academic debate and poor reasoning, we turn to political archeology.

September 26, 1867: The Initial Voter Portrait

Prior to the Civil War, Tennessee (until 1834) and North Carolina (until 1835) permitted "Free Men of Color" to vote. In Rapides parish, Louisiana, slaves were permitted to vote up until the Civil War. Arkansas, which had both Free Men of Color and slaves, permitted neither to vote. It took the defeat of the Confederacy and the military reconstruction of Arkansas to extend the ballot to the African American community. Major-General E.O.C. Ard of the Fourth Military District (Mississippi and Arkansas), complying with an act of Congress, issued a field order—General Order No. 31—to make a count of all the African Americans and whites who had registered to vote in the state, with a breakdown by counties.

Table 5.1 provides the initial list of voters in the politically reconstructed Arkansas. Here a new group of political citizens willed themselves from slavery to the pinnacle of citizenship. They now held the ballot and could as citizens exercise it in their quest for universal freedom. African Americans could now act as did other men in the state. Of the 58 counties, African Americans were the voting majority in 10 counties. African American males were one-third (35%) of the state's newly remade electorate.

The white electorate had dominant electoral power in 48 counties. As before the Civil War, whites held most of the electoral power in the state. Table 5.1 reconfigured on a map of the state (map 5.1) shows the geographical bases of power of each group. For the moment, the power configuration in Arkansas had a new demographic basis. It was a breakthrough of major proportions.

With this initial registration came a chance for these new political citizens to form alliances, affiliations, and alignments with the state's political parties. Likewise, the white electorate could either seek a new party alignment, renew an old one, or dealign from all of the parties. Both groups had the opportunity, at this critical moment in Arkansas's political history, to define or redefine, shape or reshape the nature, character, and images of the political parties in the state. Political archeology has gotten us started, yet the portrait is not complete.

If these extant voter registration data help to fix a portrait of the initial African American electorate made possible by a catastrophe—the Civil War—then further voting data provide the portrait with another time point and additional insights.

This second moment is the Nineteenth Amendment to the Constitution, which granted women their voting rights. With the ratification

TABLE 5.1 Percentage and Number of African American and White Voters in Arkansas, 1867

County	Percent of African American Voters	Number of African American Voters	Percent of White Voters	Number of White Voters	Total Voters
Chicot	77	894	23	268	1,162
Phillips	74	2,681	26	955	3,636
Jefferson	72	2,738	28	1,048	3,786
Arkansas	68	1,030	32	495	1,525
Desha	68	592	32	281	873
Crittenden	67	505	33	245	750
Lafayette	62	962	38	583	1,545
Pulaski	62	2,402	38	1,494	3,896
Little River	57	426	43	327	753
Monroe	51	551	49	525	1,076
Hempstead	48	1,195	52	1,307	2,502
Ashley	46	604	54	710	1,314
Union	46	798	54	922	1,720
Quachita	45	870	55	1,084	1,054
St. Francis	45	464	55	544	1,028
Mississippi	40	193	60	292	485
Columbia	36	740	64	1,313	2,053
Drew	35	577	65	1,079	1,656
Woodruff	35	354	65	673	1,027
Dallas	33	337	67	668	1,005
Prairie	32	512	68	1,071	1,583
Sevier	32	261	68	567	828
Cross	31	184	69	415	599
Calhoun	30	184	70	422	606
Bradley	29	368	71	908	1,276
Clark	29	464	71	1,112	1,576
Jackson	25	283	75	849	1,132
Poinsett	19	39	81	172	211
Sebastian	17	203	83	1,012	1,215
Van Buren	17	148	83	746	894
Crawford	17	148	83	746	894
Pine	14	76	86	489	565
Yell	14	131	86	831	962
Franklin	13	107	87	740	847
Conway	13	146	87	934	1,080
Hot Spring	12	102	88	723	825
Pope	11	94	89	771	865
White	11	155	89	1,279	1,434
Johnson	10	73	90	682	755
Independence	9	140	91	1,455	1,595
Randolph	7	59	93	848	907

(*Continued*)

TABLE 5.1 Percentage and Number of African American and White Voters in Arkansas, 1867 (*Continued*)

County	Percent of African American Voters	Number of African American Voters	Percent of White Voters	Number of White Voters	Total Voters
Perry	7	23	93	295	318
Craighead	7	42	93	523	565
Saline	6	42	94	712	754
Montgomery	5	27	95	491	518
Lawrence	4	43	96	971	1,014
Izard	4	31	96	763	794
Washington	4	84	96	1,834	1,918
Fulton	3	9	97	297	306
Scott	3	17	97	557	574
Marion	2	9	98	382	391
Benton	1	11	99	998	1,009
Madison	1	10	99	709	719
Greene	1	5	99	922	927
Newton	0	1	100	425	426
Polk	0	1	100	392	393
Searcy	0	1	100	574	575
Carroll	0	0	100	767	767
Total	**35**	**23,146**	**65**	**43,217**	**66,363**

Adapted from *The American Annual Cyclopaedia and Register of Independent Events of the Year 1867* (New York: D. Appleton and Company, 1869), 53. The data were checked for recording and addition errors and corrected.

of this amendment, African American women became political citizens.[13] They now had the political ballot and an opportunity to enter the state's political process and party system. With their arrival, African American women could replenish the ranks of the African American electorate depleted by disenfranchisement, denigration by Dixie demagogues like Jeff Davis, and endless obstacles such as the poll tax and white primaries, to maintain the right to vote. All of these had significantly diminished the ranks of the African American electorate. Thus when fresh troops arrived with the ballot, the few remaining African American male voters joined ranks and launched a political and electoral revolt. These old and new political citizens said to white Arkansas

Counties with an African American voting majority

MAP 5.1 POLITICAL MAP OF ARKANSAS, 1867
    COUNTIES WITH AFRICAN AMERICAN AND WHITE VOTING MAJORITIES

in 1920 that they were dissatisfied with the negative and oppressive response of the political system to their needs and wishes, and the manner in which their political rights had been circumscribed and nullified. They demanded that the state government, white electorate, and state political parties give them political recognition, full status citizenship (not Jim Crow citizenship), and human dignity. They were demanding a place in the Arkansas political process. Yet women were unable to vote in the 1920 election because the state had not ratified the amendment in time for the election.

This electoral revolt of 1920 took place in the gubernatorial general election, in which African American citizens ran their own candidate, J.H. Blount, on the Independent (Black and Tan Republican party) ticket.[14]

The Republican party in the South and in Arkansas had split into two opposing factions, the Lily-White Republicans and the Black and Tans or Lily-Black Republicans.[15] "The candidacy of J. H. Blount, 'Negro Independent,' for governor in 1920 grew out of a struggle within the Republican party between Lily-Whites and Black-and-Tan elements. Similar splits in Republican ranks appeared in other states."[16]

> After bolting the white convention Black delegates from Pulaski, Hempstead, and Phillips counties held their own Black and Tan convention (some whites joined them) at the Mosaic Temple on the corner of Ninth Street and Broadway. They chose delegates for the National Convention, raised $5,000 for group expenses, and nominated a complete state ticket headed up by a Black, J.H. Blount, . . . who was principal of a Black school in Helena [Pulaski county].[17]

Heard describes the situation: "In Arkansas . . . the lily-white Republicans 'discarded' the Black-and-Tan faction, which then met in rump session and formulated a 'Negro Independent' candidate for governor."[18]

Table 5.2 shows that more than 17,000 votes were cast for the African American gubernatorial candidate. In a four-man race these votes placed the candidate in third place behind the Democratic and Republican candidates and far ahead of the Socialist party candidate.[19] The Blount candidacy captured 9 percent of the votes cast.

If the three other parties had permitted unrestricted ballot access to the African American community, the 9 percent could have made one of the parties—particularly the Republicans—a real competitor. But with all three parties riding a platform of white supremacy, the empowerment message which the African American political and electoral revolt offered was lost and the revolt failed.

The tabular data tell us much about the demographic bases of the African American electorate after disenfranchisement. Tables 5.1 and 5.2 show that the total vote in 1920 for the African American candidate was 26 percent less than the total number of African American registered voters had been in 1867. This is a clear indication of decline.

Only two of the African American majority Black Belt counties (Pulaski and Jefferson) were significant supporters of the African American gubernatorial candidate. But before interpreting this, as many have done, as a failure of his own community to rally to Blount, the evidence must be probed further.

TABLE 5.2 Number and Percentage of Voters for the
African American Gubernatorial Candidate in
1920 by County

County	Votes	Percentage
Pulaski	1,986	11.6
Van Buren	1,617	9.4
Hempstead	1,017	5.9
Jefferson	895	5.2
Lincoln	807	4.7
Phillips	631	3.7
St. Francis	543	3.2
Monroe	527	3.1
Woodruff	508	3.0
Conway	452	2.6
Drew	424	2.5
Prairie	410	2.4
Jackson	399	2.3
Ashley	377	2.2
Lonoke	367	2.1
Clark	363	2.1
Columbia	360	2.1
Garland	328	1.9
Lafayette	317	1.8
Chicot	310	1.8
Bradley	285	1.7
Little River	261	1.5
Dallas	230	1.3
Desha	222	1.3
Miller	217	1.3
Nevada	215	1.3
Cross	208	1.2
Faulkner	183	1.1
Hot Spring	178	1.0
Calhoun	173	1.0
Mississippi	172	1.0
Quachita	171	1.0
Sebastian	168	1.0
Cleveland	168	1.0
Sevier	146	1.0
Lee	142	1.0
Howard	136	1.0
Arkansas	121	1.0
Pope	117	1.0
Crawford	112	1.0
White	110	1.0
Benton	106	1.0
Union	100	1.0
Craighead	94	1.0

(Continued)

TABLE 5.2 Number and Percentage of Voters for the
African American Gubernatorial Candidate in
1920 by County (*Continued*)

County	Votes	Percentage
Grant	66	*
Yell	62	*
Perry	56	*
Independence	55	*
Crittenden	43	*
Pointsett	38	*
Logan	36	*
Lawrence	22	*
Washington	20	*
Johnson	19	*
Franklin	19	*
Randolph	19	*
Saline	17	*
Pike	17	*
Izard	15	*
Montgomery	13	*
Polk	8	*
Greene	7	*
Sharp	6	*
Searcy	4	*
Newton	4	*
Clay	4	*
Carroll	4	*
Fulton	3	*
Baxter	3	*
Boone	2	*
Scott	3	*
Stone	2	*
Marion	1	*
Cleburne	0	0
Madison	0	0
Total	17,240	**

Adapted from Heard and Strong, *Southern Primaries and Elections, 1920–1949*,
23.

*Percentage less than .05%.

**Column does not total 100 due to rounding.

Key's classic *Southern Politics* demonstrated that as the African American population increased in a county their political participation decreased due to white political behavior. The converse was also true. As their population decreased, political participation increased. Key called this the political context variable. Table 5.3 demonstrates the validity of Key's findings 20 years before he wrote.

Table 5.3 shows that African American voter registration was significantly affected by African American population concentration. Although it is not a clearcut linear relationship as Key had argued, there is a very highly correlated relationship.

Alabama exemplified a perfect linear relation between voter registration and African American population concentration. Comparing Alabama with Arkansas over the same time period, Arkansas shows some deviation, but maintains the broad general pattern that Key found and recognized in his 1949 classic *Southern Politics*.

Figure 5.1 offers empirical evidence for this unique feature of southern politics by comparing and contrasting the fluctuating pattern in Arkansas of African American voter registration with Alabama's linear pattern.

TABLE 5.3 The Mean Percentage of African American Voters in Arkansas in 1950 and 1958 Compared with the Population Percentages

	% of African American Population	Number of Counties	Mean % of African American Registered to Vote
50+	8.0	6	21.7
40+	8.0	6	32.5
30+	14.7	11	26.3
20+	12.0	9	34.7
10+	6.7	5	24.9
0.1+	42.7	32*	20.3
0	8.0	6	0
Total	100.1	75	

For the 1950 African American population percentage see Bureau of the Census, *Census of Population: 1950*, vol. 1 Arkansas (Washington, D.C.: United States Government Printing Office, 1952), table 12.

The registration data is for the year 1958 and was taken from the *Report of the U.S. Commission on Civil Rights, 1959*, 559–560.

*There were nine counties with an African American population but no registered African American voters in 1958.

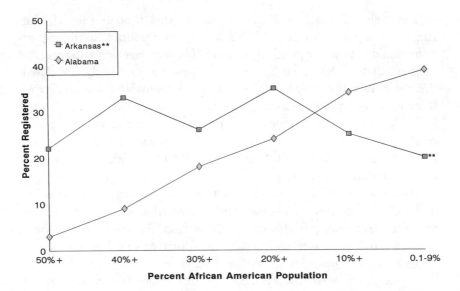

FIGURE 5.1 Percentage of African Americans Registered to Vote in Arkansas and Alabama by Percentage of County Population, 1958

Adapted from Walton and Smith, *American Politics and the African American Quest for Universal Freedom* (Boston: Allyn and Bacon, 2000), table 9.1; Bureau of the Census, *Census of Population: 1950*, Part 1: Arkansas (Washington, D.C.: Government Printing Office, 1952), table 12. The registration data for both states were taken from the *Report of the U.S. Commission on Civil Rights, 1959* (Washington, D.C.: Government Printing Office, 1959), 559–560. ‎In 1958 there were nine counties in Arkansas with no African Americans registered.

While there is a difference in the pattern in the two states, the differences are in degrees, not in kind. If we disaggregate the data even further, the degrees of difference immediately become available. Arkansas whites in the Black Belt counties were more willing to permit African Americans to register to vote than were whites in Alabama. And seemingly more African Americans in these counties were activated to register to vote.

Unlike Alabama, where a sparse African American population meant more African American registered voters, in Arkansas, the pattern was more uniform.

The number of African American registered voters in Arkansas counties did not reach the 39 percent level of certain Alabama counties. Nor did the lowest level of 0 percent match Alabama's lowest level of 3 percent. While the ranges of African American registered voters differed, in both states the number of African Americans permitted to register to vote remained very low. The differences between the two southern states remain differences in degree only.

The African American vote for Blount in 1920 tended to follow the pattern discerned by Key, as well as the thesis later advanced by him and Ralph Bunche.[20] The African American vote in this 1920 election came from counties where the African American population was moderate to small, with the exception of two counties. And in these two counties, voter registration seems to have been more difficult than in others of comparable size. The African American electoral response to Blount was inhibited by systemic factors in Arkansas's political context, most notably the poll tax, the disenfranchisement law, the climate of white supremacy and racism, and the domination of state political institutions by racial demagogues. Empirical analysis adds further insights. When the 1920 African American voting age population is correlated with the vote for Blount, the voting age population is only minimally or insignificantly associated with the Blount vote.[21] When the voting age population is used as an independent variable to see how much of the vote for Blount could be predicted, it is a mere 2 percent.[22] Despite the fact that the number of potential African American voters stood at 124,062, some 98 percent of the Blount vote must be explained by these contextual forces. Something in the state's political context suppressed the African American voting age population from registering and thereby voting for Blount.

Blount received his third highest level of support in Hempstead country, while his support in Garland country ranked it fourteenth. Nearly two decades before Bill Clinton was born, his native counties were exemplifying different degrees of African American electoral participation and support for a statewide African American candidate.

In 1944 the Supreme Court in its *Smith v. Allwright* decision outlawed the white primaries held by the state's Democratic party. Shortly after this decision the Southern Regional Council began compiling its "Negro voting registration data."[23] This systematic but not comprehensive effort produced the most reliable data (outside of Louisiana) that exists for the time prior to the Voting Rights Act of 1965.[24] Here the Federal government empowered the Justice Department to send registrars to most southern states to register African Americans to vote in federal elections. As a way of monitoring progress and the implementation of the law, registration data was to be kept by race. The 1964 Civil Rights Act launched this procedure and the Voting Rights Act merely continued the policy. The Bureau of the Census of the Commerce Department was given the Federal role and function for this task. And it is from this data that a more comprehensive and systematic portrait of the African American electorate in Arkansas emerges.

Arkansas's African American Registered Voters: A Historical Portrait

Our political archeological procedure, with its focus on four key events, has made it possible to develop a time series perspective on the shape and parameters of the African American electorate in the state, and to see patterns and trends in its evolution, devolution, and reassertion via new electoral and civil rights laws. With these insights, we move on to partisan alignment and finally some empirical sense of this second largest demographic group in the state in their support for the native-son candidate Bill Clinton.

Table 5.4 offers a composite perspective on this electorate. Such a rich archeological trove has not surfaced before. But it was discovered during the analysis of President Carter as a native-son candidate that this very rare information did exist and that it would enhance the analysis of the concept and enlarge the scope of testable propositions about the variable. Theory building was significantly enriched by the use of political archaeological research on the African American southern voter, who is a major factor in the Democratic party in the South in general and in Arkansas in particular.

Arkansas's African American Electorate: The Census Bureau Portrait

In any archaeological search for political data, particularly election data (registration and voting), state agencies, scholars, archivists, data compilers, and political scientists with a historical perspective are not the only possible sources for fugitive data.[25] Various federal agencies are potential treasure troves.

Beginning in the 1930s the Clerk of the House of Representatives issued pamphlets on the vote in presidential and congressional elections. This was followed by the Bureau of the Census issuing publications with presidential and congressional votes from 1928.[26] Since 1960, the Bureau, through its Population Reports Series, offers data on voting age population, registration, and voting. Although the Bureau has not been consistent in its reporting procedures, this series contains considerable data on the nature, size, scope, and growth of the African American electorate in Arkansas. These data sources offer another portrait of the second largest demographic group in the state. These data supplement and extend the initial and historical election data.

TABLE 5.4 Number and Percentage of African American Registered Voters in Arkansas: 1867–1990

Year	Number of African Americans of Voting Age	Number of African American Registered Voters	Percentage Registered
1867	N/A	43,217	N/A
1900	87,157	N/A	N/A
1910	111,523	N/A	N/A
1920	124,062	17,240*	13.9
1930	257,130	5,100**	2.0
1940	270,995	4,000	1.5
1946	245,013	5,000	2.0
1947	240,685	47,000	20.0
1950	227,691	N/A	N/A
1952	220,353	61,413	27.9
1956	205,676	69,677	33.9
1957	202,007	64,023	31.7
1958	198,338	64,023	32.3
1959	194,669	72,604	37.3
1960	191,000	73,000	38.2
1961	191,300	68,970	36.1
1963	191,900	77,714	40.5
1964	192,200	81,178	42.2
1970	194,000	153,000	78.9
1980	217,000	128,467	59.2
1990	195,000	99,060	50.8

Adapted from *The American Annual Cyclopaedia and Register of Independent Events of the Year 1867*, 53; Heard and Strong, *Southern Primaries and Elections 1920–1949*, 23; Luther Jackson, "Race and Suffrage in the South Since 1940," *New South* (June/July 1948); Heard, *A Two-Party South?*, 9; *Report of the United States Commission on Civil Rights, 1959*, 42 and 559–560; Arkansas History Commission, *Poll Tax Records: 1920–1967* (microfilm) (Little Rock: Arkansas History Commission, 1966). The voting age population data were taken from Statistical Abstracts of the United States (Washington, D.C.: Government Printing Office) for the years 1901, 1902, 1913, 1931, 1943, and 1972. For the years in which the Statistical Abstract did not list voting age ppopulation data-1946, 1947, 1952, 1956, 1958, 1959, 1961, 1964-the figures were estimated.
*The actual vote for the African American gubernatorial candidate is used in place of registration data.
**Voting data taken from Paul Lewinson, *Race, Class, and Party: A History of Negro Suffrage and White Politics in the South* (New York: Oxford University Press, 1932), 218.

Table 5.5 draws upon the actual number of individuals voting in the state of Arkansas and shows the estimated number of African Americans voting in each year in which Clinton sought election. It permits a comparison of the number voting with Clinton's margin of victory (or defeat) in each election. Beginning with Clinton's reelection as governor in 1980 (voting data on African Americans before this year does not exist in the reports), it is possible to see that in the 1982 primary and runoff, as well as the 1990 primary election, Clinton could not have won without the African American vote. In these three elections African Americans held the balance of victory. Without this bloc of votes he would have lost.

In 1992, the African American vote was crucial, but not critical, to Clinton winning the state and carrying its electoral votes. Without the African American vote, his victory margin would have been wafer thin and he would have been embarrassed by the low level of electoral support in his own home state. Without the African American vote, Clinton's 1992 state victory would have placed him near the bottom of the ranking of home-state support for native-son candidates.

TABLE 5.5 Number of African Americans Voting and Clinton's Victory Margins: A Census Bureau Perspective

Year	Number of African Americans Voting	Clinton's Margin of Victory in	African American Vote the Primary	Clinton's Margin in the General Contribution	African American Vote Election Contribution
1974	*				
1976	*	149,925		**	
1978	*	217,414		143,134	
1980	65,936	168,066		−32,442	
1982	71,460	70,895	565	74,359	−2,899
1982 runoff	71,460	32,851	38,609		
1984	*	197,950		222,574	
1986	74,593	140,995		191,455	
1990	67,272***	78,442	−11,167	104,461	
1992	135,000***	253,556		168,499	−33,499
1996	156,000	196,876	−40,876	149,755	6,245

Adapted from Bureau of the Census data on Voting and Registration in the Election of November 1980, 1982, 1984, 1986, 1990, 1992 and 1996, Current Population Reports, Series P-20, and Arkansas election data from the Arkansas Secretary of State. Calculations prepared by author.
*In these years, Series P-20 did not carry data on Arkansas and there was not breakdown by race.
**No general election was held.
***In these years, the Census data were taken directly from the Current Population Reports.

The Census Bureau data also permits us to see how African Americans made Clinton's comeback in 1982 successful in the primary, runoff, and general election. Diane Blair, who puts the number of African American voters in 1982 at 90,000, makes the same observation. The African American vote made his fifth election to the governorship possible, and was pivotal in the primary. This made Clinton a competitive native-son presidential candidate in 1992 and provided him a more comfortable margin than could have been achieved otherwise. The Census data tells us how active the African American electorate was and helps us understand its importance in terms of Clinton's rise as a native-son presidential candidate.

The Census data in table 5.6 show the relationship of the African American voter to Clinton's electoral victories and provide a longitudinal portrait of African American registration and electoral behavior over time. An empirical and fairly precise portrait of this electorate emerges: from 1960, when one-third of the African American voting age population was registered to vote, to about two-thirds registered in the past two decades, this electorate has been expanding its base and reach.

Slightly less than half of registered African American voters have been voting in national, congressional, and state elections. Of those registered voters who actually vote, the majority vote in presidential rather than in congressional elections. As we have seen, the African American electorate has played a critical and crucial role in state and national election outcomes. This segment of the Arkansas electorate has played a vital role in the political career and evolution of the state's native son.

The Partisanship of the African American Electorate

As recently as 1981 a group of scholars observed: "Arkansas has been the only state in the Union for which contemporary election data are not readily available in printed form."[27] Attempting to rectifying this situation, the Secretary of State, Paul Riviere, wrote: "It has been said that there is less written on Arkansas government and politics than on any other state. I agree. . . . This publication is one of several which I hope will begin to correct the problem of availability and accessibility."[28] This was written in 1980, in a publication of the 1976 election returns in the first official state election book. How then can we garner insight into the historic party affiliation of African Americans in Arkansas? Knowing the nature of their registration does not automatically tell us much about the nature and scope of their partisanship. Here, even political archaeology is of little assistance.

TABLE 5.6 The Percentage of African Americans Registered and Voting in Arkansas: 1960–1996

Year	Percentage Registered	Percentage Voting
1960	38.2	N/A
1970*	*	*
1980	62.6	50.8
1982	63.3	47.7
1984**	63.0	49.3
1986	62.5	43.3
1988	68.0	49.6
1990	50.8	34.5
1992	62.4	46.4
1994	56.0	34.5
1996	65.8	50.6

Bureau of the Census, "1960 Population of Voting Age and Votes for President, 1964 and 1960, for States and Counties," Current Population Reports Series P-23, no. 14 (14 April 1965), 2 and "Voting and Registration in the Election of November" for the years 1980 through 1996, Current Population Reports Series P-20 (Washington, D.C.: Government Printing Office, 1981–1996). Where necessary, calculations were prepared by author.

*Between 1964 and 1978, the Census Bureau reports on voting and registration did not break the data down by state but only by region. In 1980 the Bureau went back to reporting by state. It broke this pattern again in 1984 and launched a new one in 1986.

**Estimated using the rolling average method of the two preceding elections.

In this case it is necessary to employ a surrogate measure—the party vote in African American counties. Where official records are lacking, the secondary analytical approach is to find counties where the population under scrutiny is dominant, and then explore and examine the manner in which these counties (or smaller political units, such as precincts or wards) voted in presidential, congressional, state, and local elections.[29] This procedure is not only one of the oldest techniques with which to analyze election return data in political science, it is also a fairly reliable one.[30]

Of Arkansas's 75 counties, 3 have been majority African American from their creation in the pre–civil war period through the 1996 presidential election. These three counties—Chicot, Lee, and Phillips—have always had more than a 51 percent African American population. By analyzing how these counties voted for parties in diverse elections, we will provide empirical insights into the nature and significance of African American partisanship over time. Such an analysis will yield data on patterns, trends, and changes in this partisanship.

Beginning with the 1868 presidential election—the year after African Americans became registered voters in the state—the mean vote percentage in figure 5.2 indicates that these newly registered voters took on a Republican party affiliation. The 1872 election was the peak year for African American Republicanism. Although there were subsequent fluctuations in the vote for the Republican party, there was a constant decline. With the institutionalization of disenfranchisement in 1891, African American voters were eliminated and these counties went Democratic. With few African Americans to vote for the Republican ticket, the party could no longer carry these counties.

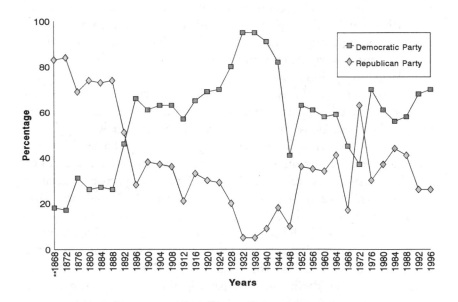

FIGURE 5.2 **The Mean Vote Percentage by Party in Arkansas's Black Belt Counties in Presidential Elections, 1896–1996**

*Adapted from Walter Dean Burnham, *Presidential Ballots 1836–1892*, 274–292; Edgar Robinson, *The Presidential Vote: 1896–1932*; McGillivray and Scammon, *America at the Polls*; Priest, "November 5, 1996 General Election Results," 17, 89, and 125.
*The Black Belt counties are Chicot, Lee, and Phillips.
**There were no data in the Burnham volume for Lee county in the 1868 and 1872 presidential elections.

Between 1892 and 1965—the period in which African Americans were banned from more than limited participation in the electoral process— these counties offered significant support for the Democratic party's presidential candidates. In 1948 and 1968, when the Dixiecrats and George Wallace's American Independent party swept these counties, the African American electorate had made its transition to and rebirth as Democrats. When Nixon carried these counties in 1972, African Americans had began a new tradition of voting Democratic. In 1968, 1972, and thereafter, we see the Democratic partisanship of these African American counties. This surrogate method, along with historical materials, indicates that African Americans in the state went from being Republicans to being Democrats, at least in presidential elections. And it was not a smooth process. In the 1880s and 1890s they coalesced with the Greenback, Populist[31], and Progressive third parties.

Below the presidential level we find a similar pattern. Figure 5.3 reveals that from the end of World War I until 1964, the Democratic party dominated the gubernatorial elections in a very dramatic fashion while the disenfranchisement of the African American electorate in the state affected the Republican party's fortunes. Only national Republican victories in the 1950s and the civil rights movement of the 1960s temporary revived the party by getting whites to switch from the Democrats to the Republicans.

The reemerge of the African American electorate rejuvenated the Democratic party's support base in these counties and restored it to dominance in state elections. In the 1960s Winthrop Rockefeller was popular with African American voters, and they strongly supported him. The empirical evidence here offers support for that contention. African American voters in Arkansas realigned with the Republican party in the state in the 1960s, while elsewhere they were aligning with the Democratic party. In Georgia, African American voters in the 1960s did not realign with or support Republican candidates for governor or other statewide offices.[32]

Raymond Arsenault, looking at the vote from 1880 to 1910, finds that these same counties not only voted significantly Republican but after 1892 underwent a major decline in voter participation.[33] With this decline in African American voter turnout, Democratic dominance was restored. African American Republicanism nearly vanished in state and national elections until the 1960s.

The African Americans in these three Black Belt counties who emerged as Republicans were eliminated from the process while the state became Democratic. This Republicanism would reassert itself in 1920 and in the 1960s, but over time it become transformed and realigned with the

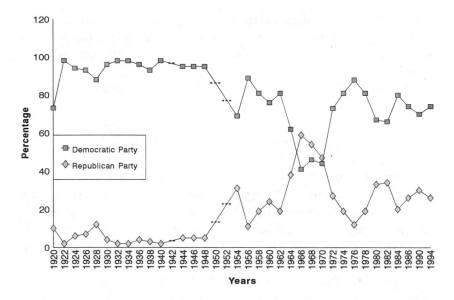

FIGURE 5.3 The Mean Percentage Vote by Party in Arkansas's Black Belt
Counties in Gubernatorial Elections, 1920–1994

Adapted from Burnham, Presidential Ballots 1836–1892, 274–292; Robinson, The Presidential Vote:
1896–1932; McGillivray and Scammon, America at the Polls.
*The Black Belt counties are Chicot, Lee, and Phillips.
**There was no general election in 1942.
***Data for 1950 and 1952 were unavailable.

Democratic party. Without this realignment these counties would have
reverted to the Republican column in the Reagan-Bush era. Thus the
African American electorate helped to sustain the state's Democratic base.

The Poll Tax and Other Attempts at Limiting the African American Electorate

Prior to 1867 the electorate in Arkansas was both lily-white and Democratic in its partisanship. From its inception as a state, voters in Arkansas voted in greater numbers in gubernatorial and congressional elections than in presidential ones. Localism predominated even after the nationalization of American politics that began in the 1840s. "Large number of Arkansans who participated regularly at other statewide elections continued to scorn voting for President."[34] Only in the 1860 presidential election did Arkansans match the level which had obtained in state elections through the previous decades. Yet even this 73 percent turnout "still fell a good way short of the impressive rate of participation which had just been witnessed in the state's gubernatorial and congressional elections some weeks earlier."[35]

Before the 1868 presidential election, the Arkansas electorate expanded to include African Americans (table 5.1). Welcomed or not, the new voters took on a partisan alignment with the Republican party. "In 1867 the black voters of Arkansas began a marriage with the Republican Party that was to last until the Franklin D. Roosevelt 'New Deal' lured the Negro away from the party of Lincoln."[36]

This is not the complete story because African American Republicans in the state party did revolt. There were revolts at state party conventions, which led to contesting Black and Tans and Lily-White delegates at national Republican conventions. But on each occasion the national convention seated the Lily-White delegates.

However, as Reconstruction ended in the state and as the Democratic party recaptured control, the party made initial overtures to this new electorate. "This wooing of black voters by white Democrats must have met with some success, for at least two black Democrats served in the Arkansas House of Representatives and another was elected county coroner."[37] The African American electorate also supported the Greenback and Populist parties. In the main, however, their partisanship remained predominantly Republican. The New Deal notwithstanding, this electorate turned out in significant numbers to support the Republican gubernatorial bid of Winthrop Rockefeller in 1966. But with the Rockefeller exception, since the New Deal, the African American electorate has demonstrated a Democratic partisanship and affiliation.

However both the Republican and Democratic parties historically attempted to marginalize this new group of voters. The transition in the partisanship of the African American electorate is only part of the story after their entrance in 1867 into the political process. The other part of the story and perhaps a major variable in shaping the historic African American partisanship in the state was the Democratic party's drive for disenfranchisement of this sector of the electorate. The party used a tripartite strategy to remove this group of new voters from its political soil.

After the revolt of the Republican Black and Tans at the 1920 national convention in Chicago, some African Americans joined with an African American physician, J. M. Robinson, in 1928 and organized the Arkansas Negro Democratic Association. Other African Americans continued to play on the periphery of the Republican party.[38] Both parties marginalized them. It would take the arrival of the national Democratic party's New Deal programs and policies to attract their affiliation at the state level in Arkansas. Until then, they voted for state parties that were not inclusive in their membership, organizational or public policies, or positions. It was political partisanship at the margins. John Graves writes: "In desperation, the Redeemers began to employ racial demagoguery. Democratic politicians used the enemy's vulnerable associations with the Republicans to invoke old memories of carpetbagger chicanery in 1888 and 1890."[39]

"In Arkansas, the first important instrument of Negro disfranchisement was the new election law enacted in 1891." This "new law created a centralized system of control which placed all of the election machinery exclusively in the hands of the Democratic Party."[40] The new technique effectively removed Republicans and Populists, except as symbolic tokens. White Democratic election commissioners found ways to keep the African American from voting.

In 1893 came the "second major instrumentality for Negro disfranchisement," the poll tax.[41] With this new device, the African American electorate shrunk considerably. Although it did not disappear, it was considerably smaller with this form of economic discrimination and oppression.

Finally, in January 1906, "the state Democratic central committee, under the leadership of Governor Jeff Davis, order the use of white primaries throughout the state."[42] This was the third instrument that the Democratic party used in repressing if not eliminating the African American electorate. The die was cast. And to spread the word beyond the state legislature and the inner circle of the Democratic Party elites, the Democratic party spawned a number of leading demagogues who launched a grassroots movement to keep the Negro in his place and establish the Democratic party as the party of white supremacy. The chief leader in this movement was Jeff Davis, the Redneck Messiah. "Elected state attorney general in 1898, he went on to serve three stormy terms as governor before moving on to the United States Senate in 1907. He was reelected to the Senate in 1912, but his career was cut short by a fatal heart attack in January 1913."[43]

By the time of his death, he had used race and white supremacy to completely remake and redefine the Democratic party. He transformed both the party and the state's white electorate. Davis's legacy, which lived on long after him, continued to cripple the African American electorate. Racebaiting and white supremacy rhetoric would continue to surface in Arkansas politics and hinder the African American voter, while mobilizing the white electorate and empowering white Democratic election officials in their efforts to slow African American registration. On this part of his legacy, there is no debate or dispute. However, on the effect of the poll tax as a disenfranchising tactic, there is some scholarly dispute.

Key declares that "the fiction has prevailed that the poll tax deters Negro participation, but the tax has counted for little in comparison with other restraints."[44] "Originally designed chiefly to discourage Negro participation, it became obsolete for that purpose with the invention of the white primary. It became simply a tax on voting by whites and nothing more."[45] To offer empirical support for this assertion, he turned to Arkansas, which kept poll tax registration records from 1920 until 1967. On analyzing these records, Key discovered a falloff of payments in off-year elections and a relationship between payments and variations in per capita income. He writes: "on the whole, however, a sharp decline in Arkansas per capita income is apt to bring with it a drop in the proportion of people qualified to vote through payment of the poll tax."[46] From the Arkansas data and that of several other southern states, Key concludes that "the poll tax has had little or no bearing on Negro disfranchisement, the object for which it was supposedly designed."[47] As far as Key was concerned, the poll tax in Arkansas was race neutral in its effects.

In the mid-1950s the Southern Regional Council sponsored a "survey of Negro Suffrage in Arkansas," prepared by African American sociologists at Arkansas Agricultural, Mechanical, and Normal College. A summary of that report appeared in a special 1957 issue of the *Journal of Negro Education*. In that summary, the authors took exception to Key's findings. "The basic requirement for voting in Arkansas is constitutional—the possession of a poll tax receipt."[48] However it was not the economic character of the poll tax that hindered African American registration and voting but its temporal character.

> The real importance of the poll tax as a deterrent to voting is not the one dollar involved, but rather the time element. The final day for the payment of poll taxes is October 1st of each year. The poll tax receipt is good for voting in all elections after October 2nd of the year in which the poll tax is paid until October 1st of the following year. Thus, the 1955 poll tax receipt was good for voting until October 1, 1956. With poll tax payment lagging one year behind voting and political issues arising in late spring or early summer, for the July or August primaries, it is too late for the issues raised to influence poll tax purchases.[49]

If African Americans did not pay their poll taxes one year before the state primary elections were held, they could not be motivated by the promises and stances of the state's demagogues and segregationists. It would be too late after the political season had started to pay one's poll taxes. Even if candidates in a political race promised the African Americans "paved and lighted streets, parks, improved schools, and removal of offensive law enforcement officers," it would be too late to mobilize, if their poll taxes had not been paid by October 1st of the previous year. The authors interviewed 38 Negro political leaders in 23 counties, counted Negro voters from each county, and analyzed demographic data, before concluding that the poll tax did disenfranchise the African American electorate.

Figure 5.4 shows the trends and patterns of African Americans of voting age who paid their poll taxes in the state. In analyzing this data, a caveat should be kept in mind. African American per capita income was lower than that of the white population. Figure 5.4 indicates that only one-third of African Americans paid their poll taxes between 1957 and 1964. There is some upward movement in the number as the Civil Rights movement starts to evolve. But while the poll tax was in effect, two-thirds of all African Americans of voting age did not pay their poll tax. Cothran and Phillips argued in their study that the poll tax along with other factors created a climate of indifference, a lack of enthusiasm, and an absence of incentives for political participation. Faced with a lack of political motivation, some African American citizens in Arkansas saw little need to pay their taxes in order to become registered voters. Beyond being a direct economic disincentive, the poll tax also served as an indirect force. Here is more evidence not supporting the position of Key.

Figure 5.5 adds more empirical evidence on the power of the poll tax as a discriminatory tool.

Using an intercounty analysis that compares the percentage of African Americans in the rural Black Belt counties with those in an urban county, a number of interesting realities emerges. Fewer African Americans in the rural Black Belt counties paid their poll taxes than in the urban county. With a greater per capita income, African Americans in the capital city of Little Rock, the state's largest urban area, out-paid and therefore out-registered their rural counterparts. By 1964 the Civil Rights movement caused rural residents to catch up to their urban counterparts. The movement had given rural residents a reason, and now 50 percent were registered to vote. This supports the Cothran and Phillips findings and suggests that Key was wrong about the tax only hurting whites.

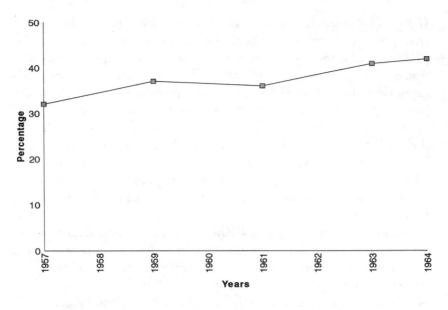

FIGURE 5.4 The Percentage of African Americans of Voting Age Who Paid
Poll Taxes, 1957–1964

Adapted from Arkansas History Commission, *Auditor of State Poll Tax Records: 1928–1973* (microfilm)
(Little Rock: Arkansas History Commission, 1985).

Before putting aside the academic debate over the Arkansas poll tax
data, it is fair to say that Key's analysis appeared before the state started to
break down the poll tax data by race. Nor should it come as a surprise that
the state auditor began a racial breakdown of the data in 1957, the year of
Little Rock and the racial crises in the city and state. This breakdown
continued until 1964, the year of the first major civil rights act. Only with
this racial breakdown of the data could a more precise understanding of
the impact of the poll tax be made. It is now correct to say that the poll
tax had direct economic and temporal as well as an indirect contextual
effects.[50] State discriminatory procedures and party leaders like Davis
provided the Democratic party with a positive image for some of the electorate and a negative image for other parts of the electorate.

African Americans in the state drew their impressions of the Democratic
party form their day-to-day, year-to-year experiences with leaders such as
Davis, with the white supremacist policies that the party pursued and promoted, and with the public policy of segregation which it legalized and

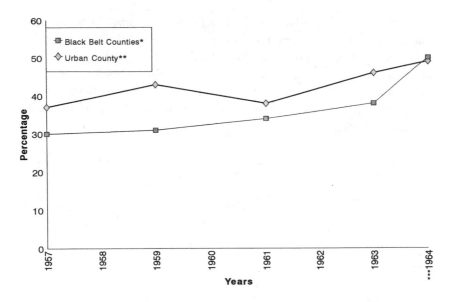

FIGURE 5.5 The Mean Percentage of African Americans Who Paid Poll
Taxes in Black Belt and Urban Counties, 1957–1964

Adapted from Arkansas History Commission, *Audit of State Poll Tax Records: 1928–1973* (microfilm).
*The Black Belt counties are Chicot, Lee, and Phillips.
**The urban county is Pulaski (which includes Little Rock).
***In 1964 the poll tax receipts in Pulaski county were not broken down by race, and have been extrapolated using the two previous years.

protected. Arkansas African Americans had to await a national image revitalization of the Democratic party before significant state affiliation could take place. But African American Democrats did not simply sit around and wait for the national party image to be revitalized, nor did they wait for the rise of progressive forces in the state and progressive leaders inside the party to rescue them. Beginning in 1930 they started filing legal suits against the party and continued straight through the era in which Governor Bill Clinton ran the state. They had both successes and failures. Even as Attorney General, Clinton did not use his office or its powers to achieve full political participation for the African American community and electorate.

Nevertheless, and despite these legal confrontations, the African American electorate supported his electoral bids, enabled his comeback, and enlarged his electoral victories in every campaign. This electorate by any yardstick clearly made possible this state's native son.

Clinton would be a force in the process of rebuilding the party image and in mobilizing this electorate in the state. Our political archaeological search has helped pinpoint this second largest demographic group in the state, and the role it played in the rise and evolution of this native-son candidate. And the transformation of this electorate from Republican to Democratic partisans came just prior to the rise of Clinton in the state's Democratic party.

Part Three

The Making of a Native-Son Candidate

The initial political steps must sooner or later be undertaken. A state based political career must be inaugurated. Then, and only then, does a political career on the national level become possible. Essential therefore to the rise of a native-son presidential candidate is the need to learn how to take those first political steps in the sundry political contests in one's home state. That is how Bill Clinton became a political candidate in Arkansas.

Bill Clinton ran for Congress in 1974, for state Attorney General in 1976, and for governor six times from 1978 to 1990. Only in 1986 did the legislature change the gubernatorial term from two years to four years. In his six races for that office, Clinton won three two-year terms and two four-year terms. He did not complete his last four-year term, because he ran for and won the presidency in 1992. In these six races for the governorship Clinton acquired not only his political legs but the endurance and stamina so essential in political contests.

In these three different types of political contests—for Congress, Attorney General, and Governor—that Clinton became a native son. In these political contests, Clinton built a friend and neighbor following. In the southern political system of a historically one-party state like Arkansas, any emerging candidate must acquire a core group of supporters and loyalists. This core group or faction starts with friends and neighbors from his own home town and then spreads out over the political terrain until it is large enough and powerful enough to elect and reelect the head of the faction. Gradually, Clinton put together his victorious faction. It did not happen at once, but it did come together by the time of his contest for state Attorney General. As has been noted, in southern politics factions are transient, fluid, and highly unstable, when not held together by matters such as race. Clinton fashioned several different factions, including in his losing effort to be reelected governor in 1980, and the new one he fashioned in 1982, by which he returned to office.

It is in the races for these types of state and local offices that the people of Arkansas, Georgia, Texas, and Alabama come to know their respective native-son candidates, and decide to support them across time and across offices. By the time that Clinton decided to run for president, he had already acquired the status of a native son. Although he did not run for president until 1992, the Arkansas political class and the media were well aware of the possibility by 1988. In that year he decided not to run for he highest office in the land, and this gave the electorate of Arkansas some time to think about supporting their native-son candidate for president.

In each of the three chapters in this section, an effort is made to determine the nature and scope of the faction behind the Clinton efforts in congressional, attorney general, and gubernatorial races. A detailed analysis is made of his electoral base and how that base shifted from office to office. Here the empirical features of a native son candidate are mapped out. For in each of these contests, there were gains and losses to the evolving Clinton faction and electoral coalition. And in the rise of a southern native-son presidential candidate, statewide office can prove crucial. For Clinton, it was the office and his long tenure as governor that finally crafted him into his state's native-son presidential candidate.

CHAPTER SIX

The Congressional Vote for Clinton

Native-son presidential candidates must be politically made. They must arise from the electoral milieu of their home state. There is simply no other way. In 1974 Bill Clinton sought the seat in Arkansas's 3rd Congressional district. It was the only seat held by a Republican in a historically one-party Democratic state. Clinton sought to recapture that seat for the Democrats. In this race, law professor Clinton would not disturb the Democratic political equation in the state, nor make enemies of powerful and entrenched Democratic incumbents. This entry into electoral politics was not a challenge to formidable party factions but a response to a deviation from the normal partisanship pattern. Such a strategy, of taking on a successful Republican in a Democratic state, was a way of soliciting and energizing the party behind a newcomer. It was a pioneering strategy and a less than confrontational path to political birth.

Another southern native-son presidential candidate, Jimmy Carter, had initially contemplated a congressional run as his means of entering Georgia politics, but decided at the last moment to emerge as a state senate challenger in a boss-controlled district.[1] Although he eventually succeeded, it was only after court and legal action.[2] The boss-controlled district engaged in electoral fraud to defeat this political upstart and novice. Carter's court challenge succeeded only at the last minute.[3]

In historically one-party Democratic systems like those in Georgia and Arkansas, longstanding partisan affiliations have permitted permanent factional groups, interests, and leaders to become entrenched at times. Political newcomers such as Carter and Clinton must find ways to break into the existing and prevailing political arrangement and structures. They must either accommodate these existing forces, directly challenge them, or find alternative routes around them. With his congressional bid, Jimmy Carter was trying an end run around entrenched political arrangements. Clinton's strategy in 1974 dramatically differed from that of Carter. But no matter their strategy for political birth, native-son presidential candidates must arise.

Congressional Candidate Clinton's Letter to President Gerald Ford

On October 6, 1974, Bill Clinton, the Democratic nominee for Congress, sent a letter to President Gerald Ford suggesting an economic strategy for the nation and proposals for his upcoming economic address to the nation and its lawmakers. He offered the President nine proposals for a "balanced budget in 1975 and work for a surplus in 1976."

The congressional candidate told the President that he had talked with nearly everyone in the 3rd Congressional District by meeting with "small farmers, small businessmen, working people, heads of large companies, retirees and almost anyone you could imagine." Claiming these people as his "economic advisers," Clinton told the President that these people wanted an economic policy "that will enable them to buy the food they need, to meet payments on their homes or to buy a new house, and to be able to live without fear that they may not be able to meet their daily economic commitments." To achieve these goals, Clinton suggested that government policies should not favor large multinational corporations or foreign governments above working people. His nine proposals offered specific mechanisms for achieving these goals.

1. We should have a balance budget in 1975 and work for a surplus in 1976;
2. I believe there should be an easing of the tight money policy at home and a tightening of the outflow of our money abroad, and that the Federal Reserve Board should alter its operation to bring the price of money down and then should vary its reserve requirements as you can authorize it to do;
3. Capital export controls should be reimposed and there should be a

    modification of foreign investment tax credits to discourage the
    outflow of dollars abroad;

4. We should terminate the insurance policies which insure multina-
    tional corporations against political reversals overseas and should
    consider giving tax relief to moderate and lower middle income
    people who have been most hard hit by inflation;

5. We should bring down food prices and reestablish the grain
    reserve program;

6. I believe you should authorize the Council on Wage and Price
    Stability to delay certain price increases when they are clearly
    unwarranted and I would also support a restraint to high wage
    increases;

7. You and the Congress should exercise general oversight over the
    operation of the Federal Reserve Board and the large banks which
    set the prime interest rate, and give them the power to keep prime
    interest rates down;

8. You should consider an end to federal subsidies to big business, as
    well as retail price maintenance, market domination by conglom-
    erates and federal regulations in transportation and other indus-
    tries which are obviously inefficient;

9. You and Congress should work to increase funding for the Small
    Business Administration and to increase the availability of loans
    to small independent businessmen.[4]

None of these nine proposals are specific to the 3rd District. Although
Clinton claimed to have derived all of these proposals from his potential
constituents, they are all national and international in scope. Not one tar-
gets the 3rd Congressional District, the state of Arkansas, or the South.
Such a set of proposals presumes constituents who are the most public-
minded and public-spirited people in the country, who have never heard
of pork barrel projects for their district. The alternative interpretation is
that the candidate was looking down the road to a time when he would be
in a position to address national economic policy.

    Nevertheless, the letter was a bold political strategy. It showed that the
candidate would work for his constituents. It gave his supporters the
impression that he was not above going directly to the top to get a hearing. The letter provided the candidate with talking points in his contest
against the Republican incumbent. And a response to the letter or the
lack thereof would also make news for the local media mill. Here was a
tool to get attention. The letter called for a balance budget and a budget

surplus. Twenty-four years later, in the second year of his second term as president, he submitted a balanced budget and asked the Republican Congress to use the budget surplus to maintain Social Security. Ideas have strange life cycles.

For the moment, candidate Clinton had a letter to the President with which he could face the incumbent congressman.

The Rise of a Republican Congressman in a One-Party Democratic State

In 1966, Republican John Hammerschmidt won election along with the Republican governor, Winthrop Rockefeller. Hammerschmidt defeated incumbent Democratic congressman James Trimble with 53 percent of the vote and a 9,920 vote plurality.[5] Congressman Hammerschmidt held one of the state's four congressional seats.

After the 1970 census, the Arkansas state legislative redrew congressional districts; on March 22, 1971 a reshaped and remade 3rd Congressional District emerged. In this new district, the Republican congressman continued to win.

Figure 6.1 indicates Congressman Hammerschmidt's continued level of electoral support. The mean vote for this Republican congressman was 67.3 percent. Only the initial incumbent, with 48 percent of the vote in 1974, offered any serious challenge in an overwhelmingly Democratic state. The mean vote for his Democratic challengers was 32.7 percent. There is a contextual reason for Congressman Hammerschmidt's success.

Like Clinton, Hammerschmidt was a native son of the state, born in Harrison, in Boone county, one of the traditional mountain counties that since the Civil War era have consistently supported the Republican party in state and national politics.[6] Unlike Clinton, Hammerschmidt grew up in a Republican context and understood the state's political discourse and debate in Republican terms. He was chairman of the state Republican party from 1964 to 1966, and a delegate to the Republican national convention from 1964 through 1984. Before this he was a wellknown businessman. In the year that Clinton challenged him, *The 1974 Almanac of American Politics* described his district political base: "The 3rd district of Arkansas is in the northwest quarter of the state. It is a region of green hills rising to mountains, of historic poverty, but recently of relative prosperity. . . . The cities of the 3rd are medium-size, and the tempo of life in them is that which many Americans seem to consider most desirable."[7] "The district . . . . contains the state's most reliably Republican territory, the mountain counties in the North, which never backed the Confederacy and have remained

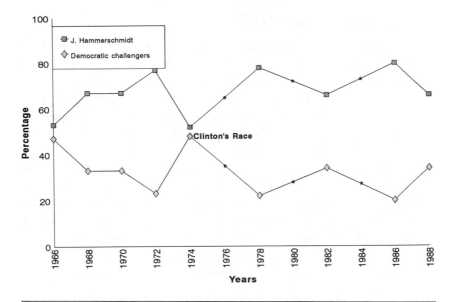

FIGURE 6.1 Percentage of the Vote for Republican Congressman J.
Hammerschmidt and His Democratic Challengers, 1966–1988

Adapted from Scammon, ed., *America Votes: 1988* (Washington, D.C.: Congressional Quarterly Press, 1988).
*Hammerschmidt faced no challenger in 1976, 1980, and 1984, and no vote was recorded in those years.

faithful to the party of the Union, the Republican party, ever since."[8]
Despite the redrawing of the district in 1970, 1980, and 1990, it still sends a
Republican to Congress.

Here is how the *Almanac* forecast the political future for Hammerschmidt in 1974:

> The lone Republican has apparently gotten on well with the other
> members of the state's delegation, having received public praise
> from some of them. Although Democratic candidates keep appear-
> ing on the ballot against him, Hammerschmidt wins by overwhelm-
> ing margins. He will almost certainly continue to do so in the
> future.[9]

The *Almanac* analysis predicted a dismal outcome for Bill Clinton's challenge: he was doomed before he started. Clinton's political strategy might
have been innovative in terms of creating his political birth, but the
incumbent Republican whom he sought to unseat was well entrenched in
this Democratic state.

The Primary and Runoff Vote

The redrawn 3rd congressional district had 21 counties—38 percent of the total number of counties in the entire state. The district had given Republican presidential candidates 74 percent of its vote in 1972 and 43 percent of its vote in 1968, with the Republican presidential candidate carrying the district. In 1968 this district gave George Wallace's American Independent party 30 percent of its vote. Democratic presidential candidate Humphrey got 27 percent in 1968 and McGovern 26 percent in 1972.

Of the redrawn district's 21 counties, in this study's demographic categorization, 7 counties (33%) fall into the rural category, 9 counties (43%) fall into the town category, 3 counties (14%) fall into the urban category, and 2 counties (10%) into the home county category—Garland county for Clinton and Boone county for Hammerschmidt. There were no Black Belt counties in the district, and African Americans made up only 3 percent of the entire district population, with most of these being in Little Rock, which was not demographically an urban center district, even though it is the state capital.

In addition to Clinton, three other Democratic challengers had their eye on this seat. A Republican seat in the midst of a Democratic state is an attractive lure. In Arkansas, the dominance of a single party means that political ambition must be played out in a crowded primary field. Factional rivalry is the order of the day.

Four candidates entered the Democratic primary for the party nomination to face the Republican incumbent in the November general election (table 6.1). Turnout in Arkansas in 1974 was down from the 1972 elections. "Of the estimated 1,372,125 persons eligible to vote (995,985 of

TABLE 6.1 Results of the 1974 Democratic Primary in
the Third Congressional District

Candidate	Votes	Percentage
Clinton	59,697	43.6
Rainwater	36,145	26.4
Stewart	34,959	25.5
Scanlon	6,121	4.5
Total	136,922	100.0

Institute of Politics in Arkansas, *Arkansas Votes 1974* (Conway,
Arkansas: Hendrix College, 1975), 15–17.

whom were registered), only 40.1 percent cast ballots in the General Election. This compared to a 50.1 percent turnout in 1972 and 52.1 percent in 1970."[10] In the primary, Clinton came in first, with 44 percent of the vote. But Arkansas, like most southern states, requires a runoff election if no candidate garners 50 percent of the vote.[11] Clinton faced the second place candidate, Rainwater, in a runoff election.

In Clinton's initial primary victory, he won 12 counties for 57.1 percent (table 6.2). Clearly his emerging electoral coalition was stronger than any of his competitors.

At least at the county level, Clinton had fashioned a rather broad electoral foundation. This can be seen in a demographic analysis of these counties. Against his Democratic primary opponents, Clinton received his strongest support from his home county of Garland, capturing two-thirds (66.7%) of the vote. This was followed by his performance in the urban, rural, and the town counties, in which he had the least support. With this base of support, he entered the runoff election.

TABLE 6.2 Results of the 1974 Third Congressional
District Election by County

Candidate	Counties Won	Percentage
DEMOCRATIC PRIMARY		
Clinton	12	57.1
Rainwater	5	23.8
Stewart	4	19.1
Scanlon	0	0.0
Total	21	100.0
DEMOCRATIC RUNOFF		
Clinton	20	95.2
Rainwater	1	4.8
Total	21	100.0
GENERAL ELECTION		
Clinton	13	61.9
Hammerschmidt	8	38.1
Total	21	100.0

Adapted from *Arkansas Votes 1974*, 17.

TABLE 6.3 Results of the 1974 Democratic Primary in the Third Congressional District by Demographic Category

Candidate	Urban Counties		Town Counties		Rural Counties		Garland County	
	Votes	%	Votes	%	Votes	%	Votes	%
Clinton	19,300	43.2	21,786	37.3	6,284	41.0	12,327	66.7
Rainwater	14,893	33.4	15,247	26.1	3,660	23.9	2,345	12.6
Stewart	8,267	18.5	19,128	32.8	4,525	29.5	3,039	16.3
Scanlon	2,185	4.9	2,188	3.7	849	5.5	899	4.8
Total	44,645	100.0	58,349	99.9	15,318	99.9	18,610	99.9

Adapted from *Arkansas Votes 1974*, 17.

TABLE 6.4 Results of the 1974 Democratic Runoff in
the Third Congressional District

Candidate	Votes	Percentage
Clinton	37,788	69.0
Rainwater	17,011	31.0
Total	54,799	100.0

Adapted from *Arkansas Votes 1974*, 17.

Usually in a southern runoff election, the candidate who placed second in the primary will win. This time it was not to be. Clinton triumphed again. Rainwater got barely half of his primary voters to support him a second time. He received only a third of the vote (table 6.4). Clinton, whose vote totals were significantly down from the primary vote, still captured 69 percent of the vote and won 95.2 percent of the counties. He overwhelmed his runoff opponent.

Demographically, as seen in table 6.5, Clinton's runoff election victory was substantial in every category. He garnered 82 percent of the vote in his home county of Garland and 71 percent in the rural counties. The urban counties were third, while the town counties remained the least supportive, yet giving him his largest vote total of the four demographic categories. Clinton had won his second election.

The General Election Vote

However Clinton could not defeat the Republican incumbent in a one-party Democratic state. Incumbency and all its advantages prevailed in the 1974 November general election. Table 6.6 reveals that Clinton came close: he lost by 6,294 votes, or 48 percent of the vote to Hammerschmidt's 52 percent. Clinton won 13 counties to Hammerschmidt's 8 counties, yet Representative Hammerschmidt won in the most populated counties, and in those with the largest voter turnout.

When the vote is disaggregated via demographic categories (table 6.7) it becomes obvious that Clinton's electoral base had shifted slightly from what it had been in the Democratic primary and runoff elections. In this election, Clinton for the first time carried the town counties and ran strongest in the rural counties. This was the reverse of his previous pattern. There was also an embarrassing reversal in his own home county of Garland. Con-

TABLE 6.5 Results of the 1974 Democratic Runoff in the Third Congressional District by Demographic Category

Candidate	Urban Counties		Town Counties		Rural Counties		Garland County	
	Votes	%	Votes	%	Votes	%	Votes	%
Clinton	12,673	68.6	15,943	66.1	5,234	71.0	3,938	81.8
Rainwater	5,809	31.4	8,183	33.9	2,140	29.0	879	18.2
Total	18,482	100.0	24,126	100.0	7,374	100.0	4,817	100.0

Adapted from *Arkansas Votes 1974*, 17.

TABLE 6.6 Results of the 1974 General Election in the
Third Congressional District

Candidate	Votes	Percentage
Clinton	83,030	48.2
Hammerschmidt	89,324	51.8
Total	172,354	100.0

Adapted from *Arkansas Votes 1974*, 17.

gressman Hammerschmidt won in Clinton's own locale. Previously the home town folks had rallied to Clinton's banner. But in the general election, the home town folks supported the incumbent over their own native son. Rarely in southern politics do home town boys lose their home town.[12]

The loss at home for Clinton was coupled with a loss in the urban counties. The Congressman captured all three of the urban counties. This was his strongest area of support outside of Clinton's own home county. While the vote from the urban areas was the highest Clinton had received in the three elections, it was well below the Republican incumbent's vote total.

The urban counties had, by Clinton's runoff victory, rallied to him and significantly increased their support. Yet they were not ready to make the switch to the Democratic party. Even in a historically one-party state, party loyalty is not the only factor that shapes the outcomes of elections. Even a promising and progressive newcomer cannot always restore party loyalties. In this case, Clinton did cause some voters to return to the fold.

> When historians look at the 1974 election year in Arkansas, there will be several candidates for mention in the history books: . . . Representative Hammerschmidt, the state's only major Republican officeholder, was pushed to the limit before emerging with a narrow 3.6 percent margin over challenger Bill Clinton, a University of Arkansas law professor.[13]

Clinton had performed much better than expected. In 1974,

> Arkansas voters were returning to their voting habits of a decade ago and focusing most of their attention on the Democratic primary rather than on the general election. The primary turnout exceeded the General Election turnout in 1974 for the first time since 1962.[14]

TABLE 6.7 Results of the 1974 General Election in the Third Congressional District by Demographic Category

Candidate	Urban Counties		Town Counties		Rural Counties		Garland County	
	Votes	%	Votes	%	Votes	%	Votes	%
Clinton	27,176	41.4	33,197	50.8	13,790	59.6	8,867	48.8
Hammerschmidt	38,492	58.6	32,183	49.2	9,334	40.4	9,315	51.2
Total	65,668	100.0	65,380	100.0	23,124	100.0	18,182	100.0

Adapted from *Arkansas Votes 1974*, 17.

While this upsurge helped Clinton capture his initial electoral victory, it did not help him in the general election.

But by launching his initial political campaign against a Republican incumbent in a Democratic state, he captured the admiration of party leaders and supporters.

> Losing the congressional election did not hurt Clinton's political status in Arkansas and enhanced his image as an emerging star of the Democratic party. He came out of the contest with what all politicians covet—an aura of inevitability.[15]

A national publication commented on his promising future: "observers of the Arkansas political scene predict a long career ahead for Clinton, whether he runs for Congress again or for some other office."[16]

The Clinton-Hammerschmidt contest "turned out to be a close race indeed, with Hammerschmidt squeaking to the narrowest victory of his career with only 52 percent of the vote. He was saved only by his strong showing in Fort Smith."[17] There political bossism and corruption carried the day and the election against Clinton. In losing this election, Clinton gained respect, sympathy, and a political following. "His race was the most talked about contest in the state. He had become the darling of the Democratic Party by taking on Hammerschmidt and coming within 2 percentage points of defeating him, by far the best showing any opponent even made against him."[18] Blair reiterates this insight by noting that Hammerschmidt's "only close challenge came from Bill Clinton in 1974; but in 1980 and again in 1984, the Democrats did not even attempt to oppose him."[19]

Examination of the congressional vote for Clinton is quite revealing not only about the shifts and changes in each election but about the very nature of a candidate's initial electoral coalition.[20] Even in a closed party system such as in Arkansas, a budding candidate can find and capture an electoral following. Personal followings and factions can be put together.

Newcomers and political novices in such states can expect serious competition in the primaries. Both serious and frivolous candidates will vie for available positions, especially when the incumbent is from the minority party. Intraparty rivalry is the norm in becoming a native-son candidate in such a state. Yet intraparty rivalry is not the only obstacle to overcome. There is also incumbency.

There are two types of incumbencies. The incumbency of the majority party in southern politics is difficult to overcome, and most challengers wait for retirement, advancement, scandal, or the advent of a popular president.

Clinton faced an incumbent of the minority party. An aberration in a one-party state, such an incumbency invites challenge. Minority party incumbents offer the hope and the possibility of a political accident in which the electorate will wake up and return to its true political moorings and partisan affiliations. Challenging this type of incumbent lowers intraparty heat and reduces partisan enemies, and allows the possibility of becoming a party hero. Challenging a minority party incumbent can be the making of a rising party star. It can instantly alert the national media. Challenging a minority party incumbent can mean a rising political wind. It is one of the ways in which one-party systems recruit future party leaders.

There is also the matter of creating an initial election coalition. A political neophyte has to mobilize and energize voters both for himself and for the party. Challenging a minority incumbent rallies the troops. It not only brings out the party faithful, it also reconverts lost political souls and attracts unattached voters.

An initial coalition like Clinton's must be tested, shaped, and structured. One way of doing this is though intraparty rivalry. Intense political contests shake out personal factions. Voters have to make up their minds about their candidates and their promised programs. Thus these initial shifting electoral coalitions start to take on stable and permanent form, at least at the core level.

Clinton emerged from the congressional election with a following, and some notice as a rising political star. He was a native-son candidate about to emerge and evolve. The political winds in Arkansas were starting to reset themselves behind a new home town boy.

CHAPTER SEVEN

The Attorney General Vote for Clinton

Clinton had to choose whether to run for Congress again or for the office of state attorney general.[1] "Although Clinton thrived on the electoral process he wanted an easier ride this time. He had lost an election, and it was always possible that he could lose again, which would greatly damage both his ego and his nascent career."[2]

Another reason for this choice was the political career ladder. In state government, the office of attorney general is often a stepping stone to the governorship.[3] This is especially true in Arkansas.

> Unlike many other states where the Lieutenant Governorship is a prime stepping-stone to the governorship . . . only one elected Arkansas governor to date was a previously elected lieutenant governor. . . . A far greater likelihood [is] the Attorney General: of the last five attorneys general four have made a [successful] bid for the governorship.[4]

Selecting this office therefore was a strategic choice for a rising native-son candidate. It offered additional options, whereas other state offices were dead ends.

> Long before he revealed his intentions publicly, Clinton began tiny
> steps helpful to the waging of a statewide campaign. The Democratic
> State Committee . . . appointed him to head its affirmative action
> committee. . . . This convenient assignment allowed Clinton to travel
> the state at party expense to meet with Democratic activists.[5]

His appointment at the law school at the University of Arkansas also
helped, as his former students returned to numerous communities around
the state to practice law. In his race for attorney general, they came out to
support him.

Another factor was the political goodwill he had earned by launching
his initial political campaign against a Republican incumbent in a Democratic state. As Martin Walker wrote of his 1974 race:

> On election day, Hammerschmidt held his seat with just over 51 per-
> cent of the vote. But Clinton had become the party's darling; thrilling
> the Democrats with an intensely tight race and the conviction that
> they had a new political star now known across the state.[6]

Clinton's loss in the congressional election had created for him an admir-
ing initial base. Now he had to test the strength and resiliency of that base
and goodwill.

The Primary Vote

On March 17, 1976, Clinton announced his candidacy for state attorney
general in the rotunda of the state Capitol, with Hillary Rodham at his
side.[7] With this announcement he expanded his political reach, moving
from a congressional district to a statewide office. Although the political
reach was greater in this second effort, the political risk lay only in the
primary whereas with the congressional seat the political risk was not at
the entrance level, but in the general election. With his announcement,
Clinton restructured the political risk to himself.

In southern states competition is most critical in the Democratic primary: victory in the primary is tantamount to winning the office. Clinton's announcement brought out other party hopefuls and contenders. On
filing day there were three candidates: Clinton, Secretary of State George
Jernigan, and Deputy Attorney General Clarence Cash.[8] The Republican
party did not put up a candidate for the position. It would be a Democratic party affair from start to finish. Clinton was well positioned, even
though his opponents were already statewide officials.

Clinton's precampaign statewide organizing, building of support, and his campaigning for the position helped him hold his initial electoral base and significantly expand it throughout the rest of the state. He had moved from a contest with only 21 counties to one with 75. This enlarged electoral base permitted him to overwhelm his Democratic opponents. These statewide officials saw their own political and electoral bases collapse. Clinton won the primary with 55.6 percent of the total vote, avoiding the need for a runoff.

Table 7.1 provides insights into the vote in the primary, and into the nature and scope of Clinton's first statewide victory. Clinton had no serious electoral competition. Jernigan captured 25 percent of the vote and ran a distant second in the overall total vote. Cash captured barely one-fifth of the vote and ran a very distant third. Clinton nearly edged him three votes to one. He was not a serious contender for the position even though he had worked in the office of the attorney general.

Jernigan and Cash did not get enough votes between them to hold Clinton under 50 percent of the vote. With a broadly based victory in the Democratic primary, Clinton was elected to office without a Republican challenger. Arkansas law prohibits the collection of election data when a candidate is unopposed, so there are no figures for the November general election.

Disaggregating the primary data into a county-level analysis, the broad base of the Clinton primary victory become even more apparent. Table 7.2 reveals that Clinton won 69 of 75 counties, or 92 percent of the counties in the state. Jernigan captured 4 counties for 5.3 percent of the total while Cash carried only two for 2.7 percent. At the county level, Clinton's victory was sweeping. He was now an electoral force in the state.

TABLE 7.1 Results of the 1976 Democratic Arkansas
Attorney General Primary

Candidate	Votes	Percentage
Clinton	273,744	55.6
Jernigan	123,819	25.2
Cash	94,384	19.2
Total	491,947	100.0

Paul Riviere, *1976 Arkansas Election Results* (Little Rock: Office of the
Secretary of State, 1980), 81.

TABLE 7.2 Counties Won by Each Candidate in the
1976 Democratic Arkansas Attorney
General Primary

Candidate	Counties Won	Percentage
Clinton	69	92.0
Jernigan	4	5.3
Cash	2	2.7
Total	75	100.0

Adapted from Paul Riviere, *1976 Arkansas Elections*, 81.

Jernigan captured only two contiguous counties—Mississippi and Poinsett. His other two counties were scattered around the state. Cash's two counties were also scattered. At the county level, Clinton's initial statewide victory was widespread (map 7.1).

Clinton won the urban, town, and rural counties by clear cut majorities (table 7.3). In none of these demographic categories did Jernigan or Cash come close to being electorally competitive. Even combined, they posed no real threat to the Clinton candidacy. Jernigan won one urban county, Mississippi, two town counties, Poinsett and Columbia, and one African American county, Lee. Cash won one town county, Independence, and one rural county, Cleveland (map 7.1). Clinton's only serious weakness was in three town counties that were scattered throughout the state.

In his home counties of Hempstead and Garland, Clinton captured 51 percent and 72 percent of the vote, respectively. He did better in the county where he grew up than in the county in which he was born. The turnout was 58 percent in Hempstead (where he was born) but only 43 percent in Garland (the county of his maturity). Jernigan and Cash together got less than a third of the vote in the home counties.

Clinton won two of the three African American majority counties—Chicot, Lee, and Phillips. He lost Lee county to Jernigan, who captured 52 percent of the vote. Cash was not competitive for the African American vote. Clinton received 55 percent, 50 percent, and 33 percent of the vote in Chicot, Phillips, and Lee counties, respectively. Overall, Clinton got a mean vote of 49.4 percent of the vote in the African American majority counties. Walker's observation that Clinton used the 1976 election to build "what was to become a formidable network of support among black voters" is clearly borne out by the analysis of these three

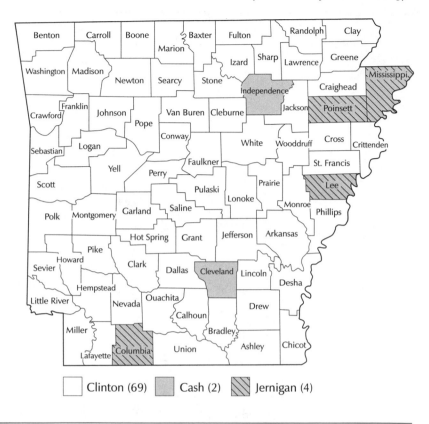

MAP 7.1 **The Number of Counties Won by the Candidates in the Attorney General's Race in the Democratic Primary, 1976.**

African American majority counties.[9] African American voters in this election began to respond to Arkansas's rising native son and political newcomer. In this initial statewide election effort of Clinton's, African American voters could build alliances and coalitions just like other groups in the Democratic party.

All demographic categories provided significant majority support for Clinton's attorney general victory in the Democratic primary. In this race Clinton projected himself into every corner of the state and built an alliance with the rising African American vote, particularly in the town and rural counties where he had been strong in his congressional race. Clinton built a significant and expanded electoral base beyond what he had set into motion during his run for Congress. He was now an elected officeholder and full fledged Democrat. This had been accomplished quickly, within the two-year period of 1974 to 1976.

TABLE 7-3 Results of the 1976 State Attorney General Primary by Demographic Category

| Candidate | Urban Counties | | Town Counties | | Rural Counties | | Home Counties | | Black Belt Counties | |
	Votes	%	Votes	%	Votes	%	Votes	%	Votes	%
Clinton	104,126	52.5	106,508	56.5	40,786	59.5	14,153	68.7	8,171	52.2
Jernigan	58,434	29.4	42,480	22.5	14,060	20.5	3,403	16.5	5,442	34.7
Cash	35,934	18.1	39,659	21.0	13,686	20.0	3,049	14.8	2,056	13.1
Total	198,494	100.0	188,647	100.0	68,532	100.0	20,605	100.0	15,669	100.0

Adapted from Riviere, *1976 Arkansas Elections*, 81.

The Congressional Base and the Attorney General Base: The Correlation

How much of the electoral base which he established in his congressional primary and runoff races held in his state attorney general race? To establish the nature of this linkage in empirical, instead of impressionistic, terms we analyze the county-level election returns from the 3rd Congressional District in the 1974 and 1976 elections.

The comparison can be seen in table 7.4 both in terms of absolute vote differences and in terms of association and the degree to which the 1974 vote can be said to have shaped and assisted in structuring the 1976 vote. In every county, save Clinton's home county of Garland, the vote rose significantly in 1976. In six counties the vote doubled. Clinton's vote increased in 20 of the 21 counties in the second of the two elections. Although the increase can be accounted for in part by the fact that the 1976 vote occurred in a presidential year, the doubling of the vote in some counties suggests the effectiveness of Clinton's campaigning.

Clinton increased his support in these 20 counties by 31,416 votes. His mean vote rose from 2,843 votes per county to 4,243 votes per county. Clinton's electoral coalition was significantly increased in these 20 counties over his initial electoral coalition. The core electoral following that Clinton built in the congressional race ballooned by his second race.

In 1974, voters were sending a congressman to represent them in Washington, while in 1976 the voters were electing a person to represent the state's legal interests both inside and outside the state. Were these two electoral coalitions linked?

A correlation analysis reveals that the two Clinton electoral coalitions in these 20 counties differed significantly. There was no statistically significant association between them. The voters in these elections had different interests, although the same candidate. Personality and candidate factors competed with other issues for the voters' attention in these two contests. And personal followings were not as strange as they had been at the time when Key wrote about Arkansas and southern politics in 1949, when he found unusual coalitions between rich and poor, urban and rural, groups.

The decline of the vote in Garland county—where Clinton grew up—offers additional evidence on this point. Home town native son issues gave way to other matters. Ordinarily the home town boy should carry the day. But Clinton lost his home town in the 1974 election and between the elections lost some more of those initial core voters. Clinton's initial

TABLE 7.4 A Comparison of the Primary Vote by County for
Clinton for Congress and Attorney General

County	1974 Congressional Vote	1976 Attorney General Vote	Difference
Baxter	2,400	4,080	1,680
Benton	3,522	3,930	408
Boone	2,040	3,738	1,698
Carroll	1,227	3,204	1,977
Crawford	2,978	4,889	1,911
Franklin	2,073	3,789	1,716
Garland	12,327	10,324	-2,003
Johnson	2,762	4,381	1,619
Logan	1,916	4,802	2,886
Madison	1,332	1,762	430
Marion	894	2,699	1,805
Montgomery	760	2,202	1,442
Newton	779	1,260	481
Perry	1,032	1,687	655
Polk	1,049	3,379	2,330
Pope	3,950	7,180	3,230
Scott	823	3,023	2,200
Searcy	664	888	224
Sebastian	8,127	9,148	1,021
Washington	7,651	7,778	127
Yell	1,391	4,967	3,576
Total	59,697	89,110	31,416
Mean	2,843	4,243	1,571

Adapted from *Arkansas Votes 1974*, 16; Riviere, "1976 Arkansas Elections," 82.

electoral coalition changed in his own home county. He lost 16.3 percent of his initial electoral coalition at home. Candidate and personality factors could not offset other issues in the voters' choice equation.

Table 7.4 shows that Clinton's initial electoral coalition underwent a profound change in the two years between the 1974 and 1976 elections. New voters were added to the initial electoral coalition, and at least in Garland county, old voters left the coalition. A new political campaign both attached and detached voters, changing the nature of Clinton's initial electoral coalition. Precisely how much did the initial electoral coalition change?

Writing in 1948 of Arkansas politics, Key noted that "whether Arkansas's fluid factionalism or its issueless politics came first or whether each fed on the other, the upshot is a politics singularly free of anything save the petty argument and personal loyalty of the moment."[10] There is no correlative association between the 21 counties in Clinton's initial 1974 race and the same 21 counties in Clinton's 1976 attorney general election (r = .27).

From the vote in these 21 counties in 1974 one could only forecast accurately 8 percent of Clinton's support in these counties in the 1976 election (r^2 = .08). "Loose and changing groupings of voters may be the cause, or the results, of a politics devoid of issues and dedicated to the choice of the 'best qualified candidate.' "[11] The correlative empirical data from these counties reveal that Clinton's initial electoral coalition was fluid, loose, and ever changing.

In the context of Arkansas politics, initial electoral coalitions possess a transient quality, a fleeting presence, an easy flowing fluidity. Electoral coalitions must be rebuilt and refashioned in every subsequent election. They need constant tending. Any initial coalition in Arkansas would lack consistency in electoral support. The "best qualified" candidate must build up "a system of alliances—in each campaign."[12]

The race in the 3rd Congressional District was a first step, a way to begin forging, but not the creation of, a permanent electoral foundation. That had to be constructed later, in a step-by-step process. In these three races, Clinton's electoral coalition continued to change and reformat itself. Even his home county, Garland, moved from initially giving him its highest support in 1974 to turning out for the Republican incumbent. Clinton's congressional election coalition was loose and fluid. At its best the initial coalition was simply a starting point, a launching pad.

Beyond creating a shifting electoral base, these races provided invaluable campaign experience. Running in 21 counties prepared emerging native-son candidate Clinton to launch his campaign for statewide office. The race in these counties provided the ground for a larger and more expansive effort. Unlike the situation Key saw in the 1940s, Clinton came of political age during a time of progressive statewide candidates. Traditionalism in Arkansas politics was fading as progressivism rose, if erratically. While the electorate embraced progressive candidates on a candidate-by-candidate basis, it had not overcome its legacy of transient and loose factional groupings. The electorate was showing signs of movement, but not in a straightforward linear manner. Clinton appeared and won office in this transitional period. Thus he had to move from electoral contest to electoral contest fashioning a new alliance every time.

For the attorney general race, Clinton had to start the process almost, but not quite, from the beginning. But in this new beginning a native-son candidate was about to be born.

The Attorney General Vote: A Summary

Clinton's primary vote was just enough for victory. A native-son presidential candidate had been born. Unlike Carter, who had decided to run for Congress as his initial effort but at the last minute filed for a state senate seat, Clinton tried a congressional campaign on his way to becoming the state attorney general. Carter won at the district level, Clinton at the statewide level. Two native sons followed two different and distinct paths to political birth. Yet both men used retail politics as a way onto the political stage.

Retail politics "in Arkansas . . . meant traveling to every town in the district and meeting as many voters as possible and asking them for their votes."[13] In Arkansas, retail politics was "a sacred political belief. . . . The political folk wisdom included a statistical component. It was estimated that 60 percent of the people vote for the candidate who met them first and asked them for their vote."[14] Clinton captured 56.5 percent of the attorney general vote. Political folk wisdom was nearly correct. In the same year that Jimmy Carter became a native-son Democratic president, Clinton won his first political office in his home state. Clinton was getting ready to follow in Carter's political shoes.

But retail politics is more than just the road to political victory in southern states. It is also a road inside the Democratic party. Here where party elites, activists, and organizational chieftains dwell, solid retail politics captures their attention, their commitment, and most important, their loyalty and support. Retail politics, in the manner that Clinton practiced it, gave him access to all the key political players and party officials. It made for Clinton a political future in the party. If the congressional effort had captured the party's attention, the state attorney general victory made Clinton a member of the Democratic party elite. Here is how southern Democratic parties replenish and renew themselves as the oldline southern segregationists fade, thanks in part to the effects of the 1965 Voting Rights Act and the newly enfranchised African American voter. Moderate and progressive candidates could now rise in these southern parties. However, "progressive and moderate in the southern context does not mean liberal, it merely means acceptance of or recognition that the law on race has changed." In fact, Clinton did see his progression as being liberal.[15] Both Carter and Clinton were forces in the transformation of southern Democratic parties and politics. They were a part of the transformation from segregationist party leaders to nonsegregationist leaders.

This transformation can be dated back in Arkansas to 1970 and the campaign for governor between Dale Bumpers and Winthrop Rockefeller.

Two political historians describe this transformation:

> The subsequent Bumpers-Rockefeller campaign was, for the Arkansas of the Faubus era, a novel gentlemanly affair, with both candidates agreeing that Arkansas's industry and its public sector should grow, that racial discrimination should stop, and that the winner should continue the policy begun by Rockefeller of appointing blacks to public agencies.[16]

They concluded that"recent state elections have suggested a shift away from the politics of Goldwater, Wallace, and racial turmoil [toward] a wave of progressive Democrats. Arkansas was such a state."[17]

These political historians came to their conclusions based on analyzing gubernatorial and senatorial elections. Clinton's victory as attorney general as well as Carter's earlier election at the state senate level suggest that this transformation was underway, at least in some states, at the lower levels of state and local politics. Clinton's initial victory provides insights into how moderate to progressive candidates can begin at the lower levels and move up the political and party ladder.

Reflecting on the scope of Clinton's victory in the attorney general race, Stephen Smith writes that "the obvious plan was to build on the organizational strength in the Third District. Clinton won clear majorities in fifty-one counties, led the field in eighteen other counties, and finished second in the remaining six."[18] One of his opponents, Secretary of State George Jernigan Jr., later quipped that he would never again run against someone with three home towns—Hope, Hot Springs, and Fayetteville. The 1976 campaign was the shortest in Clinton's career, announced in March and over in May.[19] This rapid political victory gave him time to work the party apparatus for ways to enhance his electoral base. There were, as noted earlier, soft spots in this electoral victory. Some of the counties had not climbed aboard, nor had some of the demographical categories fully embraced him. And clearly there was a way to go in maximizing the African American vote.

Single election results, no matter how impressive, leave one essential question unanswered—the stability and endurance of this electoral coalition and base. A single election, as we have noted, cannot demonstrate the depth of the winning coalition, especially in southern Democratic states notable for the unstable and transient nature of their electoral coalitions. A single election does not test the stability of the coalition over time. Thus this single election victory does not reveal much about the stability of this new statewide coalition.

Fashioning a new electoral coalition is possible in a one-party state given the transformation of the party context in the state. Carter won his first election only to lose his second, whereas Clinton lost his first but won the second. Electoral coalitions in these states are indeed transient and unstable. Multiple elections can help to give some degree of permanence and continuity to these budding and evolving coalitions. Along with these electoral coalitions, political coalitions—groups of leaders, activists, contributors, and organizers—form around the candidate and his efforts. These groups also come and go, but the nature of Arkansas politics (which until 1986 had two-year gubernatorial terms) made the constant testing of these coalitions possible. A single election victory would not help to set and fix the coalition for the next two-year term.

Clinton's victory would have to be retested for both its stability and endurance. From the moment of his political birth, a native-son candidate needs a political and electoral base that will permit him to emerge both in the political eyes of his state and in the eyes of the national electorate. So a political base is crucial. A rapidly built base, as in Clinton's state attorney general victory, gives reason to pause and consider the size, breadth, and depth of this political and electoral base.

CHAPTER EIGHT

The Gubernatorial Vote for Clinton

Of the three southern native-son presidential candidates since the 1960s, Carter and Clinton used the governorship as a springboard to the White House, while Johnson used Congress. Moving from the governor's mansion to the White House requires careful timing. Jimmy Carter's term as Georgia governor ended just as the Watergate scandal was unfolding and a political opportunity was emerging. This was not the case in 1978, when Clinton captured the Arkansas governor's mansion for the first time: a Democrat was in the White House, looking for a second term. And by the time Clinton recaptured the governor's mansion, a Republican sweep was underway that would last another full decade. The use of a governorship as a springboard into presidential politics requires careful timing. This is just the strategic reality. First there is the tactical reality.

Whatever Clinton's long term goals, the short term goal had to be the capture of the governor's office. And as Clinton would learn, losing the governorship, as he did in his 1980 reelection bid, put everything else on hold.[1] Strategic plans had to be subordinated to tactical ones. Clinton had to win the governorship. Before 1986 Arkansas granted its governor a two year term, as well as the right to successive elections. Georgia did not.[2] This right to succeed himself helped Clinton to deal with the question of timing. Arkansas election rules helped to make the governorship a strategic springboard. Yet the question remained whether

Clinton could fashion an electoral and political coalition to win the governorship.

Both Carter and Clinton felt it was possible to fashion a winning coalition, and they both left nothing to chance. Carter literally campaigned all four years between his loss in the 1966 Georgia Democratic gubernatorial primary and his victory in the 1970 race. As for Clinton, "there was never any doubt that the attorney general's office was nothing more than a brief stop on the road for Clinton. . . . It was accepted that Clinton, when he arrived in Little Rock, was the governor-in-waiting."[3] Upon his arrival in Little Rock, Clinton used the position of attorney general adroitly. "Not just as a stepping-stone to the governorship, the job of Attorney General would give him constant and undivided access to the statewide structure of county courthouses that Clinton had learned were the keystones of the Arkansas political system."[4] Here, in two years' time, he made the right political connections at the state level.

In the year in which Clinton won as state attorney general, Carter became president. Clinton used his connections and influence in both efforts, to enhance his move to the governorship. During Carter's campaign for the presidency, Clinton asked his friend and classmate, Mack McLarty, then chairman of the state Democratic party, to get Carter to name him to the position of state campaign chairman. Initially Carter wanted Clinton to chair the Texas campaign, as he had done for McGovern in 1972. When McLarty intervened, Carter changed his mind and made Clinton the Arkansas state campaign chairman. Here was a governor-in-waiting with national political connections.

When Carter became president, his state campaign chairman got not only access to the White House, but the power of state political patronage. This established him as a powerful political figure whose influence could rebound to those close to him: "President Carter appointed Hillary to the Board of the Legal Services Corporation, where she swiftly became the first chairwoman of the federally backed agency."[5] The Clintons were also invited to important White House functions. Each such event was a significant and powerful political asset for the governor-in-waiting. These national connections enhanced the political reputation of the would-be candidate, both with his electoral base and with political leaders.

Clinton was also introduced to the uses of technical expertise. In a political environment that has shifted from being party-centered to being candidate-centered,[6] candidates must rely on an array of political professionals with the technical expertise to assist them in planning, marshalling, and deploying their future political campaigns. Central among these professionals is the political pollster. Clinton had used the national political expertise and polling skills of Patrick Caddell in both his congressional race and in his campaign to become attorney general.[7] He used his connections with Caddell to connect with Dick Morris. In the fall of 1977 Morris flew down to Little Rock and met with Clinton at the attorney general's office.[8] The governor-in-waiting had taken the next step to become the next governor of Arkansas.

The Six Gubernatorial Primaries

In his initial effort for Clinton, Dick Morris conducted two polls—one to assess his prospects for the governor's race and the other to gauge his chances of succeeding Senator John McClellan. The results showed that Clinton could win the governorship and he "could possibly win" the Senate seat. But Governor David Pryor was interested in running for senator. The two men had a meeting and Governor Pryor told Clinton that "you could run for governor and be elected and serve longer than Orval Faubus," who had been in the Governor's mansion for six two-year terms from 1955 to 1967. "You could break Faubus' record."[9] In the end, Clinton came close, running six times and winning three two-year terms and two four-year terms, serving only two years of his second four-year term before leaving for the White House. Both Faubus and Clinton served twelve years as Arkansas governor.

Clinton ran in six primaries, one runoff, and six general elections (figure 8.1), a total of 13 elections for five gubernatorial victories. We now turn to these primary elections in our analysis of how this rising native-son presidential candidate built, maintained, and recaptured his electoral base so that he could make the political leap to the presidency. Prior to both Faubus and Clinton, only Jeff Davis, the Redneck Messiah, had won the state attorney general post and then the governorship three consecutive times.[10]

Clinton won all six of his primary elections for governor. His third primary victory, in 1982, netted him only 42 percent of the vote. As is typical of most southern states since Reconstruction, Arkansas election law requires a runoff election in the case of a plurality victory.[11] Clinton won the runoff election with 54 percent of the vote. Clinton was able to continually fashion a winning electoral and political coalition in all of his primary elections.

His initial gubernatorial primary took place on May 30, 1978, with a slate of five candidates. Clinton captured this race with 60 percent of the

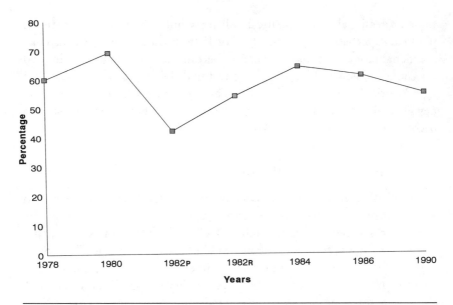

FIGURE 8.1 Percentage of Primary and Runoff Votes for Gubernatorial
Candidate Clinton, 1978–1990

Calculated from the 39 tables prepared as background material for this chapter. P = primary election,
R = run-off election.

vote, beating his closest opponent by 217,414 votes (table 8.1). By the time
of his second primary on May 27, 1980, Clinton had only one opponent,
and captured 69 percent of the vote, beating his opponent by 168,066
votes. With his comeback victory in the May 25, 1982, primary, Clinton
faced four opponents, and beat his closest opponent, Jim Purcell, by 70,895
votes. This was the only primary in which Clinton fell below 50% of the
vote.

In the May 29, 1984 Democratic primary, Clinton faced three opponents and restored his primary victory percentage by winning 64 percent
of the vote, outpolling his closest challenger by 197,950 votes.

Running for his first four-year term in the May 27, 1986 Democratic
primary, Clinton faced two opponents, one of whom was the legendary
Orval Faubus, the six-time former governor, who was trying to maintain
his record for service as governor. In this election Clinton captured 61
percent of the vote and beat Faubus by 140,995 votes.

The animosity between the two men dated back to Clinton's first term.
In 1978 Faubus was facing financial difficulties and "tried to get Governor
Clinton to buy the Faubus-Murphy property, which included more than

TABLE 8.1 Results of the 1982 Democratic
Gubernatorial Runoff Election

Candidate	Votes	Percentage
Clinton	239,209	53.7
Purcell	206,358	46.3
Total	445,567	100.0

Paul Riviere, "Arkansas Elections 1982" (Little Rock: Office of
the Secretary of State, 1983), 31.

sixty acres of prime land, and turn it into a state park and museum."[12] The
young governor turned down the former governor. When Republican
Frank White announced that he would oppose Clinton for a second term,
his chances did not look good. But "White asked Faubus for campaign
advice [and he] obliged with general suggestions on tactics and campaign
strategy. To general amazement, White won. He promptly gave Faubus a
job leading the state's Office of Veteran's Affairs."[13] After Clinton won
back the office in 1982, five days into his second term he fired Faubus. But
this was not the end of the matter.

> In 1986, still smarting from his treatment by Bill Clinton, [Faubus]
> raised seventy thousand dollars and ran against him. . . . Faubus got
> 34 percent of the primary vote—a startling show of support for a man
> of seventy-six who had lost his power base twenty years earlier.[14]

By 1990 Faubus was too old and too ill to challenge the younger man. It
was all over. But Clinton's 1986 run for governor has been touched by
forces out of the past.

Finally, Clinton sought his second four-year term when he entered the
Democratic primary on May 29, 1990. In this primary, Clinton faced five
challengers, his largest number ever. Yet he captured 55 percent of the vote
and outpolled his closest rival, Tom McRae, by 78,442 votes, in his second
lowest margin of victory.

In these six primary elections, Clinton's mean vote was 59 percent,
ranging from a low of 42 percent in 1982 to a high of 69 percent in 1980.

Figure 8.2 reveals the same story from the county level. In his first primary, Clinton won 71 counties (95%). In the 1980 primary he captured 69
(92%). In 1982 he won 50 of the 75 counties (67%). By 1984 he would get

70 (93%). In his two attempts at four-year terms he won in 65 and 53 counties (88% and 71%), respectively. Clinton always won the majority of the counties in his primary efforts. As with the vote analysis, 1982 proved the low point, and 1978 proved to be the high point at the county level.

Figure 8.3 permits us to analyze the primary vote from a demographic standpoint. Of the three categories of counties—urban, town, and rural—Clinton performed best with the urban electorate. Except in 1978, urban support for Clinton was the strongest compared to the town and rural categories. Surprisingly, his greatest support in his initial bid to become governor came from the rural and then the town counties. But after this initial election, these counties gave him less support, with the exception of the town counties in 1980 and 1984. The rural counties would after 1978 always lag behind the others in their support for him, due in part to his tag sales tax, which hurt the rural segment of the state.[15]

Collectively, the mean vote for Clinton in the urban counties stood at 59 percent, in the town counties at 56 percent, and in the rural counties at 51 percent. His best year was 1980 while 1982 was his lowest year in the demographic categories.

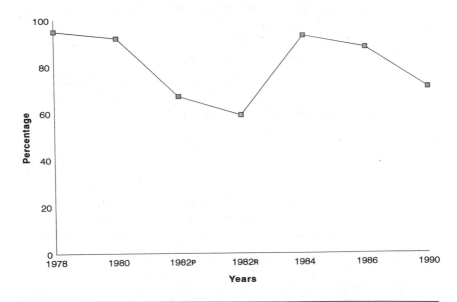

FIGURE 8.2 Percentage of Counties Won by Gubernatorial Candidate
Clinton in Primary and Runoff Elections, 1978–1990

Calculated from the 39 tables prepared as background material for this chapter. P = primary election, R = run-off election

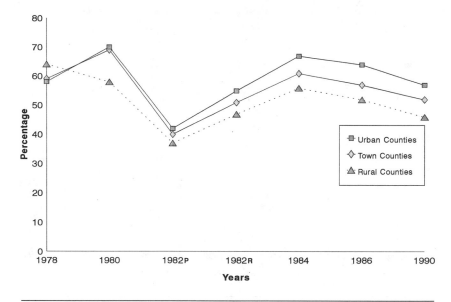

FIGURE 8.3 Percentage of Gubernatorial Candidate Clinton's Primary Vote
by Demographic Category, 1978–1990

Calculated from the 39 tables prepared as background material for this chapter. P = primary election,
R = run-off election.

In his two home counties, Clinton's greatest support came in 1980, a
year in which his reelection chances looked to be in danger. Hempstead
and Garland county voters clearly rallied to their native son by giving him
71 percent of the vote (figure 8.4). No other year approached this mark,
although 1978 and 1984 came closest with 68 percent of the vote.

Clinton's lowest level of support from these counties came in 1982, the
year of his comeback effort. Like the rest of the state, his home counties
voters seemed very skeptical of their native son, and gave him 47 percent
of the vote.

The Black Belt counties of Chicot, Lee, and Phillips rallied to his support in 1980, giving him 85 percent of their vote in the Democratic primary. This was the high water mark and 1982 was the low point, with 59
percent of the vote. Clinton's totals recovered in these counties in the 1982
runoff.

Clinton's electoral support in the Black Belt counties was significantly
higher than in his home counties, with the exception of his initial election
in 1978, where his support in the Black Belt counties was 65 percent, while
the home counties stood at 68 percent. In all his other gubernatorial pri-

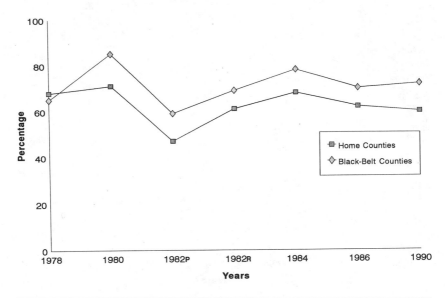

FIGURE 8.4 **Mean Percentage of Gubernatorial Candidate Clinton's Primary and Runoff Vote in the Home and Black-Belt Counties, 1978–1990**

Calculated from the 39 tables prepared as background material for this chapter. P = primary election, R = run-off election

maries, the African American electorate gave him greater support than the home counties, in several years, significantly greater. For instance in 1984 it was 10 percent greater. In terms of the mean, the home county percentage is 62 percent while the Black Belt county percentage is 71 percent. In the gubernatorial primaries African American voters supported Clinton more than his "friends and neighbors" did.

Clinton's primary victories rested upon a broad based electoral coalition that included African Americans. But after six successful primary elections, Clinton's support was starting to decline. After the 1984 highs, the vote percentage diminished at each succeeding election, even in his home counties. This suggests that there may be a point at which local primary coalitions start to slip. Before his collapsed, Clinton was able at just the right time to move on to the presidency.

The Runoff Election

Clinton's 42 percent plurality victory in the 1982 Democratic gubernatorial primary election necessitated a runoff election which was held on June

8, 1982. Clinton faced a former lieutenant governor, Joe Purcell, "a soft-spoken . . . dignified man who refused to make personal attacks against his opponents."[16] "Purcell, an elderly man, was vulnerable to Clinton's subtle hints of health problems."[17] Since runoff elections in the region generally have a low turnout, superior political organization holds the advantage. Purcell had not geared up in the same manner that Clinton had for his comeback election. Nevertheless it was a competitive race. Clinton captured 54 percent of the vote to Purcell's 46 percent. Clinton got 239,209 votes to Purcell's 206,358 (table 8.1).

The data in table 8.2 further demonstrate the competitive nature of the Purcell challenge. Clinton won only 44 counties, 59 percent of the total, while Purcell captured over a third. At the county level, Purcell was making a serious run for the governor's mansion.

From the five demographic categories, we can see the depth and dimensions of the candidates' electoral coalitions and support. Clinton ran well in the urban counties and barely won in the town counties, but Purcell beat him in the rural counties (table 8.3).

Purcell was weak not only in the urban counties, but in Clinton's home counties and particularly in the Black Belt counties. African American voters provided the margin of victory in this runoff election. Without their support—more than two-thirds of the African American vote went to Clinton—he would not have made it to the general election. Purcell would have been the opponent to Republican Frank White.

In the final analysis, Purcell lost to Clinton not primarily because of his campaign technique nor his lack of effective organization but because of his inability to mobilize the African American electorate. His age was less of a problem than his inability to overcome his generation's acceptance of segregation and white supremacy. Clinton's generation under-

---

TABLE 8.1 Results of the 1982 Democratic
Gubernatorial Runoff Election

Candidate	Votes	Percentage
Clinton	239,209	53.7
Purcell	206,358	46.3
Total	445,567	100.0

Paul Riviere, "Arkansas Elections 1982" (Little Rock: Office of the Secretary of State, 1983), 31.

TABLE 8.2 Counties Won by Each Candidate in
the 1982 Gubernatorial Runoff

Candidate	Votes	Percentage
Clinton	44	58.7
Purcell	31	41.3
Total	75	100.0

Adapted from Riviere, "Arkansas Elections 1982," 34.

stood how to overcome these for political gain. The runoff election that made Clinton's comeback possible turned on the question of how to deal with race in state politics.

With the runoff election won, Clinton moved on to complete his comeback in the general election against the Republican incumbent, Frank White.

The Six Gubernatorial General Elections

Although he won all eleven of his primary and runoff elections, Clinton lost one of his six races for the governorship, in 1980, to the Republican challenger Frank White. Clinton had learned to outmaneuver fellow Democrats in primary and runoff elections, but Republican challengers in a historically one-party state were a different political reality. Such a Republican resurgence could not always be correctly anticipated nor predicted. Thus planning and astute preparation did not always ensure victory.

Figure 8.5 tells the story. In his six races, Clinton's highest percentage was achieved in 1984 and his lowest in 1980 when he captured 48 percent of the vote. The mean percentage for all six elections stands at 59 percent.

In the general election on November 4, 1980, Frank White captured 52 percent of the vote to Clinton's 48 percent. The difference was 32,442 votes, nearly the margin of Clinton's victory over Purcell in the runoff election which was to come in 1982.

In the 1980 race, Clinton won only 32 percent of the counties—24 out of 75—for the lowest percentage of his entire political career (figure 8.6), in stark contrast to 1978, when he won 92 percent of the counties. This number would nearly be equalled in the 1986 general election in which Clinton won 91 percent of the counties.

TABLE 8.3 Results of the 1982 Gubernatorial Runoff by Demographic Category

Candidate	Urban Counties		Town Counties		Rural Counties		Home Counties		Black Belt Counties	
	Votes	%	Votes	%	Votes	%	Votes	%	Votes	%
Clinton	127,242	55.2	75,597	50.9	17,861	46.8	11,860	61.2	7,649	68.8
Purcell	103,220	44.8	71,858	49.1	20,287	53.2	7,525	38.8	3,468	31.2
Total	230,462	100.0	146,455	100.0	38,148	100.0	19,385	100.0	11,117	100.0

Adapted from Riviere, "Arkansas Elections 1982," 34.

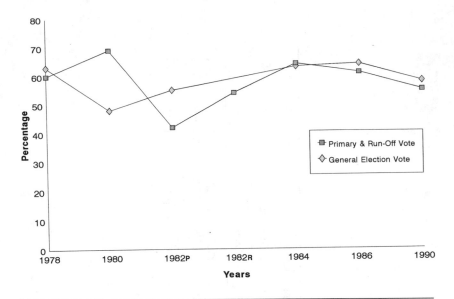

FIGURE 8.5 The Percentage of the Primary and General Election Vote for
Gubernatorial Candidate Clinton, 1978–1990

Calculated from the 39 tables prepared as background material for this chapter. P = primary election,
R = run-off election.

Figure 8.7 describes the demographic trends and patterns over time, and indicates nearly uniform voting for Clinton in the urban, town, and rural areas. Beginning in 1984, the rural counties gave Clinton a much smaller share of their vote than the other counties. This is also true to a smaller extent in the town counties. As in the primaries, Clinton in the general election was supported more strongly by the urban counties than the rural ones. The mean percentage for both urban and town counties was 58 percent, and 54 percent in the rural counties.

Clinton lost one of his home counties in 1980. Frank White won Garland county with 52 percent of the vote, by 1,126 votes (figure 8.8). The native son had lost his own home county, as he had previously in the congressional general election.

In the Black Belt counties, Clinton's vote never dropped below two-thirds of the votes cast. The mean vote for Clinton in the home counties was 59 percent, while in the Black Belt counties it was 72 percent.

Clinton's comeback effort against incumbent Republican Governor Frank White in 1982 included a conscious tactic of embracing African American voters. "Clinton wanted to be sure of a strong black vote and

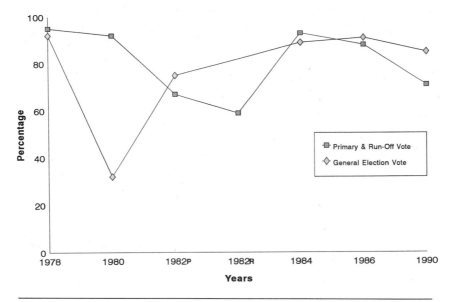

FIGURE 8.6 The Percentage of Counties Won by Gubernatorial Candidate
Clinton, 1978–1990

Calculated from the 39 tables prepared as background material for this chapter. P = primary election,
R = run-off election.

hired one of the law school students [Carol Wills] who had called him
'Wonder Boy.' "[18] Two others also joined the team, which "delivered an
unprecedented black turnout. It proved Clinton's margin as he beat White
with 55 percent of the vote."[19]

> Clinton spent most of his Sundays in black churches, and recruited
> three black organizers to help him with the black vote. . . . If there
> was an event involving black people, we were there. And we would
> get Clinton there. No one in Arkansas political annals locked up the
> black vote the way Clinton did in 1982.[20]

In 1978 "Clinton had depended on the black vote for his gubernatorial
election and . . . was rapidly gaining more support from the black community."[21]

> Arkansas's blacks constitute only 14.6 percent of Arkansas's voting-
> age population and only an estimated 13.9 percent of its registered
> voters. This means, however, that with overwhelming support from

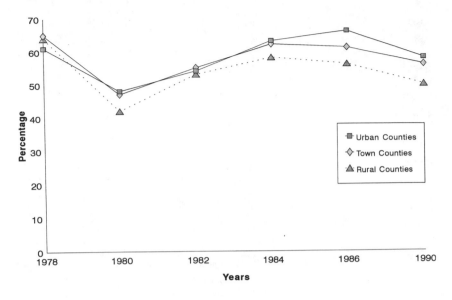

FIGURE 8.7 Gubernatorial Candidate Clinton's General Election Vote by Demographic Category, 1978–1990

Calculated from the 39 tables prepared as background material for this chapter.

the black electorate, a candidate can receive little more than a third of the white vote and still win a statewide race (and without any black support, a candidate may need nearly two-thirds of the white vote to win). Clearly, in any closely competitive race, black support can be critical. . . . Black voters . . . provided Clinton with his primary and general election winning margins in 1982. . . . It is assumed that Clinton received over 95 percent of the black vote in 1982; clearly these 90,000 or so voters were a key part of his 78,000 vote margin.[22]

These analysts and observers agree that the African American voter played a critical role in Clinton's comeback in the 1982 gubernatorial general election. Without these voters, there would have been no comeback. And our county level analysis has revealed the critical role that this electorate played in the runoff election as well. Purcell had failed to reach out to this group of voters, and Frank White made the same mistake.

In the 1960s African American voters had made it possible for Republican Winthrop Rockefeller to win his two terms as governor. African

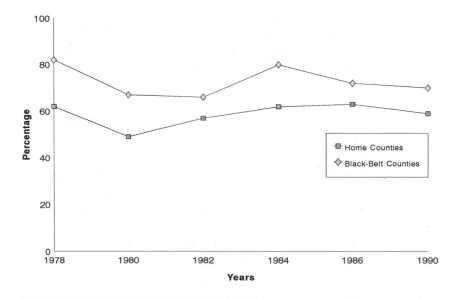

FIGURE 8.8   The Mean Percentage of Gubernatorial Candidate Clinton's
General Election Vote in the Home and Black Belt Counties,
1978–1990

Calculated from the 39 tables prepared as background material for this chapter.

Americans switched parties to support a Republican in a Democratic
state. They had proven to be the political swing vote and the balance of
power. But subsequent Republicans failed to follow up on the Rockefeller
innovation. Frank White's second bid for the governor's mansion was followed by a third in 1986. Still White had not learned to go after the
African American electorate. Republican candidates were distancing
themselves from African American voters. Without them, Frank White
lost both his second and third bids for governor.

The Clinton Coalition

These primary, runoff, and general election results tell us much about the
nature and scope of Clinton's victories and a great deal about the evolution of a native-son presidential candidate. But we can learn even more
about how this process works. By using a measure of association—"a single number whose signs and size convey information about the co-varia-
tion in a relationship"[23] —we can measure how well Clinton's electoral

coalition sustained itself from election to election and helped to shape the outcome of each following election.

By correlating one election to the next, we can ascertain what role partisan loyalties played in shaping the outcome of the election, relative to other variables such as the candidates, issues, campaign organization and finance, and the media. V. O. Key established the effect of party loyalty relative to other variables in southern elections with this measurement technique.[24] Recently, Warren Miller used similar measures of association to confirm the power of the party identification and loyalty variable in presidential elections.[25] Holmberg used the same measures to demonstrate party loyalty in Swedish parliamentary elections.[26] Here we employ these measures to help explain the Clinton coalitions in Arkansas.

The simple correlation, designated r, tells us how well the previous election is associated with the outcome in the next election. The r data tells us how strongly related and connected these two elections are with each other, while r^2, the squared correlation, indicates the extent to which the preceding election predicted the next.

Clinton's initial statewide coalition, developed in his race for attorney general, sustained itself and carried forward into his primary race for the governorship. But there was only a modest relationship between the two races. Those individuals who voted for Clinton as attorney general did not respond significantly to his primary race for governor. Only 15 percent of Clinton's primary gubernatorial vote could be predicted from his initial primary vote for attorney general. Yet enough of the attorney general electoral coalition stayed with him, while his exposure as attorney general brought a significant number of new voters and followers to him, so that he won the election without any difficulty. His electoral coalition in the initial race set the next one into motion.

But his initial gubernatorial coalition did not sustain itself into his second race for governor. There is no relationship between Clinton's 1978 primary coalition and his 1980 one. The two election coalitions were composed of different segments of the Arkansas electorate. The demographic analysis has already shown that the rural counties diminished their support along with the home counties and, to an extent, the Black Belt counties. The correlation technique offers a much more carefully measured portrait of this decline. Clinton put together a significantly different group of supporters in 1980 than he had in 1978.

The rebuilt election coalition of 1980 not only lasted but grew over the next series of elections and sustained itself until Clinton moved on to his next electoral plateau. The data show that an emerging native-son presi-

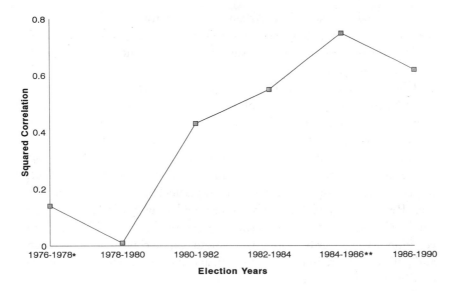

FIGURE 8.9 The Percentage of Gubernatorial Candidate Clinton's Primary
Vote Determined by His Previous Electoral Coalition: Squared
Correlation

Adapted from correlations of paired primary elections using county-level percentages.
*In this period, Clinton's county-level percentages for attorney general are correlated with his initial
gubernatorial county-level percentages, and the resultant correlation is squared.
**No votes were reported for Newton county, which was dropped from the calculations for subsequent
years.

dential candidate can fashion more than one electoral base, even in a historically one-party state. Electoral bases can be both continuous and dis-
continuous. Native-son candidates can change themselves as well as their
electoral and political bases.

In figure 8.9, r^2 indicates that 43 percent of the 1982 vote can be
predicted from the 1980 election. This figure increases, as 75 percent of
the 1986 election can be accounted for from the 1984 election. In the last
election series, 62 percent could be accounted for from the 1986 election.

The meaning here is clear. That faction in the Democratic party that
became loyal to Clinton after the 1980 election could be predicted to vote
for him in succeeding elections. Each gubernatorial primary election saw
Clinton add to his core supporters. Partisan loyalty became the dominant
variable in explaining Clinton's primary election outcomes. Other variables—such as issues, campaign strategies, opposing candidates, and media
coverage—mattered, but they had less of an effect than did loyalty to the
candidate.

Key's earlier analysis of Arkansas and southern politics remains instructive. In historically one-party systems like Arkansas, personal followings are essential to candidate success and these followings can sustain themselves over time.

Clinton's initial personal following proved to be transient and unstable; when he changed course to recapture them he was less than successful in recapturing that initial electorate. He was much more successful at creating a new following, and this following enhanced and enlarged itself (and then endured with him) until Clinton truly emerged on the national level in 1992.

Key also suggested that in the factional one-party system of the South in general, and in states like Arkansas in particular, issues are not important. Personalities and political machines hold sway. Yet in Clinton's case, the issues that beset his first term as governor diminished his electoral coalition. Even a sturdy southern electorate can be concerned about issues and policies that are important to them, and they will switch to alternative candidates in future elections.

Jimmy Carter lost in the 1966 Georgia gubernatorial primary and rebuilt a new electoral coalition for victory in the 1970 election. Clinton fashioned one in 1980 during his second run for the Arkansas governorship. Native-son presidential candidates may come to electoral power on the basis of one electoral coalition and may then move to a different position with the support of another electoral coalition. They may sustain themselves in power with a similar or growing group of supporters. Clearly native-son presidential candidates must stay attuned to their bases of power in the state's electorate.

> The fortunes of the state have rested with particular responsibility in the hands of those thirty-nine individuals elected by the people to be their governor. . . . Governors are fallible human beings. When they fail, they create profound cynicism not only about their personal capabilities but about the legitimacy of government itself. At their best . . . they not only advance the wellbeing of their state but also encourage trust and hope in our democratic institutions.[27]

Governor Clinton's reflections describe the linkage between the Arkansas electorate and the political leadership in Arkansas as well as "the social and cultural values exemplified by those elected by Arkansas voters to serve as chief executives of their state."[28]

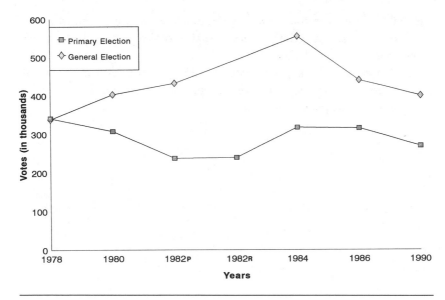

FIGURE 8.10 Total Votes for Gubernatorial Candidate Clinton in Primary
and General Elections, 1978–1990

Calculated from the 39 tables prepared as background material for this chapter. P = primary election,
R = run-off election

Our analysis of the vote reveals that the Arkansas electorate has
certain social and cultural values of its own. This is demonstrated by the
core and peripheral voters in Governor Clinton's electoral coalitions. That
coalition changed over time, with surges and declines that included
different mixtures of social and cultural values. The core voters in Clinton's electoral coalition suggest a stable attachment to the values embedded in the Democratic party. Yet there were other values, such as the
candidate's leadership and his public policies.

Except in 1978, Clinton's general election votes exceeded his primary
votes (figure 8.10). After 1978, Clinton's general election votes always
stayed above the 400,000 mark and climbed above 500,000 in 1984. His
primary votes never reached this level. In the 1982 primary and runoff,
and in 1990, his primary vote total stayed in the 200,000 vote range; on
four other occasions it went to the 300,000 range. In 1978, he got his
highest primary vote, of 341,098.

Clinton's vote pattern in the gubernatorial elections reflects in part the
mixed voting pattern of the state, where in some instances the primary
vote exceeds the general election vote, while in other elections the

general election vote count exceeds the primary. Arkansas stands in contrast to Georgia, where the primary vote almost always exceeds the general election count.

In the case of Arkansas gubernatorial candidate Clinton, with only one exception this rising native-son presidential candidate's general election vote always exceeded his primary one.

Part Four

The Southern Native-Son Presidential Candidate

Commentators could not resist mentioning Clinton's "southerness" during his presidential campaigns. After making mention of it, most found some way to relegate it to simple background information or minimize its consequences to the outcome of the 1992 and 1996 presidential elections. A few did not mention it at all in their discussions of these elections. In those cases, it is conspicuous by its very absence. One way or the other—directly or indirectly—the explanatory equation includes the words, southern native-son presidential candidate. Let us listen to some words about his 1992 presidential victory:

> One set of Clinton enthusiasts comprises the often-derided "Bubba vote": White male southerners and born-again Christians, who overlap the economically poor and less educated. Clinton had an obvious personal appeal here, supplemented by Gore, by dint of his southern roots, his accent, and his history of family poverty.[1]

The point is clear: Clinton's southerness helped him become president. Another comment:

But unlike [their] predecessors . . . Clinton and Gore came from states that were members of the Confederacy: The 1992 nominations were a strong symbolic gesture to the South, part of a successful effort to dent that now-Republican bastion.[2]

Again, Clinton's southerness. Still another opinion on this characteristic of the 1992 election:

> Clinton created a strong Democratic ticket with his selection of Senator Al Gore as his vice presidential running mate. In choosing Gore . . . he selected a fellow southerner, moderate, and baby boomer. . . . More importantly, his addition to the ticket signaled the Democrats' intention to contest the southern states seriously and generated enthusiasm for the ticket within the party.[3]

Thus Clinton was characterized not only as a product of the South, but as the architect of a new Democratic southern strategy. Clinton, like Carter before him, was a moderate southern governor relatively immune to the "liberal" label.[4] "You can take the man out of Arkansas, but you cannot take Arkansas out of the man," and Arkansas is a southern state.[5]

On the eve of the 1996 election, Bob Woodward wrote:

> When the histories of late 20th-century American politics were written, Gore believed, they would show that the only politicians capable of uniting the Democratic coalition were southern moderates such as Lyndon Johnson, Jimmy Carter, and, Gore argued, himself and Clinton.[6]

The implication here being that southern presidential candidates can make the Democratic party victorious and they can become exceptional presidential leaders, since "southern" and conservative, if not one and the same thing, are related. Combined they helped Clinton win in both and 1992 and 1996. And they had helped Carter win in 1976.[7]

This fusing of region and ideology by the Democratic candidate in 1996 led one observer searching for the meaning of the 1996 election to write:

> Contemporary Democratic policy is effectively post-liberal. . . . So-called new Democrats or neo-liberals are inclined to emphasize the limits on government. Broadly "post-materialist," they defend the individual rights associated with social liberalism and they concern themselves with "quality of life" issues like education and the environment . . . and show little interest in economic equality.[8]

Although this quote describes national realities, it can serve to direct our focus on the empirical patterns and trends that emerge from the

Arkansas election data. In such a poor state, does the "southerness" of the vote cancel out the differences in voting behavior based on economic differences between urban and rural areas? How does the electorate respond to a native-son candidate who argues that the era of big, interventionist government is over? If electoral behavior is supportive, this suggests that southerness embraces conservative economic thinking as well.

Clinton's "southerness" is pushing the Democratic party right of center. The above quote is a clever and unique way of saying it. Maybe you cannot take the man out of a southern state like Arkansas. Just as James Carter became Jimmy Carter in local southern politics, and remained Jimmy as president, so William Clinton had become Bill Clinton in his initial political race in Arkansas, and remained Bill Clinton on the national and international stage.

During his run for Congress, one of the first press releases the campaign issued referred to William J. Clinton, which is how his name was printed in a local newspaper. A restaurateur in northwest Arkansas, Billie Schneider, known as the godmother of Washington county politics, told Clinton in no uncertain terms, "What is this William J. Clinton? You're Bill Clinton. And you're gonna run as Bill Clinton." The author concludes: "She wanted to make sure Clinton understood that he was back in Arkansas. This was not Georgetown, Oxford, or Yale."[8] Since then he has run every political race as Bill Clinton.

Even as president, Clinton refers back to his Arkansas roots as he writes about the nature of community in America's future:

> Hope and Hot Springs, Arkansas, the towns where I grew up, were what we used to call tight knit communities. That's a very revealing phrase. It meant the fabric of community life was strong and whole. You not only knew your neighbor, you looked out for them and your neighbor looked out for you. . . . And that's still what we want. Americans want to be part of a nation that's coming together, not coming apart.[9]

This section searches in empirical terms at the local, state, regional, and national levels for the different dimensions of "southerness" and the native-son presidential candidates it produces. These chapters also compare this regional phenomenon by analyzing the vote for both Carter and Clinton in the South. From this perspective we can see the linkage to both state and national roots.

CHAPTER NINE

The Presidential Vote for Clinton

"Arkansas," a Clinton observer wrote, "was a small and unlikely state as a presidential springboard."[1] Just prior to Clinton's 1992 presidential announcement, one of his political advisers, former Rhodes scholar and Massachusetts judge Richard G. Stearns, noted an equally limiting feature of the state: "Arkansas, one of the country's smallest and poorest states, had a tiny financial base. Millions of dollars were required to sustain a presidential campaign."[2] Yet many had felt the same way about Georgia.[3] But both Carter and Clinton proved the pundits wrong. As has been noted, the use of the governorship of a small southern state as a launch pad to the presidency requires careful timing. Poor political timing can mean disaster for the native-son presidential candidate.

Governor Clinton initially chose 1988 as the political moment to springboard to the White House. Reelected governor in 1986, and becoming chairman of the National Governors' Association, Clinton had a series of opportunities to prepare the ground for a 1988 presidential campaign.[4] He was mentioned in national news magazines as a possible contender. Then several actual contenders withdrew. "Early on the evening of March 20, 1987, the office of Senator Dale Bumpers of Arkansas issued a brief statement announcing that he would not be a candidate for president in 1988."[5] A home boy was now out. By May 7, Gary Hart was gone.

In the wake of these withdrawals, "the Arkansas State Democratic Committee adopted a formal resolution urging him to run. His mail was running three to one in favor."[6] His friends booked a room at the Excelsior Hotel for an announcement on July 15, 1987. On July 14, Clinton told his friends and supporters, many of whom had flown to Arkansas for the announcement, that he had decided to run in 1992, as 1988 was not the correct political moment. There had been much soul searching before this decision was made. Political moments are difficult to fix and forecast.

Clinton made his official announcement on October 3, 1991 in the State House in Little Rock.

> Clinton gave a speech that lasted thirty-two minutes, the precise
> length of his ill-fated address in Atlanta. . . . Twice he evoked John F.
> Kennedy. He delivered his New Democrat riff on opportunity and
> responsibility and how he favored change that was neither liberal nor
> conservative, but bold and different [before declaring in] the first line
> of the twenty-third paragraph, "That is why today I am declaring my
> candidacy for President of the United States."[7]

With these words, the Governor of Arkansas and native-son presidential candidate sprang into national electoral politics and soon the White House. The state native son had now been fully born.

The 1992 Presidential Primary Election in Arkansas

Arkansas, which holds presidential primaries on an irregular and intermittent basis, scheduled this one for its native son on May 26, 1992. As Georgia's had been for Carter, the Arkansas primary came late in the season. Super Tuesday, the date of the regional southern primaries, had passed. By May 26, Clinton had run in 29 of the 38 state primaries, plus the District of Columbia. After his first victory, in Georgia on March 3, he won 20 more states and Washington, D.C. With Clinton's victories in the Super Tuesday primaries, the southern primary strategy had finally paid off.

> Super Tuesday emerged between 1986 and 1987 as eleven democrati-
> cally controlled southern and border state legislatures passed bills
> scheduling their 1988 presidential primaries on March 8, joining three
> southern states already holding early primaries. . . . Super Tuesday
> became the biggest one-day event in presidential primary history.

Nearly one-third of all 1988 Democratic and Republican national convention delegates would be selected on Super Tuesday.[8]

Although the Republicans went along with that date for their primaries, it was the work of southern Democratic leaders who

> wanted a different kind of presidential nominee. They wanted a nominee who was not a northern liberal. . . . To influence the Democratic party to choose [a nominee to their liking], Super Tuesday would have to be held early, before moderate and conservative candidates were knocked out of the race by losses in northern primaries.[9]

Individual southern states had attempted and failed to influence the 1984 presidential primary season: "John Glenn, whom many southern leaders supported, was so wounded by losses in Iowa [and] New Hampshire . . . that he could only limp into the Alabama, Florida, and Georgia primaries before officially calling it quits."[10]

> Senator John Glenn . . . was looking to the South and to Georgia in particular to restore life to his campaign. To help him in Georgia, the state's only Democratic Senator, Sam Nunn, several days before the primary gave him his full endorsement. . . . Glenn was also backed by Georgia Democratic Congressman Lindsay Thomas, who was serving his first term in Congress. Thomas walked with Senator Glenn through his district to introduce him to his supporters.[11]

On election day 1984, Glenn came in fourth, behind Mondale, Hart, and Jackson. He received 18 percent of the vote, and not a single delegate. This informal primary tactic had failed.

But the formal strategy would fare no better. In 1988 Jesse Jackson won these primaries and Senator Al Gore lost. Clinton's victory in 1992 made the Super Tuesday primary strategy functional. In the Arkansas presidential primary only Jerry Brown and Lyndon LaRouche, the weakest of the Democratic challengers, were left to challenge him on his own political turf. They came in third and fourth in a three man race, far behind the second place "uncommitted" vote and Governor Clinton's winning 68 percent of the vote (table 9.1).

Governor Clinton won all 75 counties in the state, something he had not been able to do as either attorney general or governor. Garland coun-

TABLE 9.1 Results of the 1992 Democratic
Presidential Primary in Arkansas

Candidate	Votes	Percentage
Clinton	344,958	68.1
Uncommitted	91,402	18.0
Brown	55,800	11.0
LaRouche	14,719	2.9
Total	506,879	100.0

Adapted and corrected from W. J. McCuen, "Arkansas Election
  Results: 1992" (Little Rock: Office of the Secretary of State,
  1993), 1–2.

ty gave him 72 percent of its vote, while his birth county of Hempstead
gave him 78 percent. In the Black Belt counties, Chicot gave Clinton 78
percent, Lee 75 percent, and Phillips 74 percent of the vote. Thus his birth
county—Hempstead—equalled one and outnumbered two of the Black
Belt counties in voter support.

The demographic analysis shows that Clinton's victory in the presidential primary was broadbased (table 9.2). In three of the demographic
categories, he captured more than two-thirds of the vote. In his home
counties, he captured just a couple of percentage points less than three-
fourths of the total vote cast. And in the Black Belt counties, he captured
a full three-fourths of the vote. The Black Belt counties gave him more
support than did his home counties, although Hempstead lead all of these
special counties with a whopping 78 percent of its vote. These special
counties in this native-son presidential election rose to support him at
their highest levels to date.

Even in this triumphant victory, the uncommitted vote was significant. The mean uncommitted vote stood at 17.2 percent across all demographic categories, ranging from 11.7 percent in his home counties to a
high of 22 percent in the rural counties. The rural counties, which had
dropped their support for Clinton in his comeback effort, were not total-
ly drawn back into his electoral orbit. In this presidential primary, one in
five rural voters was willing to remain uncommitted to him. Although
they voted, they refused to vote for their own native-son presidential candidate. Segments of the electorate which are upset over policy changes
cannot be easily placated.

TABLE 9.2 Results of the 1992 Democratic Presidential Primary by Demographic Category

Candidate	Urban Counties		Town Counties		Rural Counties		Home Counties		Black Belt Counties	
	Votes	%	Votes	%	Votes	%	Votes	%	Votes	%
Clinton	184,612	69.4	107,414	65.8	26,090	63.2	16,264	73.4	10,518	75.0
Uncommitted	44,820	16.8	32,727	20.1	9,086	22.0	2,587	11.7	2,182	15.5
Brown	29,590	11.1	17,737	10.9	4,770	11.6	2,689	12.1	1,014	7.2
LaRouche	7,144	2.7	5,267	3.2	1,348	3.2	623	2.8	337	2.4
Total	266,166	100.0	163,145	100.0	41,294	100.1	22,163	100.0	14,111	100.1

Adapted from W. J. McCuen, "Arkansas Elections Results: 1992" (Little Rock: Office of the Secretary of State, 1993), 35–41.

Former California governor Jerry Brown ran his best in the rural counties, and in Clinton's home counties Brown got 12.1 percent of the vote. Obviously there were individuals in the home counties who were sending Clinton a message. There were those in the rural and home county electorate whom "pride" could not bring back into the electoral fold at primary election time.

Lyndon LaRouche had run in the Arkansas presidential primary in 1988 and captured 2,347 votes. In 1992 he got 14,719 votes. In the home counties, LaRouche got 97 votes in 1988 and 321 in 1992.

About disgruntled voters, a keen observer of southern politics has written:

> The maintenance of a supporting majority requires governmental actions, policies, and gestures that reinforce the confidence of those who have placed their faith in the administration. Yet to govern is to antagonize not only opponents but also at least some supporters; as the loyalty of one group is nourished, another group may be repelled. [In this] interaction between government and populace . . . old friends are sustained, old enemies are converted into new friends, old friends become even bitter opponents, and new voters are attracted to the cause.[12]

Key's observation describes Clinton's gubernatorial efforts. His electoral coalition continued to shift over his five reelection campaigns. And some of his supporters who became disgruntled never returned to his coalitional fold. This occurs even in one-party states.

The 1992 Presidential General Election in Arkansas

One election postmortem cites the national effect of Ross Perot:

> In 1992 Clinton got an assist from Independent candidate Ross Perot in this double task of taking on President Bush. While Perot was persistently attacking Bush's record, Clinton was able to present himself as above the fray. Eventually, Perot's attacks on Bush's economics record and foreign policy record "softened up" Bush to the point that voters began to consider an alternative. Perot also attacked Clinton, but not so frequently or so personally.[13]

Another declares that:

Bill Clinton was the most conservative nominee of the Democratic party since at least 1976. . . . His nomination represented the first victory for the Democratic Leadership Council, a group within the Democratic party that Clinton helped to form and which aimed to push the party back to the center. . . . Bill Clinton's nomination in July, and then his victory in November, signified a major philosophic shift within the Democratic party.[14]

Another book cites antigovernment anger as a factor in 1992.

[In] a democracy elections can be considered the political equivalent of revenge: the elections of 1992 and 1994 both expressed vengeful (toward government) and punitive (toward politicians) themes, which continued into the primary and general elections of 1996.[15]

While these quotes focus on national realities, they can cue us to explore the impact of Perot, conservatism, and antigovernment anger on the patterns and trends in the 1992 Arkansas election results. Each provides a point of departure for an assessment of the election in the state.

Whatever factors were played by Perot, Democratic conservatism, or voter anger, it is certain that the Arkansas electorate played a significant role in Clinton's election. On November 3, 1992, the Arkansas electorate went to the polls to elect one of its native sons president. There were twelve other presidential candidates on the state election ballot, including an incumbent president, Republican George Bush. But incumbents had been beaten before. Incumbent native-son Jimmy Carter had fallen nationally in the 1980 presidential election. However he had not fallen in his own home state.

Clinton, as Carter had done in Georgia before him, reversed the Democratic party's electoral fortunes in his home state (table 9.3). The Republicans swept Arkansas in the 1988 election, as they had done in Georgia in 1972, the year prior to Carter's successful bid. Clinton captured Arkansas with 53 percent of the vote (505,823 votes). This was less than his highest vote total ever, in the general election of 1984, when he got 554,561 votes. Yet there was an even greater decline for President Bush.

In 1988 Bush had received 466,578 votes, for 56 percent of the total. In 1992 Bush's vote count stood at 337,324, or 35.5 percent. This was a decline of 129,254 votes and a 20.9 percent drop. The 1988 Republican victory had not just stalled, it had begun a sharp decline. The Republican incumbent had lost nearly one in every five of his previous votes.

TABLE 9.3 Results of the 1992 Presidential
         Election in Arkansas

Candidate	Votes	Percentage
Clinton	505,823	53.2
Bush	337,324	35.5
Perot	99,132	10.4
Phillips	1,437	0.2
Marrou	1,261	0.1
Fulani	1,022	0.1
Boren	956	0.1
Gritz	819	0.1
Hagelin	764	0.1
LaRouche	762	0.1
Yiamouyiannis	554	0.1
Dodge	472	0.1
Masters	327	0.0
Total	950,653	100.0

McCuen, "Arkansas Election Results: 1992," 35–42.

Clinton carried 93 percent of the counties while President Bush captured only five counties, several of which were not traditional Republican
counties (table 9.4).[16] The story is in the decline of Republican votes in
the state. In 1988, President Bush had carried 54 counties. In 1992, the
Democrats, who had won 21 counties in Michael Dukakis' effort,
increased that to 70 counties. This upsurge in county level support for
Clinton in his new role as a native-son presidential candidate was not his
best performance: He had won 71 counties in the 1978 gubernatorial primaries and captured 554,561 votes in the 1984 gubernatorial general election. This was his highest vote total in state and national elections.

A third perspective on the Clinton victory is offered by an analysis of
the demographic categories. Here we see that Clinton won more over 50
percent of the vote in all four demographic categories (table 9.5). In the
Black Belt counties, Clinton captured two-thirds of the African American vote, for his highest percentage in these categories. As African Americans had done for Carter, they were mounting their support for a
native-son president candidate. This was much higher support than these
counties had given the previous Democratic candidate, Dukakis, whose
mean percentage in 1988 was 57.4 percent in these counties.

TABLE 9.4 Counties Won in the 1992
Presidential Election

Candidate	Votes	Percentage
Clinton	70	93.3
Bush	5	6.7
Others	0	0.0
Total	75	100.0

Adapted from McCuen, "Arkansas Election Results: 1992,"
35–42.

The incumbent George Bush captured a third of the vote in four of the demographic categories but only one vote in five in the African American community. Yet the support for Bush in these Black Belt counties were much higher than the national vote for Bush from the African American community, as shown by surveys and exit polls.[17] This higher vote for Bush in the Black Belt counties does not necessarily mean a growing vote among the rural African American electorate for the Republican party, but a transition of the white vote in these counties from the Democratic party to the more anti-black and anti–civil rights Republican party, as was happening all over the South.[18]

Third party candidate H. Ross Perot garnered only one vote in ten across four Arkansas demographic categories. In the Black Belt counties, Perot's support of 6.4 percent mirrored what was happening in the rest of the nation.[19] Even in Arkansas's delta counties, the African American electorate responded to this reform third party candidate, as the community had reached out to progressive third party candidates in the past, even if they had less than a progressive position on race. Beside the Black Belt counties, Perot's strongest support came from the rural counties. Clinton's support here made only a very modest recovery. The other third party candidates barely registered in this election, with a native son at the top of the ticket. Even the African American female candidate, Lenora Fulani, barely made a showing outside the urban counties, and made her poorest showing in terms of votes in the African American counties.[20]

The native-son candidate outpolled the incumbent president by nearly 20 percent. Some of the gap was and can be explained by the presence of the Perot candidacy. Yet Perot only won 10 percent of the vote. Much

TABLE 9.5 Results of the 1992 Presidential Election by Demographic Category

Candidate	Urban Counties		Town Counties		Rural Counties		Home Counties		Black Belt Counties	
	Votes	%	Votes	%	Votes	%	Votes	%	Votes	%
Clinton	292,684	51.6	143,498	55.3	31,958	53.9	24,287	54.1	13,396	67.0
Bush	212,256	37.4	84,627	32.6	19,938	33.6	15,273	34.0	5,230	26.2
Perot	56,916	10.0	29,362	11.3	7,068	11.9	4,497	10.0	1,289	6.4
Phillips	813	0.1	442	0.2	37	0.0	127	0.3	18	0.1
Fulani	786	0.1	116	0.1	23	0.0	81	0.2	16	0.1
Hagelin	393	0.0	221	0.1	72	0.1	71	0.2	7	0.0
Boren	640	0.1	198	0.1	42	0.1	58	0.1	18	0.1
Gritz	448	0.1	288	0.1	47	0.1	34	0.1	2	0.0
Dodge	358	0.0	82	0.0	10	0.0	19	0.0	3	0.0
LaRouche	246	0.0	172	0.1	17	0.0	321	0.7	6	0.0
Yiamouyiannis	360	0.0	147	0.1	23	0.0	18	0.0	6	0.0
Masters	203	0.0	84	0.0	10	0.0	24	0.1	6	0.0
Marrou	832	0.1	266	0.1	81	0.1	107	0.2	5	0.0
Total	566,935	99.5	259,503	100.1	59,326	99.8	44,917	100.0	20,002	99.9

McCuen, "Arkansas Election Results: 1992," 35–42. Calculations prepared by the author.

of Clinton's margin is due to the "pride" factor. A native son made a much better showing than a non–native-son incumbent president. This "pride" manifested itself in the reversal of the Democratic party's fortunes in the state. Clinton became the successor to another native southerner, Jimmy Carter, in the White House.

The 1996 Presidential Primary

In the Arkansas Democratic primary on May 21, 1996, there were two challengers to Clinton, Lyndon LaRouche and Monica Moorehead, as well as an uncommitted category. President Clinton had primary competition in his home state, which he had tried to avoid on the national level. The repeat challenger from 1992 was Lyndon LaRouche. Both challengers were considered very minor candidates and no real threat. The native-son presidential candidate captured 75.8 percent of the vote (table 9.6). LaRouche got almost seven percent (6.6%) of the vote and uncommitted voters posted some 13 percent of the total turnout in the Democratic primary. The native-son candidate was absolutely strong among those Democratic voters who turned out to participate in the Democratic presidential primary.[21]

Fewer voters turned out for the 1996 primary than in 1992. In the 1992 state primary, Clinton received 344,958 votes. In 1996, only 315,503 people turned out. Of those, only 239,298 voted this time for the incumbent president.

LaRouche got 20,669 votes, compared to 14,719 in 1992. Monica

TABLE 9.6 Results of the 1996 Democratic
Presidential Primary in Arkansas

Candidate	Votes	Percentage
Clinton	239,287	75.8
Uncommitted	42,411	13.4
LaRouche	20,669	6.6
Lloyd-Duffie	13,136	4.2
Total	315,503	100.0

Sharon Priest, "May 21, 1996 Primary Election Results: Statewide Totals" (Little Rock: Office of the Secretary of State, 1996), 20.

Moorehead captured 4 percent of the Democratic primary vote. The number and percentage of uncommitted voters declined. In 1992, just under 100,000 voters in Arkansas indicated that they were not committed at that stage to their governor in his race for the Democratic nomination for president. By 1996, only 42,411 were uncommitted. The number of uncommitted votes had declined by more than half. The result reflects a mixed picture. Some people in Arkansas voted for little known minor challengers, while others were now willing to commit themselves to the native-son candidate's reelection. In Georgia in 1980, President Carter's reelection effort saw "fewer people [turn] out to vote [than in 1976]. More than 80,000 voters decided not to vote for their native son this time around." For both Clinton and Carter fewer people came to the polls the second time around.[22]

Moving from the total vote to the county level, President Clinton won all 75 counties. In both of his home counties he captured three-fourths of the total vote. In the three African American counties, the story was the same. His mean vote percentage was 78.5 percent, higher than in his home counties (75.2%). In Phillips county, the President received four of every five votes (81.4%). As before, the Black Belt counties support him at higher levels than his home counties.

Disaggregating the election data to our analytical demographic categories, an additional pattern emerges. Table 9.7 demonstrates that the President captured about three-quarters of the Arkansas vote, across the board. The rural counties, which abandoned him after his first gubernatorial election, continued to give him the lowest level of support. And the Black Belt counties continued to give the highest level of support. Uncommitted voters were found in the rural and home counties. Rural voters had not returned to his coalition by the time of his second presidential primary.

The minor Democratic challengers ran best in the urban and town counties. Such was not the case in the 1992 primary. LaRouche, who had most of his support in rural counties in 1992, improved this time in the other two major categories.

President Clinton swept the 1996 Democratic primary and smoothly outperformed his opponents. But his opponents, coupled with the uncommitted voters, took one-fourth of the Democratic primary vote; with half of that opposition vote being merely uncommitted, it was quite possible for the President to carry that vote in the general election.[23]

TABLE 9.7 Results of the 1996 Democratic Presidential Election by Demographic Category

Candidate	Urban Counties		Town Counties		Rural Counties		Home Counties		Black Belt Counties	
	Votes	%	Votes	%	Votes	%	Votes	%	Votes	%
Clinton	114,411	77.3	85,240	74.7	19,823	71.4	10,945	75.4	8,838	79.0
Uncommitted	17,415	11.8	15,434	13.5	4,980	17.9	2,627	18.1	1,955	17.5
LaRouche	9,820	6.6	8,251	7.2	1,780	6.4	574	4.0	244	2.2
Lloyd-Duffie	6,314	4.3	5,125	4.5	1,162	4.2	379	2.6	156	1.4
Total	147,960	100.0	114,050	99.9	27,745	99.9	14,525	100.1	11,193	100.1

Sharon Priest, "1996 Primary Results by County" (Little Rock: Office of the Secretary of State, 1997), 1–81.

The 1996 Presidential General Election

When the Arkansas electorate went to the polls on November 5, 1996, there were 13 candidates for the presidency on the ballot. President Clinton got about 54 percent of the total vote, while Bob Dole managed 37 percent, and Perot received about 8 percent (table 9.8). Ten minor candidates shared 1.6 percent of the vote. The Perot vote plus that for the other minor party candidates comes to 9.5 percent of the presidential vote in Arkansas. In 1992 this figure stood at 9.3 percent. This continuing surge in minor party voting is a new trend in state presidential electoral politics (see figure 4.5).

In 1996 Dole improved the Republican vote percentage by 1.3 points over the party's 1992 performance, while Clinton improved the Democratic vote percentage by only one-half of a percentage point. Perot's total decreased by 2.5 points.

Despite these slight changes in percentages, there was a significant decline in the actual number of votes cast—in 1992, 950,653 individuals voted, while in 1996, 884,262 individuals voted. Turnout was down by 66,391 votes. Clinton's vote total dropped by 30,652 votes, the Republican party vote dropped by 11,908 votes, and Ross Perot's by 29,248. Between the primary and general elections, the Clinton coalition weakened slightly.

TABLE 9.8 Results of the 1996 Presidential
Election in Arkansas

Candidate	Votes	Percentage
Clinton	475,171	53.7
Dole	325,416	36.8
Perot	69,884	7.9
Nader	3,649	0.4
Browne	3,076	0.3
Phillips	2,065	0.2
R. Forbes	932	0.1
Collins	823	0.1
Masters	749	0.1
Morehead	747	0.1
Hagelin	729	0.1
Hillis	538	0.1
Dodge	483	0.1
Total	884,262	100.0

Sharon Priest, "November 5, 1996 General Election Results"
(Little Rock: Office of the Secretary of State, 1996), 1–2.

At the county level President Clinton won 66 (88%) of the state counties, while Dole captured the remaining nine (12%). Republican candidate Dole nearly doubled the total number of counties that his party had carried in 1992. The same pattern had been the case for President Carter in Georgia in his reelection bid in 1980. Fewer counties supported that native son the second time around.

President Clinton's losses in terms of percentages of the total actual vote and the number of counties won are echoed in the demographic categories. This time President Clinton captured a little more than half of the vote in four of the five demographic categories (table 9.10). In the Black Belt counties, the President got nearly 70 percent of the total vote cast. Once again, African American voters outshone all demographic categories by giving him seven out of every ten votes. These counties rallied to his support at a greater level than did the home counties.

Dole ran best in the urban centers of the state, followed by the President's home counties. In the Black Belt counties Dole got his lowest level of voter support.

Perot ran best where President Clinton was the weakest, in the rural counties. The President had been fading in these counties since his electoral comeback and did not win back this group of voters in his final presidential contest. All of the third party candidates, including Perot, had their worst performance in the Black Belt counties. Even the African American female presidential candidate, Monica Moorehead, had a dismal showing in the Black Belt counties.[24] Although she garnered her largest number of votes in the urban centers of the state, this was not enough to lift her percentage performance above 0.1 percent.

TABLE 9.9 Counties Won by Each Candidate in the
1996 Presidential Primary

Candidate	Counties Won	Percentage
Clinton	66	88.0
Dole	9	12.0
Others	0	0.0
Total	75	100.0

Adapted from Priest, "November 5, 1996 General Election Results," 1–15.

TABLE 9.10 Results of the 1996 Presidential Election by Demographic Category

Candidate	Urban Counties		Town Counties		Rural Counties		Home Counties		Belt Belt Counties	
	Votes	%	Votes	%	Votes	%	Votes	%	Votes	%
Clinton	278,459	52.1	130,069	55.8	30,377	55.3	24,194	55.3	12,072	68.9
Dole	209,707	39.2	77,727	33.3	18,025	32.8	15,683	35.8	4,274	24.4
Perot	38,297	7.2	21,726	9.3	5,640	10.3	3,270	7.5	951	5.4
Nader	2,208	0.4	1,011	0.4	226	0.4	174	0.4	30	0.2
Browne	2,089	0.4	576	0.3	164	0.3	141	0.3	106	0.6
Phillips	1,123	0.2	656	0.1	187	0.3	80	0.2	19	0.1
R. Forbes	577	0.1	273	0.1	53	0.1	25	0.1	4	0.0
Collins	428	0.1	269	0.1	86	0.2	31	0.1	9	0.0
Masters	456	0.1	216	0.1	44	0.1	27	0.1	6	0.0
Morehead	387	0.1	263	0.1	53	0.1	22	0.1	22	0.1
Hagelin	463	0.1	150	0.1	63	0.1	43	0.1	10	0.1
Hollis	337	0.1	143	0.1	19	0.0	27	0.1	12	0.1
Dodge	317	0.1	95	0.0	25	0.1	40	0.1	6	0.0
Total	534,848	100.2	233,174	100.0	54,962	100.1	43,757	100.2	17,521	100.0

Priest, "November 5, 1996 General Election Results," 1–182.

Perot's superior resources enabled him to outperform his other third party competitors: his vote total was greater than that of all the other third party candidates combined.[25] Yet, in his second attempt in the state, his overall electoral coalition faltered, giving him fewer votes.

Demographically, Clinton's mean stood at 58 percent of the vote, Dole's mean was 33 percent, and Perot's mean was 8 percent. President Clinton's Democratic coalition in the 1996 presidential election did not permit him to set any national records for level of support, yet it did allow him to significantly defeat the Republican presidential competitor and to hold in check the surging presidential Republicanism that appeared in some of the other states of the old Confederacy.

In many ways, President Clinton's reelection bid mirrors that of President Carter when their two home states are compared (table 9.11). Both President Clinton and Republican candidate Dole lost actual votes but increased their percentage of support among the state's electorate. The incumbent President lost more ground in his home state than did the Republican challenger. With Dole at the head of the Republican ticket, the native-son candidate saw a small rollback in the state's Republican voting partisans.

Table 9.12 indicates how the African American vote compares with the President's home folks. The votes of the President's friends, neighbors, and colleagues did not reach the levels of support exhibited by African American Democrats. However both the African American and the home town folks increased their support between the 1992 and the 1996 primary elections.

TABLE 9.11 **The Difference in the Results of the 1992 and 1996 Presidential Elections**

Year	Clinton		Bush/Dole	
	Votes	%	Votes	%
1992	505,823	53.2	337,324	35.5
1996	475,171	53.7	325,416	36.8
Difference	-30,652	0.5	-11,908	1.3

Adapted from tables 9.3 and 9.8.

TABLE 9.12 Clinton's Percentage of the Vote in Presidential Elections in His Home and Black Belt Counties

Election	Black Belt Counties	Home Counties	Difference
1992 Primary	75.0%	73.4%	1.6%
1992 General Election	67.0%	54.1%	12.9%
1996 Primary	79.0%	75.4%	3.6%
1996 General Election	68.9%	53.3%	15.6%
Mean	72.5%	64.1%	8.4%

Adapted from tables 9.2 and 9.10.

In the general election African American voters increased their support while the home folks decreased theirs. This same pattern appeared in President Carter's reelection bid.[26] The mean support from the Black Belt counties was nearly three in every four voters, while two of every three voters in his own home counties supported him.

President Clinton demonstrated that a native-son presidential candidate in the region, as well as in his own home state, is a vigorous competitor to surging presidential Republican candidates. And in terms of the state electorate, the African Americans and home folks played a crucial role in his election and reelection coalition: these findings parallel earlier findings concerning another southern native-son candidate, Jimmy Carter of Georgia.

CHAPTER TEN

The Regional Vote: Clinton and Carter

Steven Rosenstone not only pioneered the multivariate measurement of the native-son variable but also empirically demonstrated that southern native-son presidential candidates have significant electoral drawing power in their region. Rosenstone further demonstrated that this was not true of the nonsouthern native-son presidential candidate.[1]

A case study of President Carter's electoral fortunes in Georgia, which followed in the wake of Rosenstone's pathbreaking work, found additional supporting evidence and corroboration for Rosenstone's insights. "Victorious presidential candidates can be influential on the subnational planes, setting whole new voting patterns and along with them new individual voting habits."[2] In 1976 and 1980,

> this reality of regional loyalties can . . . be clearly seen in Carter's presidential efforts in the state of Georgia and in the South in particular. . . . In fact, if one sees the concept [regionalism] as pertinent, then many of Carter's voters came not because he was on the Democratic party's ticket—although that helped—nor did they come because he had fashioned some unusual policy program and stance, or because of some new charisma on his part, but because he was a native of the region.[3]

This regionalism inherent in the Carter vote seemingly stalled or stopped surging Republicanism in Georgia and the South,[4] as did the later Clinton-Gore vote in Arkansas, Tennessee, and the South.[5]

It also repositioned the southern African American voter vis-a-vis his northern counterpart. After the disenfranchisement of the African American voter in the South, the northern African American voter played the leadership role in the Democratic party coalition, since southern African Americans were mostly voteless and, with the arrival of all-white primaries in the Democratic party, were told to stay out of party politics.[6] Southern African American Democrats had little power or influence in national party affairs or the national organization, and no chance at the southern level. The best that these presidential Democrats could do was to file suits, as did Dr. J.M. Robinson of the Arkansas Negro Democratic Association, which was formed in 1928 to contest the party's all-white nature and the closed lily-white primaries.[7] Southern African American Democrats were forced to abandon the leadership role to their northern counterparts. By the time that Carter came on the national scene, here is how the process worked.

> Usually, the process was one where several *northern* black leaders and heads of national civil rights organizations would coalesce with the most liberal Democratic candidate in the primaries and urge southern blacks to support him in the general election.[8]

Northern African American Democrats selected from the field of Democratic hopefuls the one candidate who seemed most sympathetic to the African American plight and endorsed him for the African American community. Bishop Alexander Walters and his National Colored Democratic League set this into motion in the 1912 election of Democrat Woodrow Wilson.[9]

Later, W.E.B. DuBois institutionalized this leadership selection procedure by making the NAACP a chief player in the process.[10] When it was initially established, this first and major African American civil rights organization was little more than an informal mechanism to influence the major political parties and the Democratic party in particular. While this procedure was modified over time, it would remain in place from 1912 until the Carter presidential candidacy. But in 1976 and 1980, the pattern completely reversed itself as new heroes and heroines in the African American community came from the South and the civil rights movement.

A southern politician with the aid of key local black civil rights leaders such as Andrew Young, Ben Brown, Coretta Scott King, and Daddy King, spearheaded drives in both the North and South to get black voters to support not the most liberal candidate of the Democratic party but a born-again southerner. [The leaders'] endorsement first took root in the South and later in the North—as they bypassed northern black electoral leaders and went directly to the masses of the black voters through the churches.[11]

This reversal of the leadership role took place in 1976 and 1980 rather than in 1964, when national figures such as Roy Wilkins, Whitney Young, James Farmer, and Floyd McKissick were still active players. By the initial Carter win, they were older and their successors had not achieved heroic status.

The analysis suggests that part of the reason that African Americans moved to support Carter—and later the Clinton-Gore ticket—is due to the regional factor. Many of the northern African American electorate were transplanted southerners, and indirectly affected by this southern regionalism.

In this second case study of a southern native-son presidential candidate, we can continue to look for the existence of this variable's dominant characteristics, its influence in the stalling of resurgent Republicanism, and the support it garners from the southern African American electorate. The exploration of this factor is essential if the study is to generate testable propositions for a more general theory of the native-son presidential candidate variable.

Regionalism: An Overview

In the wake of the passage of the 1964 Civil Rights Act, the Republican presidential candidate, Barry Goldwater, initiated a resurgence of voting in the South at the presidential level for the Republican party with his endless attacks on the Civil Rights Act and his cleverly designed appeal to state's rights.[12] His anti–civil rights stand instantly converted numerous Democratic southerners to the Republican party.[13] This was his southern strategy. Following his defeat, Nixon revised this southern strategy. Instead of appealing only to hardline segregationists, Nixon combined race with other hot button social issues such as busing, school prayer, abortion, taxes, family values, and patriotism. With this approach, Nixon created a solidly Republican South.

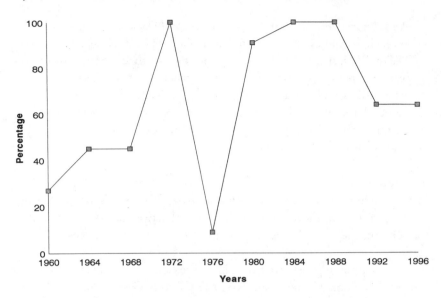

FIGURE 10.1 The Percentage of Southern States Won by the Republican
Party in Presidential Elections, 1960–1996

Scammon and McGillivray, eds., *America Votes 1996* (Washington, D.C.: Congressional Quarterly
Press, 1997). The states are the eleven states of the Confederacy: Alabama, Arkansas, Florida,
Georgia, Louisiana, Mississippi, North Carolina, South Carolina, Tennessee, Texas, and Virginia.

Both Reagan and Bush continued this approach based on an anti–civil
rights posture and racial cleavage. The end result was that individual
southerners switched, voting for the Republican presidential candidate,
and their states gave these candidates their electoral votes. Among these
was the once-Democratic state of Arkansas. However Democratic native-
son presidential candidates stalled and in some instances reversed this
process.

Figure 10.1 shows the percentage of southern states that the Republicans won with the Nixon candidacies of 1960 and 1964. In 1976, Carter
reduced the number of these states voting for the Republican candidate to
one, and Clinton in his two elections reduced it to 7. Clinton regained
one-third of the southern states while Carter regained nine-tenths in 1976.
Even when Carter lost in 1980, he kept his native state of Georgia in the
Democratic column. Carter and Clinton both reversed the Republican
trend in the southern states to different degrees.

As the native son candidates reversed Republican party fortunes in the
region, they also did so in the state of Arkansas (figure 10.2). Both Clinton

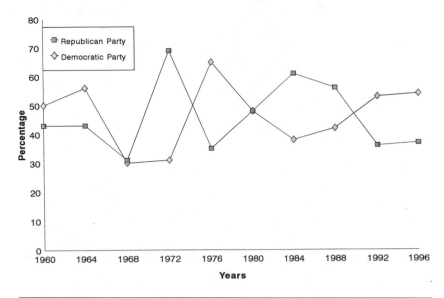

FIGURE 10.2 The Percentage of the Vote in Arkansas for Democratic and
Republican Presidential Candidates, 1960–1996

Adapted from Scammon and McGillivray, eds., *America Votes 1996.*

and Carter changed the percentage of the state vote in favor of the Democratic party. Clinton increased this marked Democratic tendency in 1996, while Carter made it the largest that the Democratic party had captured since the Goldwater candidacy. In fact, Carter outpolled Clinton in his own home state.

Figure 10.3 presents the mean percentage of the vote for Republican presidential candidates in the states of the old Confederacy. The two Democratic presidential candidates, Clinton and Carter, as well as the American Independent Party candidate George Wallace, significantly reduced the mean vote for the Republican party. Even when these candidates lost, as did Wallace in 1968 and Carter in 1980, they still lowered the mean Republican vote in the region. Clinton, who carried only four states in the region in both of his presidential electoral bids, significantly lowered the mean Republican vote from its 1988 peak by 14 and 10 points, respectively.

Embedded in this regionalism and its vote are negative feelings and values about race. The Wallace candidacy demonstrated this characteristic through a third party effort which had an effect on the major parties,

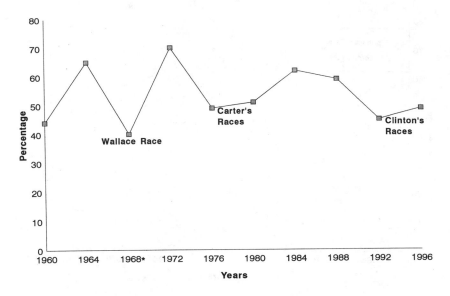

FIGURE 10.3 The Mean Percentage of the Presidential Vote for the
Republican Party in the Southern States, 1960–1996

Adapted from Scammon and McGillivray, eds., *America Votes 1996.*
*George Wallace ran as a southern native-son candidate on a third party ticket, winning Arkansas and
four other southern states, and rolling back the Republican resurgence in the region.

energizing and mobilizing this emotion in the southern electorate. "The
Wallace campaign served as a political 'conveyer belt,' helping to transport
millions of Southern and working class white Democrats into the Republican party's presidential coalition."[14] The Democratic party has not yet
escaped the Wallace influence. Carter's meld of fiscal conservatism and
racial liberalism helped outpoll Wallace in the region in 1980. Clinton,
learning from Carter, dropped the racial liberalism: as noted by one
observer, he rose 10 points in the polls the week after he cut Jesse Jackson
down to size.[15] At the moment, to capture the region's vote, candidates
must take into account one of its main features, racism.

One more empirical indicator of this regionalism is the percentage of
the southern electoral vote captured by Republican presidential candidates with their southern strategy.

Figure 10.4 permits us to see how a southern native-son presidential
candidate influences the electoral vote of the region in the face of the
Republican anti–civil rights strategy. With Nixon's revised southern
strategy, the Republican party captured 100 percent of the region's

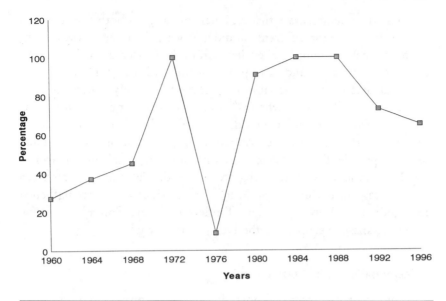

FIGURE 10.4 The Percentage of the Southern Electoral Vote Won by the
Republican Party, 1960–1996

Adapted from Scammon and McGillivray, eds., *America Votes 1996*.

electoral vote in 1972. With Carter running in 1976, the Republican party captured only 9 percent of the southern electoral vote. In 1980, Reagan gains 91 percent of the southern electoral vote. The resurgence continued in 1984, and in 1988 with Bush. However, Clinton reduced that resurgence to 73 percent in 1992 and 65 percent in 1996.[16] Although Clinton only won four southern states in each of his two victories, the four states in 1996 had fewer total electoral votes than the four states he won in 1992.

Together these southern native-son presidential candidates demonstrated that they could arrest or reverse the surging Republicanism in the South at the state level, at the vote level, and at the electoral vote level. These southerners clearly changed the fortunes of the Republican party in the region. And this empirical evidence, albeit at the aggregate level, suggests that regionalism is clearly a variable shaping political behavior in the eleven states of the old Confederacy. Southerners responded to the native son candidate not only in the respective states of Georgia and Arkansas, but regionally. The cultural matrix affects its people—both black and white.

These data demonstrate that regionalism varies at both the state and regional level and for different candidates, yet it is nevertheless present and functional. The empirical evidence from the Carter and Clinton elections corroborates the finding of professor Steven Rosenstone that southern candidates have a regional influence. And the analysis permits us to view the vote in the region when nonsoutherners ran for president in 1972, 1984, and 1988. Clearly the region did not respond with as great a level of support as it did when southerners ran in 1964, 1972, 1976, 1992, and 1996. Southern presidential candidates brought out the regional vote in favor of the Democratic party. And having a vice presidential running mate from the same region, as Clinton had in 1992 and 1996, obviously strengthened this regionalism: in both elections Tennessee, Albert Gore's home state, joined Arkansas in supporting the Democratic party.

Regionalism: The State Portrait

The comprehensive regional portrait provides a broadbased collective dimension of general trends and patterns. But this collective dimension can be disaggregated into smaller units for analysis and additional insights. Our initial question is how did native-son presidential candidate Carter perform in Arkansas and its counties? The data offer some intriguing insights as well as some linkages between Carter and Clinton.

In both of Carter's presidential races, in 1976 and 1980, Arkansas held Democratic primaries, and in both years Bill Clinton was a candidate for statewide office. He ran in the 1976 primary for the state attorney general post, while in 1980, he was in both the primary and general elections seeking reelection as governor. These simultaneous races provide an opportunity to see connections between these two recent southern native-son presidential candidates, as Carter's presidential efforts overlapped with Clinton's emerging native-son efforts.

The May 25, 1976 Democratic presidential primary brought before the Arkansas electorate two regional native-son candidates, Georgia's Carter and Alabama's Georgia Wallace; a liberal, Arizona's Morris Udall; and a moderate centrist, Henry Jackson of Washington. Wallace was best known in Arkansas for his bedrock defiance of federally supported integration. In 1968, as a third party candidate under the banner of his own American Independent party, he had won the state and its six electoral votes with 39 percent of the vote: the second place Republican captured 31 percent of the vote and the Democrat 30 percent. By the 1972 Democratic primary Wallace still had a significant following in the state, although an assassination attempt during the Maryland primary campaign left him paralyzed and in a wheel chair.[17] By 1976 he was no match for Carter (table 10.1).

Wallace received less than half the 240,982 votes he won in 1968, as Carter won every one of the state's counties. Carter swept the primary with about two-thirds of the total vote cast. Carter's victory over Wallace in Arkansas helped to end Wallace's native-son presidential aspirations and career. Yet, even in his twilight, Wallace proved that even in Arkansas race was still a salient feature of the regional vote, this time within the Democratic party ranks.

Disaggregating the Carter victory by demographic categories shows that Carter's performance was balanced across all the different categories (table 10.2). He did very well in the home counties of the state's incipient attorney general, Bill Clinton. Clinton, as the state chairman of the Carter campaign, had galvanized the electorate for his candidate. Even the African American voter gave more support to Carter than to the liberal Morris Udall, who was backed by civil rights leader and Georgia legislator Julian Bond. Udall got less than 5 percent of the vote in the Black Belt counties. The centrist Henry Jackson performed even worse.

In the general election in November, facing the Republican incumbent President Gerald Ford, Carter won 65 percent of the popular vote and all six of the state's electoral votes (table 10.3). In 1972, Nixon had carried the state for the Republican party. Carter's victory over Ford reversed the emerging Republican tendency in Arkansas. A native-son candidate was clearly having regional influence.

TABLE 10.1   Results of the 1976 Democratic Presidential
Primary in Arkansas

Candidates	Votes	Percentages
Jimmy Carter	314,277	62.6
George Wallace	83,005	16.5
Uncommitted	57,145	11.4
Morris Udall	37,983	7.5
Henry Jackson	9,554	1.9
Total	501,764	99.9

Riviere, "Arkansas Elections: 1976," 4.

TABLE 10.2 Results of the 1976 Democratic Presidential Election in Arkansas by Demographic Category

Candidate	Urban Counties		Town Counties		Rural Counties		Home Counties		Black Belt Counties	
	Votes	%	Votes	%	Votes	%	Votes	%	Votes	%
Carter	126,630	61.5	121,338	64.0	43,145	62.7	12,793	61.3	10,371	62.9
Wallace	31,323	15.2	31,862	16.8	13,655	19.9	3,315	15.9	2,850	17.3
Uncommitted	23,274	11.3	22,075	11.6	6,910	10.0	2,701	12.9	2,185	13.3
Udall	20,602	10.0	10,844	5.7	3,917	5.7	1,692	8.1	728	4.4
Jackson	4,054	2.0	3,600	1.9	1,176	1.7	378	1.8	346	2.1
Total	205,883	100.0	189,719	100.0	68,803	100.0	20,879	100.0	16,480	100.0

Adapted from Riviere, "Arkansas Elections: 1976," 4.

TABLE 10.3 Results of the 1976 Presidential Election in
           Arkansas

Candidate	Votes	Percentage
Jimmy Carter	499,614	64.9
Gerald Ford	268,753	34.9
Eugene McCarthy	647	0.08
John Anderson	382	0.04
Total	769,396	99.9

Riviere, "Arkansas Elections: 1976," 19.

In the county level analysis of the general election, we see that Carter captured 96 percent of Arkansas counties, including some of the 19 traditionally Republican counties (table 10.4).

In each of the demographic categories, the Carter effort, orchestrated by Clinton, captured about two-thirds of the total vote (table 10.5). In Clinton's home counties and in the Black Belt counties, the combination proved powerful. These two southerners put the Ford campaign at a great disadvantage. Some of the voters who had embraced the Nixon southern Republican strategy in 1972 now shifted back to the Democratic party or simply dropped out and refused to vote in this election. President Ford received barely one-third of the vote.

There is one more suggestion in this empirical evidence about the 1976 presidential primary and general election in Arkansas. This southern native-son presidential candidate clearly got a significant boost from a rising native son. After Georgia, Arkansas gave Carter his highest level of electoral support, 65 percent to Georgia's 67 percent.

Clinton also played a role in Carter's reelection bid in 1980. But in 1980 Clinton was up for reelection as governor, and the two men's friendship had become very strained. Clinton would in fact blame Carter for his reelection defeat. One key factor was that President Carter had sent Cuban detainees to Fort Chaffee in northwest Arkansas.

[On] June 1, 1980, a bad situation deteriorated [as] several hundred Cuban refugees who had come to the United States in the Mariel boatlift rioted and broke out of their resettlement camp . . . nearby residents were alarmed this time by reports that the Cuban contingent included criminals and mental patients.[18]

TABLE 10.4 Counties Won by Each Candidate in the
1976 Presidential Election

Candidate	Number of Counties	Percentage
Carter	72	96.0
Ford	3	4.0
Total	75	100.0

Riviere, "Arkansas Elections: 1976," 22.

There was a serious confrontation in Barling, Arkansas. The local newspapers picked up the matter. Little help was forthcoming from the White
House, and Clinton could not get Carter on the phone. When White
House aide Eugene Edenberg came to Arkansas to resolve the matter, he
promised Clinton that no new detainees would be sent to the state. However, "On August 1st . . . word came from the White House that all Cuban
refugees still being housed at resettlement camps in Wisconsin, Pennsylvania, and Florida would be transferred to a single consolidated camp at
Fort Chaffee."[19]

Clinton came to believe that his own president was among those
"killing him for reelection as governor."[20]

> The decision, Clinton told reporters, was the most politically damag-
> ing one Carter could make. Placing the final resettlement camp in
> Wisconsin, Pennsylvania, or Florida would have been smarter, he
> argued, because Carter had a better chance of carrying Arkansas in
> the fall election than any of those states. Now, he shared [Senator
> David] Pryor's assessment that Carter's chances in Arkansas were
> shot.[21]

The Republican gubernatorial candidate made extensive use of the Fort
Chaffee situation. "Republican challenger Frank White and his handlers
. . . replayed footage of the Fort Chaffee riot to associate Clinton with
images of disorder and bad times."[22] The footage implied that a southern
native-son president had betrayed the people of his own region by pushing unwanted people of color upon them. Arkansas rejected both the
Carter and Clinton reelection bids. However Clinton fared better than
did Carter.

TABLE 10.5 Results of the 1976 Presidential Election by Demographic Category

Candidate	Urban Counties		Town Counties		Rural Counties		Home Counties		Black Belt Counties	
	Votes	%	Votes	%	Votes	%	Votes	%	Votes	%
Carter	225,135	61.8	175,259	68.5	63,011	68.4	21,104	61.4	15,105	69.8
Ford	139,393	38.2	80,440	31.5	29,130	31.6	13,253	38.6	6,537	30.2
Total	364,528	100.0	255,699	100.0	92,141	100.0	34,357	100.0	21,642	100.0

Adapted from Riviere, "Arkansas Elections: 1976," 22.

In the 1980 primaries Clinton got 306,736 votes, while President Carter received 269,290. In the general election Clinton captured 403,242 votes to President Carter's 398,041 (table 10.6). The Arkansas electorate favored their own native son over the other regional candidate. Clinton had not mobilized the presidential vote as he had in 1976. In both the primary and general election, President Carter ran considerably behind the state's governor. There might not have been a public break between the Governor and the President, but there was an electoral break in the final analysis.

The decline of support for President Carter had been presaged in the primary election, in which the number of uncommitted voters rose significantly to almost one in five. Southern Democrats were refusing to support one of their own regional candidates at the level that they had in 1976. This was one indication that the Arkansas electorate was moving away from a regional position.

In 1980 President Carter's support dropped noticeably in all of the demographic categories (table 10.7). In the Black Belt counties there was a sizable shift in the primary from President Carter to the liberal challenger Senator Edward Kennedy. However President Carter still captured a majority of the African American vote.

The larger Arkansas electorate in the primary, faced with a questionable regional incumbent versus a known liberal, opted across all demographic categories for the native son. The Arkansas electorate did not shift votes to a nonsoutherner: they simply stayed away from the polls.

The evidence from the primary was fully confirmed in the general election (table 10.8). President Carter lost the state's six electoral votes to

TABLE 10.6 Results of the 1980 Democratic
Presidential Primary in Arkansas

Candidate	Votes	Percentage
Jimmy Carter	269,290	60.1
Uncommitted	80,895	18.1
Edward Kennedy	78,530	17.5
Cliff Finch	19,459	14.3
Total	448,174	100.0

Riviere, "Arkansas Elections: 1976," 22.

TABLE 10.7 Results of the 1980 Democratic Presidential Primary by Demographic Category

Candidate	Urban Counties		Town Counties		Rural Counties		Home Counties		Black Belt Counties	
	Votes	%	Votes	%	Votes	%	Votes	%	Votes	%
Carter	128,303	59.5	97,095	61.5	23,009	59.2	13,857	60.5	7,026	55.9
Uncommitted	41,203	19.1	25,978	16.4	7,077	18.2	4,720	20.6	1,917	15.2
Kennedy	37,108	17.2	27,349	17.3	7,236	18.6	3,677	16.1	3,160	25.1
Finch	9,186	4.3	7,575	4.8	1,579	4.1	646	2.8	473	3.8
Total	215,800	100.1	157,997	100.0	38,901	100.1	22,900	100.0	12,576	100.0

Adapted from Riviere, "Arkansas Elections: 1976," 6.

Republican Ronald Reagan. Governor Clinton lost his reelection bid to Republican Frank White. Democratic anger was shifted to support of the Republican party. Although they were close defeats, they were defeats nevertheless. The electorate simultaneously rejected both its own native son and a regional native son.

At the county level, President Carter won two-thirds of the counties (table 10.9), but the counties which Reagan captured carried enough votes to win the state.

Turning from the county analysis to a demographic one, Carter's best performance came in the Black Belt counties, where he captured 61 percent of the vote (table 10.10).

President Carter also won the town and rural counties. Reagan outpolled the President in the urban areas and in Governor Clinton's own home counties. Reagan's poorest performance came in the Black Belt counties.

The demographic and county analysis reveals that President Carter's loss was not broadbased. The Republicans did not sweep the state. Presidential Democrats were still alive in the state, but at a reduced level of turnout and intensity than in the 1976 election.

Had President Carter received the same number of votes as Governor Clinton, Carter would have won the state and captured its six electoral college votes. But the regional variable was less potent in the 1980 election than it had been just four years earlier. The regional variable does fluctuate in strength and intensity across local and national issues. Both types of issues played a strong role in this election.

TABLE 10.8 **Results of the 1980 Presidential Election in Arkansas**

Candidate	Votes	Percentage
Ronald Reagan	403,164	48.1
Jimmy Carter	398,041	47.5
John Anderson	22,468	2.7
Ed Clark	8,970	1.1
Barry Commoner	2,345	0.3
Benjamin Babar	1,350	0.2
Gus Hall	1,244	0.2
Total	837,582	100.4

Paul Riviere, "Arkansas Elections: 1980" (Little Rock: Office of the Secretary of State, 1982), 15–16.

TABLE 10.9 Counties Won by Each Candidate in the 1980
Presidential Election

Candidate	Number of Counties	Percentage
Carter	50	66.7
Reagan	25	33.3
Others	0	0.0
Total	75	100.0

Adapted from Riviere, "Arkansas Elections: 1980," 19.

Regionalism: The Vice Presidential Dimension

The two native-son presidential candidates played the vice presidential card in different ways. The most obvious difference is that Clinton's vice president is yet another regional native son, Al Gore of Tennessee, while Carter's choice was a liberal from Minnesota, Walter Mondale. Former President Carter used his regional connection to support Mondale in 1984. Mondale, who was also backed by Bert Lance, Hamilton Jordan, and several black leaders, narrowly won the Georgia state primary. With this victory in Georgia, Mondale's campaign gained the momentum for him to capture the party's nomination. Former President Carter's hold on regionalism turned the tide in the primary.

Carter's influence seems to have been strongest in his home county and weakest in the black majority county of Hancock. It was modest in the other demographic categories in the state. Carter was unsuccessful in transferring his African American support, which went to Jesse Jackson.[23]

> Mondale's slim primary victory in Georgia, he later indicated to the press, revitalized his sagging campaign and gave him the momentum to hold off his two rivals, Jackson and Hart, and to win a first-ballot nomination at the Democratic convention in San Francisco.[24]

But the state support that Carter generated for Mondale in the primary disappeared by the general election: President Reagan won Georgia for the Republican party. Reflected primary regionalism gave way to a transference of this regional vote to a Republican.

The question can be raised: would Carter's regional influence have been greater had Mondale not been a liberal? The election of 2000, in which a southern vice president will most probably run, will surely provide some empirical insight into this matter.

TABLE 10.10 Results of the 1980 Democratic Presidential Primary by Demographic Category

Candidate	Urban Counties		Town Counties		Rural Counties		Home Counties		Black Belt Counties	
	Votes	%	Votes	%	Votes	%	Votes	%	Votes	%
Reagan	230,177	49.6	119,719	46.4	25,457	46.4	19,591	51.1	8,220	37.7
Carter	209,998	45.3	130,119	50.3	27,548	50.2	17,186	44.8	13,190	60.5
Anderson	14,340	3.1	5,619	2.2	1,159	2.1	1,114	2.9	236	1.1
Clark	5,491	1.2	2,514	1.0	564	1.0	281	0.7	120	0.6
Commoner	1,819	0.4	383	0.1	90	0.2	47	0.1	6	0.0
Babar	989	0.2	254	0.1	32	0.1	65	0.2	10	0.0
Hall	905	0.2	225	0.1	37	0.1	61	0.2	16	0.0
Total	463,719	100.0	258,833	100.1	54,887	100.1	38,345	100.0	21,798	100.0

Adapted from Riviere, "Arkansas Elections: 1980," 15–16.

President Carter's approach in choosing Walter Mondale as his running mate had been the traditional one of balancing the ticket regionally. Clinton, on the other hand, refused the balanced ticket approach and chose another southerner, Tennessee Senator Gore. Tactically, it would help Clinton win at least one more southern state if regionalism was still potent at the state level, as the 1980 election in Arkansas had shown.

Tennessee had voted Republican in the 1968, 1972, 1980, 1984, and 1988 presidential elections. Only Carter's election in 1976 had pulled the state back to its historical Democratic voting pattern. The choice of Senator Gore was a strategy to break the Reagan-Bush Republican hold on the South. In 1980, 1984, and 1988, the Republicans swept all of the states of the old Confederacy, with the exception of Georgia in 1980. Clinton was faced with a solid Republican phalanx over the stars of Dixie.

In 1992 and 1996 both Arkansas and Tennessee shifted back to the Democratic fold.[25] Two native sons reversed the Republican presidential tide in their two states. The regional variable was once again working and was aided this time by a southern vice presidential candidate. And while the Clinton-Gore ticket did not recapture the entire South, four states did break from the Republican bloc and drift back into the Democratic presidential column. Things did change in at least two elections, proving that the regional variable was still alive and well in the old South. Localism in presidential elections still had influence and impact.

In sum, there are two approaches to the use of the vice presidential candidate to stimulate the regional variable in voting behavior. The native-son candidate can try to directly rally his electoral troops around the candidate if he is not from the region; the tactic might work in the primaries, given the nature and scope of the candidate field. It seems less likely to work in the general election if the candidate is a liberal.

The other tactic is to select a southerner as vice president. Table 10.11 shows that nonsouthern Democratic presidential candidates have selected a southern vice presidential running mate eight times this century. Four of these times the Democratic party won the presidential election: and each of these times the party has won with more than half of the solid South. On the four occasions that it lost, only once, in 1988, did it not win a single southern state.

When southerners headed up the Democratic ticket, a significant number of southern states were won, except in 1980.

When the Democratic party is competitive in the rest of the nation, it only needs to win about one-third of the solid South to be victorious. And if it is not competitive elsewhere, it can win up to seven states of the region and still lose the presidency.

The selection of a native-son southerner as vice president does more than capture regional electoral votes for the Democratic party. It positions the Democratic party to become competitive with the Republicans in the region. And it sets into motion the possibility of a native-son Republican presidential candidate from the region. The next presidential election might provide a window on this possibility. At the moment, the vice presidential candidate tactic has revived regionalism for the Democratic party.

There is a regional variable in southern presidential politics. Empirical evidence for the influence of this variable is found in the Carter and Clinton presidential elections. Southern native-son presidential candidates Wallace, Carter, and Clinton stalled, reversed, or slowed Republican gains in the South. A native-son vice presidential candidate, Gore, stalled southern Republicanism in his home state of Tennessee.

Carter in two elections won in Arkansas once, in 1976. Clinton in two elections won in Georgia once, in 1992. This demonstrates that the regional variable does shift and change with candidates, events, and party competition. This regionalism can shift parties as the Nixon, Wallace, Reagan, and Bush candidacies revealed. However there is an underlying Democratic tendency that can be activated by a combination of other factors and forces.

The African American electorate has strongly supported the native-son candidates, with the exception of Wallace, over more liberal white candidates. This electorate has also supported an African American candidate, Jesse Jackson.[26] Race influences the African American as well as the white electorate. A liberal African American candidate seems to sway the African American electorate as a conservative white candidate can the white electorate.

When an African American presidential candidate is not running, the regional variable seems to influence both races in a similar fashion. Carter and Clinton were major beneficiaries of the African American Democratic vote and of party activists. They won with and because of this aspect of regionalism. It was a political asset that made a difference.

Lastly, regionalism as a variable offers the future possibility of a southern native-son Republican presidential or vice presidential candidate. The year 2000 offers just such a prospect, with the potential of new insights into this variable in the offing.

The conclusion from the evidence must be that "Southern Republicanism at the presidential level has at least one major flaw: It can be significantly reduced by a native son presidential candidate. Both the Carter and Clinton candidacies provide evidence that this flaw exists."[27]

Part Five

The Native-Son Candidate and the Democratic Party

V. O. Key Jr. raised an interesting question in his article "The Future of the Democratic Party": "What about the South? How should it be weighed in a set of calculations on the long-run balance of power between the parties?"[1]

By the time Bill Clinton became a native-son candidate in Arkansas, the Democratic party no longer enjoyed "the great advantage of the ingrained loyalty of most Southern voters."[2] Clinton decided, while still in law school, that he would transform and reinvent the Democratic party and reposition it to be more acceptable to his region and to the country. He set about this transformation of the Democratic party in stages.

Stage one began after the 1984 Mondale loss, when he and other southerners formed the Democratic Leadership Council (DLC), a conservative Democratic organization, to help reshape the party.

> Bill Clinton, [five term] governor of Arkansas and founding member and former Chair of the Democratic Leadership Council, . . . framed his candidacy for the Oval Office largely around the strategy advocated by the DLC.[3]

The DLC was conceived and organized as "a supplementary policy-oriented organization, with a membership consisting of elected officials only."[4] The point of origin of this organization was the Committee on Party Effectiveness (CPE) formed by a group of House Democrats after President Carter's 1980 loss. Representative Gillis Long, a member of the Long dynasty of Louisiana, offered his top aide, Al From, to lead the committee, which was disbanded after Long's term ended in 1984.

> Al From was looking for a job, so he launched the DLC in 1985. The 1984 election created a "market" for membership in the DLC among Democratic elected officials who believed the party's national message was too liberal and who worried about the impact of the national party identity on their own political careers. . . . The initial DLC leadership cadre consisted of elected officials who stood to gain from the achievement of the organization's political goals, and those who had worked closely with From in the House Caucus . . . joined . . . because of the personal influence of Gephardt.[5]

The presence of these House and Senate members attracted others outside of Congress, like Clinton. By 1988 the DLC had more than 200 members and a firm financial basis in contributions from these elected officials. In the following year, Ron Brown, who became the Democratic National Committee chairman, assisted the DLC in becoming accepted within the national party. The previous Democratic National Committee chair, Paul Kirk, had not been as helpful to the group as Brown would become.

The DLC created a think tank, the Progressive Policy Institute (PPI), to develop policy; established state and local chapters with other elected officials; published a bimonthly magazine, "The New Democrat"; and began a major fundraising effort. By the late 1980s it could claim half of the Democrats in Congress and Democratic governors as members.

In 1989 the DLC initiated its annual conference. The DLC saw "liberal fundamentalism" as the problem and sought to develop a new and different policy stance by thrashing out new ideas at these conferences. As these ideas started to emerge, the organization needed a message carrier.

> [Al] From set out to recruit a chair for the DLC in 1991 who would be considered a plausible 1992 candidate. At the very least, the chair needed to be someone who could command the attention of other potential candidates. Bill Clinton quickly emerged as best suited for the task.[6]

Governor Clinton became chairman of the DLC in 1991 and traveled with From to more than two dozen states to set up state DLC chapters.

The connection continued: when Governor Clinton announced his presidential candidacy in the fall of 1991, his speech included the twin DLC themes of opportunity and responsibility. Much in the speech was taken from DLC policy and idea papers. Governor Clinton picked up the DLC message and ran with it. Shortly thereafter he had the party's nomination. At the 1992 Democratic National Convention, the DLC captured the platform.

> Of 51 subheadings in the Democratic Platform, 37 were in agreement with agenda items in the DLC's New Choice Draft and the other 14 items were in rough accordance with the DLC document. Nothing in the Democratic Platform was in disagreement.[7]

L. Sandy Maisel, in a detailed analysis of the 1992 platform writing process, noted that the party platform in a candidate-centered era belongs to the nominee. "Platforms in 1992 were candidate, not party, platforms . . . we should not be surprised that victorious candidates attempt to implement their platforms and that congressional parties of victorious candidates support major items in the platform."[8]

Thus, in 1991, the interests of the Democratic party's newest organization, the DLC, and those of a southern native-son presidential hopeful coincided, despite the fact that central to the DLC's New Democrat policy and philosophy was the distancing of the party from African Americans and other minorities.

The second stage of this strategy came in the nomination process, in which Clinton distanced himself from Jesse Jackson by criticizing Sister Souljah's statement about the Los Angeles riots.[9]

Clinton had been invited to speak at Jesse Jackson's Rainbow Coalition convention in Washington, D.C. on June 13.

> None of his senior advisers felt an urgent need to court the controversial reverend. On the contrary, [George] Stephanopolous and [Paul] Begala saw an opportunity for Clinton to distance himself from Jackson.[10]
>
> At the end of a routine address to Jackson's group, Clinton criticized Jackson and his Rainbow Coalition for providing a forum the night before for a black rap singer named Sister Souljah, [after] Jackson had just mentioned approvingly that she had been on the previous day's panel.

After the speech, Jackson tried to hand Clinton a long memo out-
lining the assets he would bring to the Democratic ticket should
Clinton choose him as his vice-presidential running mate.

Clinton declined. "I'm not going to put you through what Fritz
Mondale or Mike Dukakis did."[11]

Not only did Clinton refuse to accept Jackson's memo, he rejected him
outright and belittled him before his own organization. The New Democrat not only distanced himself from Jackson, but Jackson from the remade
party. Clinton's first biographer noted that, during an interview, Clinton
"took a phone call from Jesse Jackson on his cell phone, all uh-huhs and
southern whispers, then got off the phone and sarcastically disparaged
Jackson as a pest."[12] Clinton's strategy involved not only face-to-face techniques but behind-the-back tactics as well.

Clinton moved to displace Jackson by supporting other African American leaders from his own state, and those such as Congressman Mike
Espy of Mississippi. Other African American civil rights leaders were distanced from the new Democratic party. In addition Clinton chose another
southerner, Senator Al Gore, to be his running mate and heir apparent.
Gore, if elected president in his own right, could continue to help transform and reinvent the party.

At the Democratic National Convention, Clinton described himself as
a New Democrat who sought a new direction for the Democratic party, a
"third way" between traditional Democratic liberalism and Republican
conservatism. This was a strategy called triangulation, developed by his
long time political consultant Dick Morris.

Essentially stage two gave the party a new ideology and ideological
stance by displacing the old ideology and its leadership and constituency
group in the electorate, the African American voter. This was the group
in the party most visibly identified with the ideology of liberalism. Clinton linked his new ideology to another base, the white middle class.

Once Clinton was elected, the transformation of the party was temporarily halted, since liberal Democrats controlled the House of Representatives and the Senate. Initially Clinton offered liberal policies, but by
the midterm 1994 Congressional elections these policies had failed and
the Democrats were swept from Congressional power. Stage three began.

The Republican capture of Congress weakened Congressional
Democrats who "were eventually forced to look to Clinton as a party
leader far more than they did during Clinton's first term. . . . The 1994
elections created a vacuum in the Democratic party that only Bill Clinton

was in a position to fill."[13] The liberal Democratic congressional party found itself following the President's lead in 1996 and this gave Clinton another opportunity to reshape the party.

By the 1996 elections, "incumbent Democrats increasingly took their cues from the White House, both in policy and tactics; most Democrats running for Congress for the first time faithfully repeated the presidential line . . . on the issues."[14] Stage three saw "Clinton's rightward move . . . abetted by his growing influence over his party's congressional contingent."[15] Liberal congressional Democrats became policy moderates and shadow conservatives. The transformation was taking place.

Stage four of the transformation began with President Clinton's reelection in 1996. He remade the Democratic National Committee and appointed new leadership in tune with his centrist philosophy, in preparation for an eventual run for the presidency in 2000 by Vice President Al Gore.

This part of the book explores the future of the Democratic party in presidential elections from the standpoint of what the native son theory tells us about cracking the Republican party's hold on the region. The Republican party hold has both strengths and weaknesses and the native-son theory suggests ways in which the Democratic party can take advantage of those weaknesses. The theory also suggests ways in which the Republican party's strengths might be neutralized.

To quote Key:

> Republicans have replaced the image of a South of moonlight and
> magnolias by a fond dream of a balance-of-power South, a South
> reactionary to a man, almost unanimously opposed to every major
> congressional enactment since 1933, ground under the heel of a Feder-
> al tyrant, and awaiting only a propitious moment to embrace the
> Republican liberation.[16]

But how long will the idea of the Republican party as liberator of the South endure, if it runs counter to the concerns of the country? Once the opposite pertained—the Democratic party as liberator of the South—until it ran into serious difficulty with the needs of the rest of the country, and as a result collapsed, and transformed both itself and the region. Such new balance-of-power hopes run essentially the same risk, under a new partisan label. A native son candidate might or might not prevent this from happening. Yet one thing is certain. The transformation of the Democratic party to date has come at the expense of the party's and native-son Clinton's own electoral savior, the African American electorate.[17]

CHAPTER ELEVEN

The Democratic Party in Presidential Elections: The Native-Son Theory Revisited

If the reelection of President Clinton had any consequences, these included changes for both major political parties, a different contour for the party system, and an alteration of southern politics. There were also cries, whispers, and signs about the future of the Democratic party.

> The world in which Bill Clinton came of age had a definite geopolitical cast. His native South in particular had a political character all its own. It was, stated simply, Democratic. Two years before he was born, 71 percent of all voters in the region still considered themselves Democrats [but Republican candidate] Reagan won a healthy victory among southern voters in 1980, and Reagan and Bush both took the South in 1984 and 1988, respectively.[1]

This new geopolitical cast has been significantly influenced by the reelection in 1996 of the comeback kid from Arkansas.

Political parties, if they are to survive electoral defeats and political disasters, must surmount domestic and foreign crises wrought by the changing political context.[2] The American political process is dynamic, ever evolving and ever transforming itself. Political entities and institutions must be resilient, adapting to swiftly moving currents, surging political tides, rapid economic fluctuations, and widespread electoral movements at both the state and national levels. Political parties face continual change in the American political environment.

Party scholar L. Sandy Maisel has written that:

> Parties in the role of institutions have adapted as the nation has changed over two centuries. But as parties are not monolithic, any analysis must take into account not only their complexity but also the various points at which they affect the American polity.
>
> The Democrats and the Republicans have not always responded in the same way to these changes in American politics; partisan differences on some reforms have been pronounced.[3]

But respond they must if they are to survive: "as the nation has undergone dramatic changes, the political parties, as institutions that must function within this changing context, have had to respond."[4]

The Black Freedom movement, in both its civil rights and Black Power manifestations, created a major crisis for the party system in general and the Democratic party in particular. During the Great Depression the Democratic party put together a New Deal coalition with a major fault line in the electoral coalition between southern whites and African Americans of the urban areas of both the North and the South.[5] Economic issues initially papered over this major gap as the financial crisis set into motion by the collapse of Wall Street in 1929 took priority over the antagonistic race relations embedded in southern regionalism. President Roosevelt did little to assist African Americans except in a symbolic manner, while placating southern politicians and their race hatred and fears by adopting a policy of ambiguity.[6]

At the time of the New Deal coalition African Americans had little national political power either in Congress, in the president's electoral coalition, at the Supreme Court, or in the federal bureaucracy.[7] Southern whites had significant national as well as regional power. Economics, combined with the lack of electoral and political power, made one member of the New Deal coalition a junior member. Southern whites dominated, giving the Democratic party a southern base at the presidential and congressional levels. The 1960s exposed the racial divide in the Democratic party, wrenched the Republican party to a hard shift to the right, and engendered a new set of race-based third parties like George Wallace's American Independent party.

How did the Democratic party handle its crisis? Slowly it has developed a southern native-son presidential candidate strategy to stay its eroding southern electoral base. President Clinton's reelection is only the most recent step in that strategy. The recent history of the Democratic party's success in presidential elections cannot be fully grasped without reference to the southern native-son candidacies of Johnson, Carter, and Clinton. Without these individuals, the Democratic party would not have had a presence in the White House since the passage of the 1964 Civil Rights Act.

The central question still pertains: what does a southern native son theory tell us? Drawing upon the empirical data from Carter and now Clinton, we can learn with a high degree of certainty about party transformation and gain insights into how parties attempt to resolve crises. We can discern problems inherent in party literature and scholarship, and reflect on how parties remap their state and regional electoral bases. Finally, the theory offers some ability to forecast the future of the Democratic party in presidential elections and, by extension, the future of the Republican party. Overall, the native son theory, with the additional data from the Clinton experience, offers a previously ignored window on Democratic elections in America. Its absence in the exploration of the American political process and the party system has left much unexplored and unanswered. Thus it was time to revise the theory and enrich its skeletal nature with new insights from President Clinton's reelection.

The Party Literature: Missing the Native-Son Presidential Variable

Popular and scholarly literature have left readers bereft of essential insights on several critical issues concerning American political parties and regionalism. Native son candidates such as Wallace, Johnson, Carter, and Clinton are all manifestations of the southern regional reality. These men, particularly Wallace and Johnson, have had significant influence on the fortunes of the Democratic party. They have in one way or other altered the course of party politics in American life. But the standard textbooks and academic musings on political parties have both given short shrift to these compelling forces in the life and history of American political parties.

The party literature can be divided into two categories—traditional and behavioral—to explore the roots of this missing variable. In the traditional era, from 1900 to the 1960s, parties were analyzed in historical, institutional, and structural terms. This literature emphasized the fact that the president was the titular head of the party and directed it from the

White House, with his handpicked chairman running the national organization. Leadership was seen from the standpoint of the presidency or Congress, and little else. Regionalism, and the role of regionally based leadership, was rarely a consideration in this literature.[8]

Behaviorism, in the 1960s to 1980s, and the postbehavioral era which followed, focused on roles and functions, and individual attributes such as perceptions, candidate qualities, and partisan attachment and identification. Although regionalism was an indirect concern in terms of how different regions of the country shaped voting behavior, the role of regional leadership in remapping the party's identity was not a central feature of the literature. Notice was taken when these regional candidates appeared, but no systematic view was made of this new variable in the party process.

> Like Johnson, [Carter] benefited from his regional identification, and he momentarily slowed the southern white flight from his party with his 1976 campaign when he ran against the Washington establishment. He did not appear to hurt his party—at least at the grassroots level, where party identification flourishes—but he scarcely took honors as the revitalizing leader of the party-in-the-electorate.[9]

This perceptive remark, rare for discussing the nature of regional party leadership, introduces one of the dominant features of party analysis in the current literature, namely, the party-in-the-electorate aspect. This feature is one of the reasons why the party literature has devoted so little time, space, and reflection on regional leadership as a transforming element in the Democratic party's revitalized role in presidential elections.

On the eve of the behavioral era in political science, V. O. Key Jr. broke the traditionalist paradigm and developed a functional typology based on behavioral roles and functions as a new and more rewarding way in which to perceive and understand political parties. It is this typology that has come to dominate both the popular and scholarly assessment and portrayal of current American political parties.

By the time of the fifth edition of his popular textbook on political parties, Key had redefined and fully developed a four-fold theoretical typology for interpreting American political parties. His typology consisted of (1) party-in-the-party-system, (2) party-in-the-organization, (3) party-in-the-electorate, and (4) party-in-the-government.[10] The initial aspect of this typology was that American political parties reside in the two party system that has emerged and evolved over time. It includes the battles between parties, including minor parties and state parties.

Party-in-the-organization focuses on and describes the essential structural features of American political parties such as the nature of party organization at state, local, and national levels, and how the parties nominate their candidates at national conventions as well as in primaries. Embedded in this aspect of parties are the party machines that run local, county, and sometimes state governments.

The party-in-the-electorate probes party voters' loyalty, participation, and characteristics; party finances and campaign techniques; and the electoral system of ballots and registrations. Here one could see the party at the individual and collective levels.

Finally, there is the matter of the party-in-the-government. After the political party has acquired political power it has the task of organizing and administering the government. Here the focus centers on party sponsored legislation and party led governmental performance.

Key hoped this division of political parties into four discrete and separate functions would aid empirical analysis and fact based interpretation. Although Key included all of these features in the initial edition in 1942, they were not as refined and as well structured and organized as in the last edition, of 1964. Subsequent textbooks on political parties adopted three of the four typologies. The standard textbook model has come to rest on features 2, 3, and 4.[11] The party-in-the-party-system has traditionally been omitted from the literature. This feature includes the combative, clashing, and contentious warfarelike aspects of parties. Since 1945, political science, with its emphasis on stability, order, and cooperation, looked away from social and political conflict.[12] Thus this aspect of the typology was quietly set aside in the standard textbook model on political parties. But it was in this dropped typological feature that Key discussed the impact and influence of sectionalism on American political parties.

Key noted that from colonial America until the 1940s, sectionalism was a major factor via political parties.

One of the recurrent and persistent cleavages of interest in politics has always been between people living in different territorial areas.[13]

    As for the post-civil war Democratic party, we have one of the major parties dominating and dominated by a region, the South. . . . For sectionalism to exist in its most extreme form, it is essential that an economic interest, or some other interest, dominate a geographical region. Regional homogeneity of interest, then, is a durable basis for sectionalism.[14]

By the time of the fifth edition, Key had polished his discussion of this sectionalism thesis. Here he stated emphatically:

> Sectional interests have constituted important building blocks for the American parties. Each party has had its roots deep in sectional interest and each has sought to built intersectional combinations powerful enough to govern.
>
> For its two-party form and for the persistence of that form, American politics owes a considerable debt to an underlying dual sectionalism, which for well over a century contributed to a partisan dualism; and undoubtedly in the earlier decades of the Republic mightily aided in molding enduring political habits.[15]

For Key, sectionalism began with the advancing frontier. "Even the debate over the adoption of the Constitution took the form of a dual sectional conflict, a dispute between the frontier and the seaboard."[16] The sectional contest between the frontier and the eastern seaboard gave way to the contest between the North and the South when the issue of slavery exploded on the political scene. For Key sectionalism did not disappear from American political parties, it merely was replaced by a new sectionalism. This new sectionalism left a lasting pattern on American political parties in general and the Democratic party in particular. Here is how he describes it:

> Since the South has been our most cohesive section, the factors underlying its solidarity deserve special mention. For many decades it formed the bedrock of the Democratic party. It stood for the party and the party spoke for it.[17]

And the source of this cohesiveness, says Key, is the Negro.

> The unity of the South is generally exaggerated, yet on one set of issues—those relating to the status of the Negro—a high degree of political cohesion prevails. Concern about the Negro may, in fact, be about all there is to southern solidarity.[18]

Key's insightful discussion of southern regionalism as a factor shaping the Democratic party disappeared when this first aspect of his typology was dropped from the standard textbook model. Although it has been redeployed and discussed in terms of the party-in-the-electorate, it has been reduced to essentially psychological attributes and described in the popular and scholarly literature as the "angry white male" syndrome, with the focus on the individual voter and not on southern native-son leaders. Leadership is presumed to be driven by the electorate and not by party leaders such as Johnson, Wallace, Carter, and Clinton. There are no insights into the relationship between party leaders and the electorate.

A careful reading of Key and of the empirical data on Clinton suggests not only the need for the restoration of the lost typological feature, but possibly the addition of a new one. Given the role and function of Johnson, Wallace, Carter, and Clinton, it is possible to expand the typology to include party-in-region leadership. The literature could be urged to explore this new feature. But this is just one element that the native son theory postulates.

Party Crisis and Transformation

It was widely reported that as President Johnson signed the 1964 Civil Rights Act, he remarked to an aide that he had just handed the South to the Republican party. Many analysts, commentators, and pundits have agreed, and it became the conventional wisdom that providing African Americans their constitutional rights disrupted the old New Deal coalition, polarized whites and African Americans, and led to Republican presidential victories in the last third of the twentieth century. One political observer declared that the Democratic party would win no presidential elections before the year 2000.[19] Race became the reason for everything: party polarization, party failure, party electoral defeats, party volatility, party extremism.

Yet President Johnson's remark did not take into account what Johnson himself symbolized for the region and the socializing effects that he would set into motion for other southern native-son candidates. Unlike Carter and Clinton, who rose to the presidency from southern gubernatorial positions, Johnson came to the presidency via the vice-presidency, in which he had balanced the national ticket for the Democrats in 1960. In 1964 he proved that a southerner could win not only in the South, but nationally.

At first, there was no southern political rebellion at the signing of the 1964 Civil Rights Act. Then George Wallace created a grassroots party rebellion. With his forays into northern Democratic primaries, Wallace did what Thurmond and the Dixiecrats had not been able to do. Goldwater pushed the grassroots rebellion into the Republican party. By 1968 and

Wallace's American Independent party run, southern white Democrats splintered and broke their alliance. The schism was in the open. Wallace, Goldwater, Nixon, and later Reagan and Bush made party conversion and realignment in the South possible. For the media and many in the academic world, this is the story. But it is only half the story.

How did the Democratic party transform itself to handle the crisis? How did it deal with both intraparty factionalism and interparty regional rivalry and competition? It stumbled upon its transforming techniques. President Johnson had shown the way, followed by Carter and Clinton as southerners who captured the party's nomination and then the White House. It was done in intermittent steps: Johnson in 1964, Carter in 1976, and Clinton in 1992 and 1996. Only Clinton had consecutive victories. Of the nine presidential elections since the signing of the 1964 Civil Rights Act the Democrats have captured four to the Republicans' five. The Democratic native-son southern candidates have clearly been competitive. They have disrupted the Republican party's southern strategy.

At the presidential level, the South has not been completely transformed, but it has been turned into an active battleground between the two parties. The Republican party has had to fight for the southern vote when southern native sons have appeared as presidential candidates (except for President Carter's reelection effort in 1980). At best the Republican party has won a fractionated South in presidential elections. Aside from African Americans, there is a significant core of white Democrats in the region still voting for the party. At the grassroots level, Johnson, Carter, and Clinton continued to attract white Democratic voters, if in reduced numbers.

Parties find ways to transform themselves and survive social and political upheavals. Parties can find ways to meet interparty challenges rooted in sectionalism. Such strategies may not be developed purposefully. In an era of candidate-centered politics such strategies evolve through a series of candidates' trial-and-error and not in some centralized fashion developed at the national level. Party transformation in a candidate-centered era may only be possible though a succession of regional candidates.

Finally, native-son candidates make it difficult for their opponents to implement regional electoral strategies. President Nixon and his political strategists learned this about George Wallace in 1968 and in 1972 before they came to an accommodation with him.[20] President Bush would later make a similar discovery about how difficult it is to capture the South against a native son.[21] Winning the South against a northern Democrat such as Mondale or Dukakis was a much easier task for Republican strategists and nominees. A native son of the same region make for serious party competition. Thus the native son theory provides evidence for the nature and scope of party reaction to crisis, how transformation takes place, and how interparty challenges are met on the regional level.

The Regional Political Opportunity Structure

During Governor Clinton's sixth and final race for governor in 1990,

> Clinton's campaign was burdened with a sense that he was stretching his time in office. . . . His opponent in the Democratic primary, a liberal policy analyst named Tom McRae, played on this mood with an anti-Clinton ad that showed a line of clocks stretching into infinity.[22]

Clinton had declined to run in 1988 for the Democratic presidential nomination but had to maintain a high profile until the opportunity presented itself again in 1992. Another race for the governorship was inevitable. Native son theory tells us about the nature of such realities in an obscure southern state, and how that state may be used as a springboard to the White House.

Historically, southern states had for the most part let their political, economical, social, and cultural systems ossify. Progress in any field was first judged in terms of how it would affect white racial domination in the South. Modernization was put off or slowed to a snail's pace. By the time of the African American freedom movement of the 1960s, modernization had occurred only in a few small enclaves in the South. Almost concomitantly with the rise of voting rights for African Americans, the South saw a new wave of Southern white politicians[23] who called themselves progressives.[24] These were men who preached moderation in race relations, or who subordinated race to economic issues. They urged upon their fellow southerners the need to improve a backward society. This new wave of leaders, aided by newly enfranchised African American voters, became governors and members of Congress.

The African American freedom movement widened the political opportunity structure. Southern politicians who sought to reform their state's economy, taxation system, education, prisons, and the social culture could now be called progressives. And the voters in the region approved such policy positions and stances. Everyone knew the need for such internal improvements and reforms. Many who were concerned with the race issue preached that modernization and urbanization would eliminate the region's burdensome and costly system of segregation.[25] But they did not. Modernization followed the collapse of segregation. And it was the African American freedom movement that brought about the collapse.

> The effect of the achievements of the civil rights movement was to free southern governors and gubernatorial candidates from the shackles of the past. They no longer were chained to the old rhetoric and posturing needed to win elections or succeed in office. Instead, perhaps for the first time in the twentieth century, governors could focus on real problems of their states and regions— poverty, health, education, environmental protection, economic development, crime, governmental accountability, responsiveness, ethics, and so forth.
>
> The change was immediate and noticeable. Even governors caught on the cusp of the changes had to alter their political style and message.[26]

This rise of the new southern progressive at the state and local level evolved with Carter and Clinton to the presidential level. As a candidate for the Democratic nomination, Carter declared that as governor, he helped to modernize his state, improved the budgetary process, and brought the state into the twentieth century.[27] He also claimed to be progressive in race relations. This assessment won him the cover of *Time* magazine and its endorsement for president.[28] Minor changes became big deals. Infrastructure improvements provided the opportunity for Carter to promote himself among the national electorate as a progressive. The Carter candidacy was the first to take this progressive and reform image outside the region to a national audience. Although Carter ran for both his party's nomination and the presidency as a progressive reform candidate, he did not run as such in Georgia for the governorship. While the African American freedom movement altered the legal basis of the South, it did not overnight unleash a progressive electorate. Nor could it, given the role that Wallace, Lester Maddox, Ross Barnett, and other diehard segregationists played in the reconstructed South of the 1960s.

During Carter's second, successful run for Governor in 1970, George Wallace campaigned with him throughout southwest Georgia and in its Black Belt counties.[29] Georgia and Alabama share a border and Wallace was popular in both states. Carter reached out to the old Georgia in the campaign as well as reaching out to the new Georgia by installing Martin

Luther King Jr.'s portrait in the State Capitol. With this mixed strategy, Carter defeated the more progressive Democratic candidate, Carl Sanders. As he would later do at the national level, Carter innovated at the state level. Carter made maximum use of the new political opportunity structure and became an instructive native son for future regional candidates. Enter Bill Clinton.

Unleashed by the African American freedom movement, this new southern political opportunity structure also affected Arkansas. Professor Diane Blair tells us:

> There is, then, the possibility that Arkansas's preference for progressive leaders in recent decades is neither a peculiar twist on its provincialism nor the accidental product of personality politics. Rather, it is the expression of at least mildly progressive impulses that were suppressed or diverted in the traditional political system but have been able to flourish in contemporary times.[30]

Here in why reform-progressives succeeded in the state:

> Arkansas has been destitute since it became a territory of the United States in 1819. . . . The state took a disastrous course when it joined the Confederacy. Its treasury was emptied. After the war, national economic pains and depressions further sapped the state's strength.
>
> The Depression of the 1930s again robbed the state of what little money it had accumulated. Thousands of Arkansans joined their Oklahoma neighbors in the trek to California. In the 1940s, mechanized farming began to replace human labor in east Arkansas. This forced another migration as blacks moved north to Chicago and Detroit to find industrial jobs.[31]

Economic catastrophes were not the only factors. Segregation also sapped the state of its spiritual and human strength. In 1957 Governor Orval Faubus decided to make Little Rock the site of a civil rights showdown. The consequences were staggering.

> Little Rock and Arkansas were to be marked indelibly by the events of 1957. The state was yanked backward again, lumped with Mississippi and Alabama as a monument to inequality. It is still struggling to recover.[32]

By the 1960s Arkansas, like much of the South, was in serious need of reform. Leadership was provided in the late 1960s and early 1970s by a succession of progressive governors.

> Winthrop Rockefeller [replaced Faubus] in 1966. . . . A liberal Democrat, Dale Bumpers, replaced Rockefeller after a couple of terms. Moderate Democrat David Pryor replaced Bumpers when Bumpers went to the U.S. Senate. Pryor joined the U.S. Senate soon after, leaving the governor's seat to the young idealist, Bill Clinton.[33]

But before Clinton could step into the reform-progressive gubernatorial role, he lost Garland county, which included his home town of Hot Springs, in his losing congressional race of 1974. His campaign staff "knew that Garland county was conservative, but assumed that the favorite son could at least break even there."[34]

"By midnight, every county had reported except the largest and most conservative one, Sebastian county, home to Fort Smith. Clinton was still leading by several thousand votes."[35] After the vote was counted, Clinton lost by 6,294 votes. The rising native son learned, as had gubernatorial candidate Carter, that the New South had not yet completed its transformation.

So Clinton's gubernatorial campaigns, like Carter's, reached out to both the Old South as well as the New South, particularly to African American voters. His policy changes in education, environmental matters, and the economy marked him as one of the state's most progressive governors. He had brought change and reform—even at the price of personal defeat in his second bid in 1988.

So when Clinton announced his bid for the Democratic party nomination in 1992 he, like Carter, could have run under the reform-progressive label. However, the political opportunity structure remolded the progressive into a New Democrat with a New Covenant for the party-in-the-electorate, to replace the much maligned label of liberal.

Permitting the rise of a new candidate and a new image is only one feature of this new political opportunity structure. Both Georgia and Arkansas fixed their presidential primaries so as to help their native sons in the scramble for convention delegates.

Journalists, political scientists, media consultants, and pundits tell us that the New Hampshire primary creates media coverage and electoral momentum and how vital this is to candidates in a crowded field.[36] But this focus on New Hampshire overlooks how the southern regional primaries and the home states of Carter and Clinton have deployed their presidential primary elections to benefit these candidates. Another feature of the opportunity structure is the role and function it plays in the presidential primary sweepstakes.

Finally, the new opportunity structure gives the southern African American voter a new role. Previously in presidential politics, the major roles were played by northern African American elected officials and national civil rights leaders. Now the African American electorate in Georgia and Arkansas has made it possible for both Carter and Clinton to evolve as native-son candidates. In the case of Clinton, this electorate has helped him endure the political context and make a comeback.

Beyond their balance-of-power role in state electoral contests, southern African American leaders have helped regional candidates in their rivalry with liberal northern candidates. Andrew Young travelled to northern cities and used his civil rights contacts to help shift the traditional linkage between northern African American voters and liberal Democratic hopefuls.[37] Carter has credited Andrew Young as the person most responsible for his election to the presidency.

Clinton also used local African American notables to help legitimize him to northern African American voters and maintain the break between these voters and liberal candidates. He deployed them during the crucial New York primary.

> The Clinton machine was in full operation at this point. A busload of black supporters from Arkansas headed for New York to fan out throughout the city to draw up minority support.
>
> With help from New York City blacks they covered sixty leading black churches. . . . [Lottie] Shackelford [a Little Rock city director] alone spoke from five pulpits Sunday morning. She and others extolled Clinton's commitment to blacks and his record of appointments to boards and commissions.
>
> Wherever a minister would balk at giving time to the Clinton campaign, [Carol] Willis would telephone a black preacher in Arkansas, who would call and give Clinton a strong reference.[38]

The southern native-son presidential candidate not only survived multiple state electoral challenges, but northern and western presidential primaries, thanks to the African American voter. And after his election, Clinton appointed more African Americans to cabinet positions than had Carter.[39]

The new political opportunity structure now lets southern African Americans play visible leadership roles in the Democratic party after having elected white southerners to the White House.

The native son theory offers insights into the new political opportunity structure in the South and through it, additional insights into the transformation of African American electoral and activist leadership circles.

The Remapping of the Geopolitical Terrain

The native son theory empirically reveals the changes and transformations that native-son presidential candidate Clinton wrought in both the state and presidential electoral base of the Democratic party. On the national level, there was "great stability of the vote in Clinton's two victories." Pomper also asserts that

> the state pattern also shows remarkable stability in the vote. [Clinton] held twenty-nine of the states (and the District of Columbia) that he had won in 1992 and added the previous Republican strongholds of Florida and Arizona, while losing closely his 1992 majorities in Colorado, Georgia, and Montana.
>
> Clinton did well in 1996 in precisely those areas where he had run successfully in 1992, and his strength is based on the same geographical coalition as that of other recent Democratic candidates.[40]

Figure 11.1 illustrates this stability in Clinton's 1992 and 1996 electoral victories in his home state, where the Democratic vote shifted up from 54.8 percent to 56 percent. Although at glance this increase seems small, 47 counties reported an increase in the 1996 election, 27 reported a decrease and in one county there was no change. President Clinton improved his election coalition over the prior election, thus the coalition was stable and increased slightly.

When correlated, these two elections show a remarkably high degree of similarity ($r = .93$). Clinton's party loyalists in the 1992 election could have been used to predicted 88 percent of the vote in the 1996 election. Only 12 percent of the 1996 election in Arkansas's counties were decided on factors other than Democratic party loyalty. To a stable set of core voters, Clinton's reelection added a few more. Democratic one-partyism in Arkansas was strengthened in the presidential terrain.

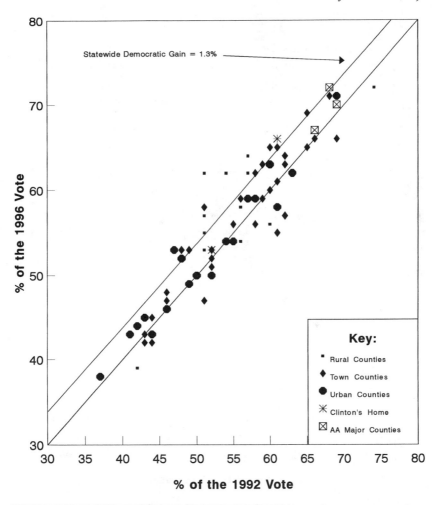

FIGURE II.I **The Relationship Between County Percentages in the 1992 and 1996 Arkansas Presidential Vote for Clinton.**

Adapted from W. J. McCuen, "Arkansas Election Results, 1992," (Little Rock: Office of the Secretary of State, 1993) and Priest, "November 5, 1996 General Election Results."

At the national level, figure 11.2 offers additional empirical evidence for stable growth. Clinton's two presidential elections are highly related and associated with one another (r =.88).[41] He kept his core voters or party loyalists who came to him in 1992 and expanded upon this base for 1996. He lost some of that initial group of voters while his strength rose due to a large replacement by new loyalists. One could have forecast that 77 percent of his 1992 voters would follow him forward to the 1996 elections (r^2 = .77).

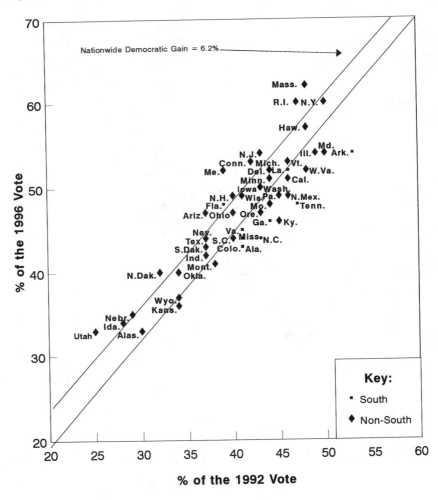

FIGURE 11.2 The Relationship Between State Percentages in the 1992 and
1996 Presidential Vote for Clinton.

Adapted from Scammon and McGillivray, *America Votes 1992*, 11, and "Official 1996 Presidential
Election Results," *Congressional Quarterly Weekly Report* (18 January 1997), 188.

Only 23 percent of his 1996 voters join the coalition or stayed with it for
reasons other than Democratic partisanship. Analysts have noted this is a
very high level of party identification.[42]

Moving beyond the measurement of the correlation coefficients, the
percentage summary measures reveal that Clinton improved his mean
from 43 percent to 49.2 percent. Clinton increased the Democratic party
percentage in all fifty states, as well as in the District of Columbia.[43]

Pomper tells us that "this pattern suggests that the election reflected short-term forces moving all groups in a Democratic direction, not a fundamental change in the parties' electoral foundation."[44] But we do not know if these increases are just short-term, nor do we know whether or not a fundamental change in the party's electoral foundation has taken place.

The native son theory allows us to look beyond the increases in Democratic partisanship at the national and home state levels to a regional exploration. In the South, Clinton won Arkansas, Tennessee, Louisiana, and Florida but lost Georgia. This state level analysis suggests that the Republicans basically kept their new base in the region. The Democratic party made at best a partial comeback. Stability again prevailed.

Yet table 11.1 reveals movement, serious movement, in the region. While Clinton may not have won back the solid South for the Democratic party, he, like Carter, began the process of erosion. Democratic partisanship grew in all of the states—those he won, as well as those he lost. The greatest increase (9%) came in Florida, which switched to the Democratic party, and the least came in Arkansas, with a one half of one percent increase. Even in the new Republican bastion of Mississippi, the Democratic increase was 3.3 percent, which was also the median. The mean increase was 3.8 percent, while the modal increase of 2.3 percent occurred in both Georgia and Alabama. The smallest increases came in the home states of native-son candidates Gore and Clinton. Neither state gave its native son a one percent increase, with Arkansas ranked last. But even these varying degrees of increase indicate both stability and growth at the regional level.

Using the summary measure of correlations, the two presidential elections in the South are highly associated and related ($r = .80$). Clinton's Democratic partisans in the region were loyal and quite stable. These followers stayed with him throughout both elections. Almost two-thirds of the 1996 voters ($r^2 = .64$) had remained loyal and had returned to vote for him on the basis of Democratic partisanship. One-third joined his electoral coalition for reasons other than party identification. Republican partisanship, even while it remained strong, lost electoral ground, at least in this presidential election.

Clinton as a native-son presidential candidate remapped the geopolitical terrain in his own state, in the South, and at the national level. While the degree of dynamism might not have been large in all three geopolitical sectors there was change in the direction of the Democratic party.

Whether this change proves to be short- or long-term will most likely be tested by another native-son candidate, Vice President Gore, in 2000.

TABLE 11.1 The 1996 Percentage Vote Increase for the
Democratic Party in the Southern States by Rank

State	% Increase 1992–1996
Florida	9.0
Texas	6.7
Louisiana	6.4
Virginia	4.5
South Carolina	4.1
Mississippi	3.3
Georgia	2.3
Alabama	2.3
North Carolina	1.3
Tennessee	0.9
Arkansas	0.5
Mean	3.8

Adapted from Richard Scammon and Alice V. McGillivray, eds., *America Votes 1994*
(Washington, D.C.: Congressional Quarterly, 1995), 11 for 1992 and "Official
1996 Presidential Election Results," *Congressional Quarterly Weekly Report* (18
January 1997), 188 for 1996.

Gore inherits a political terrain different from the one Clinton received
from Dukakis and Carter. Clinton's selection of Gore ensures that a
regional native son is in place to inherit the new Democratic wind in the
southland.

Table 11.2 offers a composite of the empirical findings from both this
study and an earlier study on President Carter. Each of these case studies
adds to the body of knowledge about this variable and the composite permits us to build an overall theory about how native son candidates from
any region of the country shape presidential election outcomes and individual and group political behavior. Such a table advances the knowledge
equation and stream.

Forecasting the Future: The New Democrat

After the 1960s the Democratic party became known as the party of lib-
erals. A succession of liberal Democratic candidates—Hubert Humphrey
in 1968, George McGovern in 1972, Walter Mondale in 1984, and Michael
Dukakis in 1988—all met electoral defeat. It appeared that the Democratic party could not find a way to remake and restructure its image.

TABLE 11.2 The Testable Propositions for a Southern Native-Son Candidate

Contextual Factors

The party system is a one-party or modified one-party system
Partisanship in this party system is of a Democratic nature
The Republican party or its candidate has a southern strategy
The Republican or third party candidate is competing for the southern vote
Partisan competition involves a conservative stance on race
Partisan competition promises a reversal on civil rights
Partisan competition uses race or religion as a wedge issue
A regional candidate has captured the presidency

National Factors

Rise of a supplementary party organization focused toward the South
The Democratic party has lost one or more presidential elections
The Democratic party hopefuls include an African American
The Democratic party has supported civil rights policies
The Democratic president has links with southern leaders
There is an electoral base outside the South for regional racial concerns

State Factors

Elected state leaders have launched presidential campaigns
The state's partisan character determines the partisanship of the native son
The native son must win office at the local, district, and statewide level
The statewide office can be won in either a national or statewide election
Segments of the state electorate can be marginal in their support of the native-son
  candidate as long as other segments are highly supportive
In winning state elective office, the native-son candidate builds a network with
  political technicians, pollsters, media experts, etc.
Evolving native-son candidates need to build linkages with large campaign
  contributors
The political timing of the native son becoming a presidential candidate must be
  propitious
The state alters its election laws governing presidential primaries to enhance the
  chances of its native son

Racial Factors

The African American electorate has supported progressive/reform candidates
The African American electorate strongly supports Democratic candidates
The African American electorate shows little support for Republican and third party
  candidates
African American politicians gain cabinet or sub-cabinet positions
A southern native-son Democratic president who follows a civil rights innovator does
  not sponsor any new initiatives
A southern native-son Democratic president does not support strong protection of
  African American civil rights through regulation
The collapse of once-dominant party coalitions permits a southern native-son
  Democratic presidential candidate to fashion a new policy image and public policies
The southern native-son Democratic president can attempt to continue his legacy
  with a vice president from the region

Electoral Factors

The southern native-son candidate raises the voter turnout in his state
The southern native-son candidate raises the voter turnout in the region
The southern native-son candidate raises the voter turnout in the African American
  Democratic electorate

After the 1988 defeat, "a faction of moderates, many of them from the South, who sought to reorient the party toward the white middle class," formed the DLC.[45] Clinton became chairman of this group of elected party leaders in 1990. Whether one calls it a moderate or a conservative organization—and there were elements of both, though the latter group was more dominant—the organization sought to recapture the party from the Jesse Jackson influence of the 1984 and 1988 presidential primaries. Jackson, the DLC argued, was moving the party to the left, when it had to be repositioned to the right.

Almost all of Clinton's biographers stress that Clinton had been moving from liberal to centrist positions for a long time; he saw the failures of the liberal wing of the party as threatening its future. The new Democratic party would rest on the middle class. The first step toward this future would be to embarrass Jackson at his own Rainbow Coalition convention.

The agenda that Jesse Jackson had advanced would be jettisoned for the one that Clinton had adopted over the years. Thus Clinton's 1992 campaign ignored race altogether, both in the primaries and in the general election.[46] Race and racial matters with which Jackson was so closely associated disappeared, while Clinton simultaneously courted the African American vote.

Once in office, President Clinton only responded to racial issues raised by the Republicans or which evolved from conflicts in race relations.[47] He neither made nor took any bold legislative initiate except the abandonment of welfare. Yet by the time of the 1996 election, Clinton would reach out to the liberal wing of his party, minus Jesse Jackson.

> In the north since November [1996], most analyses of Clinton's reelection victory have referred to Clinton as having moved to the right to emphasize the traditional Republican issues of taxes, crime, welfare, and the federal budget. But to a considerable extent Clinton followed [Senator Edward] Kennedy's advice. He did effectively neutralize the Republicans' issues, but the real foundation of the wing's strategy was a liberal agenda, not a conservative one.[48]

This interpretation of Clinton's reelection rests on interviews with both men, as well as a three page memorandum which Senator Kennedy gave to President Clinton following the 1994 congressional elections, in which the Republicans won control of both houses of Congress. "The largely unnoted 1996 election alliance between Clinton and Kennedy began on

December 13, 1994 in the President's private office, in the Treaty Room on the second floor of the White House."[49]

Kennedy had prepared rigorously for the meeting. Aware that Clinton and the Democratic party were at a turning point, he had spent the previous month meeting with academics, historians, economists, and political experts, exploring the broad question of what the Democratic party's future should be.

In that memo at the meeting:

> Kennedy offered a different kind of political advice from the kind
> that Clinton had offered him. Instead of emphasizing the future,
> Kennedy urged the President to campaign on a number of themes
> that had long been identified with traditional Democratic party liber-
> alism: protecting Medicare, Medicaid, and education, and raising the
> minimum wage.[50]

Thus the New Democrat could combine the past with the future minus one central issue—race. Removing race from the old New Deal agenda might carry the country and the region into the Democratic column in the future. This position is still in the process of evolution, and the reaction to the President's proposed apology for slavery has set off the racial divide once again. Led by the Republican southern congressional leadership of former Speaker Newt Gingrich and Trent Lott, the current fractionated South could become solid again. And southern Republican native sons, congressional or presidential, might or might not lead the Republican party back to victory.

There is another interpretation of the remade Democratic party. Robert Smith, after a careful appraisal of the 1992 polling and election data, says:

> What is puzzling about the Clinton election is that he received
> roughly the same or in some cases even less support among white
> ethnic and regional groupings than Dukakis . . . Clinton did a little
> better than Dukakis among southern whites but all in all the white
> ethnic and regional votes were basically the same as in other post-
> civil rights era presidential elections. Essentially, then, the election of
> 1992 was not so much a gain in voter support by Clinton and the
> Democrats but rather a loss in support by Bush and the Republicans,
> a loss not so much to Clinton but to Perot.

This suggests that perhaps an openly generic Democrat like New York Governor Mario Cuomo might have won in 1992, contrary to the conventional wisdom that the election of Clinton represents a vindication of the DLC's centrist ideology and the new orthodoxy's strategy of disengagement from blacks and the poor.[51]

Smith suggests that the New Democrats and the tactics of President Clinton may be short-term and that the wave of the future is not a remade party but a "generic" Democrat. The New Democrats and their policies have not resolved the racial, economic, and social divides that still haunt the country. Southern Democratic native-son presidential candidates might just be passing phenomena.

Overall, the native son theory as enlarged by the Clinton presidential victories offers a powerful set of insights into regional politics, American political parties, African American politics in the South, the possible future of the Democratic party, and what a New Democrat might include in his or her public policy agenda. Clinton in his role as a southern native son has pushed the frontiers of the theory even further. He has put into place a vice president from the region. Unlike Carter, this native son is trying to promote a successor and thereby shape the future of his party in subsequent presidential elections.[52]

CHAPTER TWELVE

Epilogue: Scandal, Public Support, and the Native-Son Variable

In an era in which elections have been transformed from party-centered to candidate-centered, the inevitable question becomes how political corruption and scandals influence, shape, and reshape public support for parties, candidates, and presidents. Yet this has been the least addressed question in the discipline.[1] Political scientists—with their focus on the determinants and causes of individual political behavior—have rarely if ever reduced political corruption and scandals to measurable variables and modeled their influence on voting behavior and electoral outcomes. Nor have political scientists tried to analyze pre-election attitudes to discern if variables such as corruption and scandals reduce or enhance public support at even the vote choice level.

Yet both political corruption and scandals have been major forces in the American political process.[2] Since hardly a decade goes by without either public or private scandals, they have continually energized the reform impulse in American life and politics.[3]

If behavioral scholars have generally ignored or downplayed these factors, political campaign strategists have not: they have long made great use of both corruption and scandal to shift public support for their party and their candidate. Inherent in the very nature of a competitive party system is both the need and desire to modify and alter public support to enhance one's chance of winning. Each side is looking for advantage even if it means using less-than-savory information and materials.

Such realities are not unknown to southern native-son presidential candidates and presidents. Yet for both Johnson and Carter they were not the deciding factor: the perceived quality of their job performance and crisis management eroded public support for their presidencies and their party. President Johnson withdrew his reelection bid in 1968 because of public opposition to his Vietnam and to a lesser extent his civil rights policies. President Carter tried for a second term in 1980 but double digit inflation and the Iranian hostage situation reduced public support for him and he lost his job.

For the third southern native-son president, it is not a question of job performance or crisis management that threatened the loss of public support, as much as a scandal involving personal morality and behavior in the White House. Would this personal scandal reduce public support for his party at the 1998 midterm elections? All the political pundits thought it would, as did the congressional leadership of the Republican party when the scandal broke in January 1997. Republican congressional leaders and party advocates seized on the personal scandal and shaped from it a second, embryonic, party strategy to penetrate the South and the rest of the nation.

Public Support and the Southern Native-Son Democratic Candidate

Changing public support for the party of a southern native-son president or presidential candidate is only one part of the electoral equation. Altering this public support in his region, state, and home county is the other side. As noted earlier, President Johnson predicted that his signing of the 1964 Civil Rights Act would significantly change public support for the Democratic party in the South until it would no longer be competitive and successful there. Signing the law merely set the stage. It was the necessary but not sufficient condition. Clearly the Republican party exploited the situation to its advantage. Using race as a wedge issue, it penetrated the region and captured the once-solid Democratic bastion. Race eroded public support for the Democratic party. It lost offices at every level in the region in 1968, 1972, 1980, 1984, and 1988. This was the Republican party's initial strategy to penetrate the region and the nation.

Yet, as Robert Speel writes: "When the Republicans began to gain votes among Southern white voters, the Democrats gained in reaction many votes among the historical political opponents of the South, Northern Yankees."[4] This is the electoral realignment in support of the Democratic party that President Johnson did not foresee when he made his astute observation in 1964.

Southern native-son presidential candidates seeking to reconvert the region have had not only to escape from the hot-button issue of race, but they have also relied upon their "southerness" to split the Republican hold on the region. To date, Johnson, Carter, and Clinton have been able to do precisely that in presidential elections.

Race is a group attribute with a long and turbulent history in the region. It is not an individual characteristic of southern native-son presidential candidates, nor of those who have become president. Hence it is substantively different from personal morality. In the political context, the South is the Bible Belt. Personal morality—like race—matters, and it cannot easily be sidestepped. Republican congressional leaders who were also southerners knew how important religion is to the region and how such a personal morality scandal might enable them to make further electoral inroads into this region and maybe the nation; in a sense, they were equating the two forces—race and religion. Race had enabled earlier national Republican leaders to successfully penetrate the region. Here was a new political strategy to expand the Republican revolution: the personal morality scandal would find potential support based in the religious culture of the region. But this new political strategy, like the one based on race, was not without its shortcomings and weaknesses.

> The southern strategies of Republican presidential candidates to emphasize their conservative stance on civil rights, religious, and patriotic issues compared with the liberalism of the national Democrats has had the frequently unnoticed effect of losing many traditional northern Republican voters. But the strategy has certainly had success among its intended audience. White Southerners are now one of the most Republican groups in the nation in presidential elections.[5]

Beginning in 1964, a major dual realignment occurred both in the South and the rest of the nation. Courtney Brown was the initial electoral scholar to pick up this voting reality.

In 1964, there were actually two landslides [realignments]. The first occurred in the areas outside of the Deep South, in favor of Johnson, and the second occurred in the Deep South, in favor of Goldwater. A comparison of the two landslides [realignments] offers an extraordinary chance to begin to discern, in more general terms, differences in the internal structures of landslides [realignments].[6]

How and why did this unseen electoral realignment occur? Speel, once again:

In most of the Northern U.S. areas that have trended Democratic, racial issues have been fairly unimportant to most voters, partly because of the absence of any significant African American populations. This is one reason that national Republican appeals to southern views on racial issues have been something of a turnoff for traditionally Republican northerners.[7]

Thus the use of the racial strategy by the Republican party to erode public support for the Democratic party and Democratic southern native-son presidential candidates and presidents has had both costs and benefits.

Race is a group attribute with a long and turbulent history in the region. It is not an individual characteristic of southern native-son presidential candidates, nor of those who have become president. Hence it is substantively different from personal morality. In the political context, the South is the Bible Belt. Personal morality—like race—matters, and it cannot easily be sidestepped. Republican congressional leaders who were also southerners knew how important religion is to the region and how such a personal morality scandal might enable them to make further electoral inroads into this region and maybe the nation; in a sense, they were equating the two forces—race and religion. Race had enabled earlier national Republican leaders to successfully penetrate the region. Here was a new political strategy to expand the Republican revolution: the personal morality scandal would find potential opposition based in the religious culture of the region. But this new political strategy, like the one based on race, was not without its shortcomings and weaknesses. What are the problems in using regional concern about personal morality and elevating it to the larger national context to erode public support for the president's party? Are there intraregional problems?

Personal Morality as a Character Issue

In a candidate-centered electoral process, the candidate's presentation of self is critical in gathering and mobilizing the electorate. "A candidate is helped by being thought of as trustworthy, reliable, mature, kind but firm, devoted to family, and in every way normal and presentable."[8] A presidential candidate's character counts in the political equation of garnering or losing public support. But in our times the question of personal morality as a character issue did not first emerge on the presidential level. It arose at the congressional level.

From the 1950s through the 1970s *Washington Post* journalists Drew Pearson and Jack Anderson wrote a column titled "The Washington Merry-Go-Round." The column named names and described in detail financial and sexual misdeeds of congressmen and other officials. Eventually, these stories made their way into two books: Drew Pearson's *The Case Against Congress* and Jack Anderson's *The Washington Expose*.[9] The rather shotgun approach of these two journalists evolved into a major national story in 1968 when Congress unseated Harlem Congressman Adam Clayton Powell Jr. using personal morality as one of its charges against him. Congressman Powell sued and the Supreme Court declared that the House could not unseat a duly elected representative. Before the Supreme Court decision, New York state held a special election for the vacated seat and Powell won that election. After the Court's ruling, the House voted to strip the Congressman of his seniority and committee chairmanship, and reduced his privileges. Instead of fighting, the Congressman flew to the island of Bimini and went fishing. Appalled that he would not fight, his constituents failed to turn out on his behalf in the 1970 Democratic primary and he lost the election by less than 200 votes to the current Congressman from Harlem, Charles Rangel. When the character issue involves questions of personal morality public support can erode for an incumbent no matter what his or her previous accomplishments.[10]

The same fate befell Democratic Congressman Wayne Hays of Ohio, who had led the charge to unseat Congressman Powell over the character issue. After an expose about his sexual relationship with his secretary appeared in the Sunday paper, Hayes denied the charge, before being admitted to a hospital after a suicide attempt. He later resigned his seat in Congress. In their own turn, Arkansas Congressman Wilbur Mills, Senator Robert Packwood of Oregon, and the former Speaker of the House, Robert Livingston of Louisiana all faced accusations of sexual misconduct. All of these personal morality matters were congressional. When did the question of personal morality become a fixture in presidential contests? Most would point to the 1988 race and Gary Hart. In fact, it surfaced in 1976 with a southern native-son presidential candidate, Jimmy Carter.

During that campaign the former governor of Georgia gave an interview to *Playboy* where he mentioned that he lusted after women in his heart. The remark and the furor that it generated, Wilson Carey McWilliams says, undoubtedly hurt Carter.[11] He continues:

> The 1976 election was almost unique in the intrusive attention devoted to the private lives and personal beliefs of the candidates [who] were subjected to a scrutiny that went far beyond a concern for personal integrity. Carter felt compelled to discuss his code of sexual behavior. Mrs. Ford discussed premarital sex and marijuana, as did Mrs. Carter, and the candidates' children commented, with apparent frankness, on their parents' ideas.
>
> It is . . . notable that such questions should be asked and answered. Until quite recently, it would have been assumed that presidential candidates held traditional beliefs about private morality and in the unlikely event that they held differing views, would not offend the electorate by saying so. In any case, such matters were *private*, not appropriate subjects for public prying and discussion, and a reporter who raised them openly would have been seen as intolerably impertinent. . . . In 1976 candidates and voters alike considered that "private" moral beliefs had become public issues.[12]

The Gary Hart scandal in 1988 only further dramatized that private behavior had become a permanent fixture of presidential contests and that it could erode public support for the candidate and possibly for his party. In the rising furor over Hart's character, he withdrew from the campaign, re-entered, and eventually lost.

One observer stated that "in 1988 . . . Gary Hart's derelictions shattered his candidacy . . . private proprieties may now outweigh public virtues."[13] Despite the fact that the final outcomes were different for Carter and for Hart, both character issue problems occurred in Democratic presidential primary seasons. In such contests the voters can directly respond to the candidate. In the case of President Clinton, the voters would not be able to take their anger out on him, but on his party in the 1998 midterm elections.

Public Support and the 1998 Midterm Elections: The Fate of the Clinton-Led Democrats

On November 3, 1998 the electorate registered it degree of support for or opposition to the president's political party. Democrats gained and the Republicans lost 5 seats in the House of Representatives. Democrats went from 206 seats to 211 while Republicans dropped from 228 to 223. "It was the first time since 1934 that the party controlling the White House gained seats in an off-year election—and the first time since James Monroe in 1822 that the president's party picked up House seats in his sixth year in office."[14] The Republicans maintained control of Congress but their margin in the House was so reduced that Speaker Newt Gingrich of Georgia was forced to step down.[15]

At the state level, Democrats captured two Republican governorships, in South Carolina and Alabama, and they also captured an open seat gubernatorial post, in Georgia. None of the party's incumbent governors were defeated. At this level the bright spots for the Republicans were the elections of former President George Bush's sons, Jeb Bush in Florida and George W. Bush in Texas. Two southern native-son Republican governors now stand on the presidential horizon. "Republicans, however, lost ground nationwide in state legislative elections, breaking the historical axiom that the president's party loses state legislative seats in midterm elections. . . . Democrats gained about 45 legislative seats nationwide and made a net gain of three legislative chambers, leaving them in control of 53 legislative chambers to the Republicans's 45."[16]

Using the congressional and state elections as indicators, it is clear that in light of the scandal over the president's personal morality, public support shifted toward a net gain for the president's party. An analysis of individual attitudes can tell us more about the nature and scope of public support for the president's party in these elections.

Keating Holland, the director of polls at CNN, found in the final CNN pre-election poll that "23 percent said they were going to support Clinton, 23 percent were going to oppose Clinton, and . . . a majority (52%) said that the [scandal] was not really going to affect their vote."[17] When Holland reviewed the post-election CNN exit poll, he found that "only 1 percent of voters actually switched their vote to the Republican party in 1998 because of an expressed desire to vote against" the president, while "another 1 percent switched their votes to the Democratic party in 1998 because of a desire to show support for Clinton." The 2 percent of the voting public that switched parties "represented 1.4 million of 72 million votes cast on November 3."[18] According to Holland, the shift in public support at least at the individual attitudinal level was a wash. But if there was no net movement in either direction, what explains the electoral outcome favoring the president's party? According to Holland, many of the races were decided by narrow margins, implying that these slight changes were not picked up by the CNN exit poll. He goes on to say that "the Republicans did not get their core voters out . . . The Republicans miscalculated in holding to a strategy that concentration on impeachment would get their base out."[19] In his estimation this was a losing strategy. Yet this interpretation of the election results does not quite explain the results. That the shift in public support was a wash and part of the Republican base did not mobilize cannot be the entire story.

The personal morality scandal was not the only factor shaping public support for the president's party in these midterm elections. There was also his job approval rating. Kathleen Frankovic, director of polling at CBS News, discovered, in analyzing the polls:

> One of the most striking findings to emerge in public opinion polls this year is the stability of Bill Clinton's job-approval rating. Prior to the State of the Union message in early January, about 58 percent of Americans said they approved of the way President Clinton was doing his job, about the same number who said they approved of his job performance throughout both the 1996 campaign and 1997.
>
> After the State of the Union message, Clinton's approval rating peaked at a high of 73 percent, and ever since it has stayed between 60 and 70 percent.[20]

Frankovic finds that throughout the scandal the public had been making

> a distinction between Bill Clinton the president and Bill Clinton the person. When Americans are asked whether the charges against Bill Clinton have to do with his job or whether they are private and have to do with his personal life, by 2 to 1 they answer that it's his personal life. This answer has been consistent from February 1998 through the fall.[21]

So the full impact of the scandal on public support for the president's party was mitigated by the public's level of approval of his performance in office. And most importantly, the public drew a distinction between the president's personal morality and his job performance.[22]

Taken collectively, what do the polling data on individual attitudes tell us about the midterm election results? The information is anything but clear and precise. At best these polls provide a limited hint, a clue toward an incomplete answer. In terms of public support, a segment of the Republican party's electoral coalition was demobilized. But in light of the president's high job approval ratings, was a segment of his electoral coalition mobilized or remobilized? On this crucial matter, the national polling data do not provide information. But one election postmortem notes:

> In state after state the Democrats shamelessly played the race card, alarming African-American voters and openly calling Republicans racists.
>
> The get-out-the-[black]-vote effort provided yet another fascinating demonstration of Clinton's uncanny ability to turn adversity into advantage.[23]

Here we are told that mobilization did occur in these midterm elections. This insight is missing from the analyses of the polls. The president and his campaign strategists consciously targeted their mobilization efforts to remobilize the African American electorate. In the 1992 and 1996 presidential elections, as well as the 1994 midterm elections, the African American voter had been systematically demobilized by the DLC philosophy that urged the party to distance itself from this voter and to prioritize middle class America. African American turnout declined and the result in the two presidential elections was victory without a majority of the vote and loss of control of both houses of Congress in the midterm elections. In the scandal-laden atmosphere of the 1998 elections, the African American base of the president's party had to be remobilized. And the African American electorate needed to express itself about the Republican revolution. Here was a time and place of entrance.

The Republican revolution led by Presidents Reagan and Bush and Speaker Gingrich played the race card to the hilt for its own purposes. In the years of the Republican presidencies and the four years of Gingrich's control of Congress, the African American community suffered defeats, setbacks, and continual humiliation. The symbolic initiatives on civil rights of the Clinton administration did very little to relieve the crisis. The 1998 midterm elections permitted African Americans to act as agents on their own behalf. It was not the mobilizing tactics of the White House as much as the contextual forces that helped to energize this group of voters.[24]

Did demobilization, mobilization, and possible remobilization occur?

TABLE 12.1 A Comparison of the Vote in Two Statewide Races in the 1994 and 1998 General Elections

Office	1994 Total Vote	1998 Total Vote	Decline in Vote	Percentage Decline
Governor	716,840	706,011*	-10,829	-1.5
Secretary of State	698,543	687,590	-10,953	-1.6

Adapted from Sharon Priest, "Official Tabulation of the Results of the General Elections Held in Arkansas on November 3, 1998" (Little Rock: Office of the Secretary of State, 1998).
*Total includes 11,099 votes (1.6%) for Keith Carle, the Reform party candidate for governor.

Since the polling data provide insufficient empirical insights, let us turn to the president's home state and home communities in Arkansas and to the South, particularly Georgia. A comparison of the total number of voters in the 1994 midterm elections with those in the 1998 elections can be seen in table 12.1, using two different statewide Arkansas races—the gubernatorial race where no incumbent ran in 1998 and the Secretary of State race where the 1994 incumbent ran again in 1998. In 1998 fewer people came out to vote in these races. There was a decline of 1.5 and 1.6 percent respectively, or 10,829 and 10,953 fewer votes. At first blush, the scandal demobilized a small percentage of the electorate in the president's home state.

Table 12.2 offers some interesting insights on how the president's party fared at the voting booth. Between these two midterm elections, the Democratic party lost 21 percent of the vote, and it lost the governorship to the Republicans, who gained almost 20 percent. A new third party emerged in the state, the Reform party, and its candidate for governor captured 1.5 percent (11,099) of the vote. The decline in voters, the switch in voter support, and the capture of votes by a new third party in the gubernatorial race suggest that the scandal demobilized support for the president's party and mobilized support for the Republicans.

Disaggregating the gubernatorial election outcome by demographic categories shows where the erosion and shift took place (table 12.3). The Democratic winner in 1994 saw a substantial decline in his party's fortunes in every area of the state in 1998, while the Republican winner in 1998 saw an almost equal increase in support across the state. In the president's home counties, the Democratic party's demobilization is nearly matched by the Republican increase in support. Even in the traditionally loyal Black Belt counties, the vote for the Democratic party declined. African Americans were demobilized.

TABLE 12.2 A Comparison of the Party Vote in the 1994 and 1998 General Elections for Governor

Year	Democratic Gubernatorial Votes	Democratic Vote Percentage	Republican Gubernatorial Votes	Republican Vote Percentage
1994	428,936	59.8	287,904	40.2
1998	272,923	38.7*	421,989	59.8
Difference	−156,013	-21.1	134,085	19.6

Adapted from Priest, "Official Tabulation of the Results of the General Elections Held in Arkansas on November 3, 1998."
*The votes for the third party candidate are not included in this table.

Turning to the Secretary of State race, candidate Sharon Priest won in 1994, and in 1998 there is evidence not of demobilization but of mobilization and remobilization. Table 12.4 demonstrates that between 1994 and 1998 the Democratic party increased its public support by nearly 18 percent, amounting to an additional 109,385 votes, while Republican party strength was eroded by nearly the same percentage. Here the vote shifted to the president's party and away from the opposition.

Further analysis of the Secretary of State election result reveals that the support for the Democratic incumbent increased in every demographic category, including in the president's home counties and the Black Belt counties (table 12.5). In this statewide race, the Republican party lost public support.

The overall election data from Arkansas indicate that the influence and impact of the scandal depended upon the office and upon the candidate. Local factors and the local context mattered. They either enhanced or mitigated the effect of the scandal. Clearly it was not a wash, nor merely a story of only demobilization. And despite White House efforts to mobilize the African American electorate, there was no uniform response to these efforts in the president's home state. Nor was there uniform support for the presidential party in his own home communities among his friends and neighbors. For more empirical insights it is necessary to go outside Arkansas.

We can see how the scandal influenced public support in Georgia, another native-son state. In the 1998 elections nearly 14 percent more people voted than in 1994 (table 12.6). In addition to this rise in voting, for the first time two African Americans won two statewide offices—Attorney General and Secretary of Labor.

TABLE 12.3 Demographic Comparison of 1994 and 1998 Gubernatorial Vote in the General Election

Year and Candidate	Urban Counties Vote	Town Counties Vote	Rural Counties Vote	Home Counties Vote	Black Belt Counties Vote
DEMOCRATS					
1994, Tucker	245,790	122,782	28,926	18,588	12,850
1998, Bristow	157,680	78,332	17,069	11,939	7,903
Difference	−88,110	−44,450	−11,857	−6,649	−4,947
REPUBLICANS					
1994, Nelson	175,573	75,305	18,936	13,225	4,865
1998, Huckabee	259,658	108,255	26,811	19,859	7,414
Difference	84,085	32,950	7,875	6,634	2,549

Adapted from Priest, "Official Tabulation of the Results of the General Election Held in Arkansas on November 3, 1998."

TABLE 12.4 A Comparison of the Party Vote in the 1994 and 1998 General Elections for Secretary of State

Year	Democratic Votes for Secretary of State	Democratic Vote Percentage	Republican Votes for Secretary of State	Republican Vote Percentage
1994	366,620	52.5	331,923	47.5
1998	476,005	69.2	211,585	30.8
Difference	109,385	16.7	−120,338	−16.7

Adapted from Priest, "Official Tabulation of the Results of the General Elections Held in Arkansas on November 3, 1998."

TABLE 12.5 Demographic Comparison of 1994 and 1998 Vote for Secretary of State in the General Election

Year and Candidate	Urban Counties Vote	Town Counties Vote	Rural Counties Vote	Home Counties Vote	Black Belt Counties Vote
			DEMOCRATS		
1994, Priest	210,610	103,870	25,614	15,528	10,998
1998, Priest	277,029	133,830	30,869	21,819	12,458
Difference	66,419	29,960	5,255	6,291	1,460
			REPUBLICANS		
1994, J. Jones	201,134	88,259	20,882	15,744	5,904
1998, R. Jones	135,830	50,771	12,227	9,890	2,867
Difference	−65,304	−37,488	−8,655	−5,854	−3,037

Adapted from Priest, "Official Tabulation of the Results of the General Election Held in Arkansas on November 3, 1998."

TABLE 12.6 Comparison of the Vote in Three Statewide Races in Georgia in 1994 and 1998

1994 Total Vote	1998 Total Vote	Difference	Percentage Difference
	GUBERNATORIAL GENERAL ELECTION		
1,545,2971	1,792,808	247,511	13.8
	ATTORNEY GENERAL*		
1,445,745	1,737,086	291,341	16.8
	SECRETARY OF LABOR*		
1,451,688	1,696,902	245,214	14.5

Adapted from Max Cleland, "Official State of Georgia Tabulations by Counties, General Election, November 8, 1994" (Atlanta: Secretary of State, 1994) and Lewis A. Massey, "General Election November 3, 1998: Votes by County for Candidates" (Atlanta: Secretary of State, 1998).
*African American candidates won these statewide posts, for the first time.

Since more individuals were mobilized to vote in Georgia in the midst of the scandal, which party benefitted? Which party lost? Both parties captured increased support (table 12.7). The scandal mobilized voters in both parties, although the rise in support for the Democratic party dwarfed that for the Republican party. The polling data claim that the Republican party failed to mobilize its core base is simply not the case either in Georgia nor in some elections in Arkansas. But the mobilization of Republican partisans in the home state of Speaker Gingrich failed at the statewide level to cause a shift in power. In Georgia, more Democrats came out to vote and significant among them were African Americans. In this state, they were remobilized.

Table 12.8 provides a portrait of the urban and rural African American voters' remobilization. In Atlanta, one in every four previously inactive voters came to the voting booth. In Savannah, a full 16 percent of previously inactive voters were remobilized, while in the rural area of Hancock county, nearly one-third of inactive voters became involved. In every precinct more African Americans turned out in this election than had in 1994. And in all of these areas, the vote for the Republican party fell. Urban or rural, African Americans came to vote for the Democratic ticket.

On the other side of the political ledger in Georgia, the seven Republican congressional incumbents and the Republican Senator all won reelection. The Republicans continued to hold the majority of seats—7 of 11—in the state's congressional delegation. Yet when Georgia is compared with Arkansas, the president's party at the state level was victorious. Mobilization of the state's Democrats and remobilization of the state's African Americans kept the party in power at the state level. Here the scandal caused an across-the-board increase in public support.

TABLE 12.7 A Comparison of the Party Vote in the 1994 and 1998 General Elections for Governor of Georgia

Year	Democratic Gubernatorial Votes	Democratic Vote Percentage	Republican Gubernatorial Votes	Republican Vote Percentage
1994	788,926	51.1	756,371	48.9
1998	941,076	52.5	790,201	44.1
Difference	152,150	1.4	33,830	−4.8

Adapted from Cleland, "Official State of Georgia Tabulations by Counties, General Election, November 8, 1994" and Massey, "General Election November 3, 1998: Votes by County for Candidates."

TABLE 12.8 **A Demographic Comparison of the African American Party Vote in the 1994 and 1998 General Elections for Governor in Georgia**

| Year | Urban | | Rural |
	Atlanta	Savannah	Hancock County
	DEMOCRATIC PARTY		
1994	19,888	10,020	1,326
1998	26,678	11,906	1,961
Difference	6,790	1,886	635
	REPUBLICAN PARTY		
1994	1,680	2,257	431
1998	1,376	1,687	347
Difference	−304	−570	−84

Adapted from Cleland, "Official State of Georgia Tabulations by Counties, General Election, November 8, 1994" and Massey, "General Election November 3, 1998: Votes by County for Candidates." The Atlanta data are derived from precincts which were over 90 percent African American in both elections; the Savannah data, from three majority African American districts in Chatham county. Hancock county is 75 percent African American, and African Americans control county and local government.

Elsewhere in the South, the president's party captured the gubernatorial office from Republicans in Alabama and South Carolina and the state house in North Carolina. Clearly, the religious base of the Republican party in the region was not strong enough to cost this native-son president substantial losses in his own region nor did it offset the remobilization of a segment of the presidential party's electoral coalition.

At this point we can reconsider the embryonic Republican party strategy based on religion, and reflect on its strengths and weaknesses in this personal morality scandal. Like the race-based strategy, it had cost and benefits. At least in the short run, the strategy had significant cost to the party at the state and local level in the very region of the country that the party had hoped to further penetrate. At the national congressional level, there were modest costs to the party. They lost a few seats and did not continue to penetrate the rest of the nation. Significant miscalculations were made with the strategy. As the southern native-son president mitigated the race-based strategy of the Republicans, the remobilization of the African American electorate helped to moderate this religious strategy.

TABLE 12.9 The Measure of Party Loyalty in the Midterm
Elections for Governor and Secretary of State in
Arkansas in the Period 1994–1998

Party	Office	r^2
Democratic	Governor	.55
Republican	Governor	.50
Democratic	Secretary of State	.66
Republican	Secretary of State	.67

r^2 is expressed in the percentage of party loyalty in the vote.

Yet in the president's home state and home counties, there were benefits for the Republicans from this strategy. Overall, the president's party
lost support in Arkansas. Despite the differences in various electoral contests there was a small decline in voter enthusiasm for his party. In the
gubernatorial race, only 55 percent of the Democrats voted purely on the
basis of party loyalty and partisanship and 45 percent cast their vote for
other reasons (table 12.9). Among Republicans, 50 percent voted purely on
the basis of party loyalty and half voted for other reasons. In the Secretary
of State race, two-thirds of voters of both parties cast their ballots on the
basis of party loyalty and partisanship. Comparing these data for the
Democrats with the data in figure Part 2.1 shows a major decline in the
role that party loyalty and partisanship played in determining the party's
vote in this traditionally one-party Democratic state. Elsewhere, the elections in Florida and Texas positioned the Republican gubernatorial win-
ners to become future southern native-son presidential candidates and
possibly accelerate the Republican penetration of the region and the
nation.

Two Republican strategies and two Democratic responses: This recent
response by Clinton to the impact of his own personal morality scandal
on the electoral fortunes of his own party suggests that the more recent
religion-based Republican strategy, like the race-based one before it, can
be counteracted, at least in part, on different electoral levels and in different political contexts. Even in a candidate-centered electoral process,
scandals, personal or otherwise, can be moderated in terms of their influence on voter support.

The Election Data: A Research Note

Although the authors of *The Elusive Executive* do not include nor do they consider the native-son presidential variable, they do insist on the need for researchers of the presidency to concentrate on systematic description. For them, data that is "systematically acquired and analyzed" reduces dependence on speculative anecdotal observations and provides order

> with a patterned cognitive structure that permits anticipation of future developments. . . . Systematic description reduces the information overload that precludes meaningful understanding and paves the way for the next important step: the move from systematic description to explanation.[1]

They suggest that researchers seek to discover statistical patterns in the presidency.

To explore the native-son variable in President Clinton's elections, this book has used essential aggregate election return data from national, regional, state, county, and local sources. While this might seem a straightforward question of data collection, it is anything but. Arkansas has not always collected and reported its election return data in a systematic and comprehensive fashion. The record in Arkansas is at best scattered, fragmentary, and incomplete. As recently as the early 1980s, contemporary information about election results in printed form was not readily available. "Since 1924, Arkansas has been the only state in the Union (with the possible exception of Texas) for which contemporary elections are not readily available in printed form."[2]

A historian of late nineteenth century elections states that:

the choice of counties was dictated partly by the availability of electoral data (local newspapers are the only source for Arkansas precinct returns from the period 1892–1912; unfortunately, many precinct returns were never published, while others were published in newspapers which are no longer available to historical researchers).[3]

Prior to the findings of Burnham and Arsenault, an article appeared in the *American Political Science Review* also reflecting upon the problems of getting published election data for Arkansas. After canvassing all the states, the author reported that in 1933 Arkansas had published no report in eight years.[4] There were "returns on file in the office of the secretary of state [yet] information regarding state [elections] was incomplete."[5] The study concluded that "the published returns are so irregular or so incomplete as to be of little value."[6] The state had created its own problem.[7]

But these are comments about late nineteenth and early twentieth century election data sources. In 1980, the Arkansas Secretary of State, Paul Riviere, published the data for 1976 with the following remarks:

It has been said that there is less written on Arkansas government and politics than on any other state. I agree and I have been concerned about the lack of material on these subjects. . . . Many people contact this office requesting information about election results and voter turnout. . . . It has been generally inconvenient to obtain.[8]

His sincere efforts were a start. At this writing, neither the Secretary of State's office nor the Arkansas History Commission have data available for the 1974 election, which was Bill Clinton's first. The director of the History Commission wrote that "we never received 1974 election books from the Secretary of State, and we could not find Third Congressional District totals for 1974 in newspapers."[9]

With such gaps in election data sources, a massive data collection effort and significant historical work in the form of political archeology had to be undertaken before analysis could begin. The data set which resulted will be available from the Inter-University Consortium for Political and

Social Research (IUCPSR). Similar efforts were required to gather election return data for Jimmy Carter in Georgia, although Georgia has a better data reporting system than Arkansas.[10]

Once gathered, the Arkansas electoral data provided not only meaningful information about the native-son presidential variable in the state, but numerous statistical patterns that undergirded the testable propositions that emerged from this study. We are now on the road to generalizations about this variable.

In addition to the aggregate election data, this study also collected and analyzed the Bureau of the Census data on Arkansas's voting-age population, voter registration, and voter turnout. Such data is based on current national population surveys. Although such surveys are not as accurate as the election return data, the estimates derived from such public polling are quite informative, particularly when used in a supplemental fashion, as they were here.[11]

Thus the dataset for this work is twofold: the survey data provide insights into participation levels, while the election return data reveal the nature and scope of electoral behavior. These two major quantitative data sources provide this study with its statistical patterns and trends as well as its empirical foundations.

The National Election Data

Arkansas's published data on President Clinton's elections in the state covers the two decades from 1976 to 1996. This information offers contemporary insights and does not provide a significant time dimension to Arkansas politics. Nor does it provide an analytical context for Arkansas politics. To situate President Clinton's 21 elections in a contextual timeframe the author turned to *Historical Statistics of the United States* for election data for Arkansas. The 1996 data came from the *Congressional Quarterly Weekly Report*, the Arkansas Secretary of State, and Michael Nelson's *Guide to the Presidency*. These data sources provided the material for figures 4.1, 4.2, 4.3, 4.4, 4.5, and 4.7, tables 5.1, 5.2, 5.5, and 5.6, and map 5.1.

The absence of information on voting patterns in Arkansas's 75 counties in presidential elections made it necessary to refer to Walter Dean Burnham's *Presidential Ballots, 1836–1892*, Edgar Robinson's *The Presidential Ballots, 1896–1932*, Alice McGillivray and Richard Scammon (eds.), *America at the Polls, 1920–1956* and *America at the Polls, 1960–1992*. The 1996 data came from the Arkansas Secretary of State. Collectively, these data sources provided the county level returns for figures 4.5, 4.10, 5.2, 5.3, and 6.1.

Election return data for the senatorial and congressional races shown in figures 4.1, 4.5, and 4.7 were taken from Congressional Quarterly's *Guide to U.S. Elections*, 3d edition. Where necessary, these data were supplemented by information found in the *America Votes* series, Volumes 1–21, and materials provided by various Secretaries of State in Arkansas for figures 4.1, 4.5, and 4.7.

The Regional Election Data

In exploring the native-son presidential variable at the regional level of all eleven states of the old Confederacy, election data were taken from Alexander Heard and Donald Strong's *Southern Primaries and Elections: 1920–1949*, Numan Bartley and Hugh Graham, *Southern Elections: County and Precinct Data, 1950–1972*, and Richard Scammon's *America Votes*, vols. 1–21. These regional data were the sources for tables 1.1, 10.1, 10.2, 10.3, 10.4, 10.5, 10.6, 10.7, 10.8, 10.9, 10.10, and 11.1 and figures 10.1, 10.2, 10.3, and 10.4.

The Heard and Strong volume contains numerous recording and additive errors in the county level data which were corrected here.

The State Election Data

Since the Arkansas Secretary of State and the Arkansas History Commission do not have county level election returns for Bill Clinton's initial run for the 3rd Congressional District in 1974, this information was obtained from *Arkansas Votes 1974*, published by the Institute of Politics at Hendrix College in Conway, Arkansas. These data were gotten through interlibrary loan and are reported in tables 6.1, 6.2, 6.3, 6.4, 6.5, 6.6, 6.7, and 7.4.

For the Attorney General race in 1976 and the six gubernatorial races between 1978 and 1990, the electoral data were provided by the various Secretaries of State for tables 7.1, 7.2, 7.3, 7.4, 8.1, 8.2, and 8.3, and figures 8.1, 8.2, 8.3, 8.4, 8.5, 8.6, 8.7, 8.8, 8.9, and 8.10.

These same sources provided the county level returns for tables 9.1, 9.2, 9.3, 9.4, 9.5, 9.6, 9.7, 9.8, 9.9, 9.10, 9.11, 10.1, 10.2, 10.3, 10.4, 10.5, 10.6, 10.7, 10.8, 10.9, 10.10 and figure 11.1.

Data for the gubernatorial races were found in Heard and Strong, Bartley and Graham, Scammon's series, the *Guide to U.S. Elections*, and the materials provided by the Secretaries of State. Table 4.1 and figure 4.8 reflect this information.

A word about the combined data in chapter 8: Clinton's six elections for governor provide something of a short time series. The analyses of these six elections were presented in a longitudinal fashion rather than as a series of single analyses. The longitudinal data were a result of some 39 initial tables created by the author, covering each election in detail. The results of these 39 separate analyses are summarized in a short time series. This collective portrait permits the reader to fully and easily compare the governor's electoral performance in full detail. Thus all of the tables and figures in chapter 8 are a combined data synthesis of the 39 tables developed for the chapter.

The Local Election Data

The author had hoped to use election return data from Little Rock, the state capital, located in Pulaski county. Officials at City Hall were quite helpful in providing what data they had, but directed me to the Pulaski County Election Commission for additional data. The Commission has data available for elections between 1972 and 1996. Despite two visits to the Commission office and numerous telephone calls, the promised data was not forthcoming, and therefore no analysis could be performed.

The African American Election Data

In my previous study of President Carter in Georgia, I benefitted from the help of Numan Bartley and Joseph Brend, who have made concerted efforts over their academic careers to collect, record, and analyze the African American vote in that state. They graciously provided me their data for the Carter study.

In Arkansas, I did not have such resources. The Arkansas History Commission did have a microfilm copy of poll tax receipts from 1920 to 1967, broken down by race from 1957 to 1967. This official document was very valuable since Arkansas did not have an official voter registration list. Poll tax receipts were usually seen as being equivalent to voter registration. These microfilm data show how African Americans registered in the state between 1957 and 1967. Given this limited timeframe, these data had to be supplemented.

The number of initial African American voters who registered after the Civil War is recorded in the 1868 *Annual Cyclopedia*. Such data were checked for recording and additive errors and used in table 5.1 and map 5.1. Heard and Strong recorded the vote by county for the African American gubernatorial candidate J. H. Blount in 1920. This is shown in table 5.2.

The Civil Rights Commission captured more information about these voters in their 1959 Report, the source for table 5.3 and figure 5.1. These empirical insights were supplemented by data from the Bureau of the Census reports on voting and registration and the report on "Projections of the Voting Age Population for States." These were based on surveys of the African American population in Arkansas. Data on African American voters in Arkansas were also taken from monographs published by the Southern Regional Council. Lacking prior compilations, a fairly reliable portrait of these voters was developed from these various data sources.

The Survey Data

In order to capture the participation context in Arkansas, the author had to turn to the Bureau of the Census publications on registration, voting, and turnout. Using survey research methodology, the Bureau has been reporting such data for decades and by race since 1964. From these data statewide estimates were made, making it possible to analyze racial participation in Arkansas over time.

The Arkansas Native-Son Vice-Presidential Candidates

Table A.1 lists the individuals from Arkansas who have run as vice presidential candidates since the founding of the state. This table demonstrates that long before Bill Clinton became a native-son presidential candidate, four native sons offered themselves for the vice presidency. Three ran on minor third party tickets, while one, Senator J. T. Robinson, ran on the Democratic party ballot.

TABLE A.1 Arkansas Native-Son Vice Presidential Candidates,
1888–1960

Year	Party	Vice Presidential Candidate
1888	Union Labor	Charles E. Cunningham
1928	Democratic	J. T. Robinson
1932	Liberty	William H. Harvey
1960	National State Rights	Orval E. Faubus*

Adapted from Nelson, *Guide to the Presidency*, 1447–1451.
*Former governor Faubus eventually declined the nomination and withdrew his name.

Collectively, these various sources of election data permit a systematic and comprehensive description of the native-son presidential variable in Arkansas and the South. The statistical patterns arising out of these empirical data makes possible the systematic comparison with other presidents, and initiate the theoretical basis for future discussions about this variable. With such an approach, this variable will not continue to be elusive in the study of American presidents. And with such knowledge will come a greater understanding of this major American political institution.

Foreword

1. Katharine Seelye, *New York Times*, 16 February 1998.

2. *The New Yorker*, 5 October 1998, 32.

3. Katherine Seelye, "Embraced by Forgiving, Clinton Talks of Forgiveness," *New York Times*, 29 August 1998.

4. I discuss the politics of redemption in detail in my forthcoming book, *Something Within: Religion in African-American Political Life*, Oxford University Press.

5. Jonetta Rose Barrass, *The Last of the Black Emperors: The Hollow Comeback of Marion Barry in the Age of New Black Leaders*, (Baltimore: Bancroft), 1988, 55.

6. Katherine Seelye, "Embraced by Forgiving," *New York Times*, 29 August 1998.

7. Mike Wilson, Craig Pittman, and David Barstow, "I have sinned," *St. Petersburg Times*, 4 December 1997.

8. Waveney Ann Moore, David Barstow, Mike Wilson, and Monica Davey, "Ouster Attempt Fails; Lyon Wins," *St. Petersburg Times*, 4 September 1997.

9. Mike Wilson, David Barstow, and Waveney Ann Moore, "Lyons' backers successfully use race as a political strategy," *St. Petersburg Times*, 4 September 1997.

10. Hugh Gurdon, *The Sidney Morning Herald*, 21 September 1998.

Prologue

1. According to CBS/New York Times exit poll data and using a slightly different definition of the South, Pomper found that Clinton captured only 41 percent of white two-party support in the South. Even by this measure he did much better

than Dukakis, who gained the support of only 32 percent of southern whites. Gerald F. Pomper, Christopher Arterton, Ross K. Baker, Walter Dean Burnham, Kathleen A. Frankovic, Marjorie Randon Hershey, Wilson Carey McWilliams, *The Election of 1992: Reports and Interpretations* (Chatham, N.J.: Chatham House, 1993), 139.

2. Walter Dean Burnham, "The Big Bang of 1994," in Colin Campbell and Bert A. Rockman (eds.), *The Clinton Presidency* (Chatham, N.J.: Chatham House, 1995), 364.

3. Gary Jacobson, "Reversal of Fortune: The Transformation of U.S. House Elections in the 1990s." Paper presented at the Annual Meeting of Midwest Political Science Association, Chicago, Illinois, April 10–12, 1997, 5.

4. Jessica and Maria Puente Lee, "Female and Minority Turnout Helps Dems," *USA Today*, 5 November 1998.

5. Laura Tolley, " 'It's Time For Doing Right For Texas'; Bush Dodges Questions About Presidential Bid," *Sun Sentinel*, 5 November 1998, 8A.

Preface

1. Hanes Walton Jr., *The Native Son Presidential Candidate: The Carter Vote in Georgia* (Westport, Conn.: Praeger, 1992), 26–33.

2. Hanes Walton Jr., "Black Voting Behavior in the Segregation Era: 1944–1964," in Hanes Walton Jr. (ed.)., *Black Politics and Black Political Behavior: A Linkage Analysis* (Westport, Conn.: Praeger, 1994), 115–134.

3. Nancy MacLean, *Behind the Mask of Chivalry: The Making of the Second Ku Klux Klan* (New York: Oxford University Press, 1994), xiv.

4. Benjamin E. Mays, *Born to Rebel* (New York: Charles Scribners, 1971), 40–88.

5. Numan Bartley, *From Thurmond To Wallace: Political Tendencies in Georgia, 1948–1968* (Baltimore: Johns Hopkins Press, 1970), 5–17.

6. Herman Talmadge, *You and Segregation* (Birmingham: Vulcan, 1955) and *Talmadge: A Political Legacy, A Politician's Life: A Memoir* (Atlanta: Peachtree, 1987).

7. Lerone Bennett Jr., "Swifter Than Eagles, Stronger Than Lions," in F. Thomas Trotter (ed.), *Politics, Morality, and Higher Education: Essays in Honor of Samuel DuBois Cook* (Franklin, Tenn.: Providence House, 1997), 71–77.

8. Letter from John L. Ferguson to Hanes Walton Jr., 18 November 1996.

1. Elections

1. V. O. Key Jr., "The Politically Relevant in Surveys," *Public Opinion Quarterly*, vol. 24 (Spring 1960), 55–56.

2. Angus Campbell, Philip Converse, Warren Miller, and Donald Stokes, *The American Voter* (New York: Wiley, 1960).

3. Such studies of elections prior to 1960 include C. Thompson and F. Shattuck, *The 1956 Presidential Campaign* (Washington, D.C.: Brookings Institution, 1960), and Ruth Silva, *Rum, Religion, and Votes: The 1928 Election Reexamined* (University Park, Pa.: Pennsylvania State University Press, 1962).

4. See Nelson Polsby and Aaron Wildavsky, *Presidential Elections*, 9th ed. (Chatham, N.J.: Chatham House, 1995), 18–45.

5. Key, "The Politically Relevant in Surveys," 56.

5. V. O. Key Jr., "Social Determinism and Electoral Decision: The Case of Indiana," in Eugene Burdick and Arthur Broadback (eds.), *American Voting Behavior* (Glencoe, Ill.: Free Press, 1959), 298.

7. M. Kent Jennings and Thomas E. Mann, "Warren Miller and the Study of Elections" in M. Kent Jennings and Thomas E. Mann (eds.), *Elections at Home and Aboard: Essays in Honor of Warren E. Miller* (Ann Arbor: University of Michigan Press, 1994), 8–9.

8. Larry Sabato, "The November Vote: A Status Quo Election," in Larry Sabato (ed.), *Toward the Millennium: The Elections of 1996* (Boston: Allyn and Bacon, 1997), 143.

9. Wilson Carey McWilliams, "The Meaning of the Election" in Pomper (ed.), *The Election of 1976: Reports and Interpretations* (New York: David McKay, 1977), 115.

10. Ibid., 161–162.

11. William Schneider, "The November 4 Vote for President: What Did It Mean?" in Austin Ranney (ed.), *The American Elections of 1980* (Washington, D.C.: American Enterprise Institute, 1982), 218.

12. Ibid., 247.

13. Wilson Carey McWilliams, "The Meaning of the Election" in Gerald Pomper (ed.), *The Election of 1984: Reports and Interpretations* (Chatham, N.J.: Chatham House, 1985), 159.

14. Ibid., 179.

15. Wilson Carey McWilliams, "The Meaning of the Election" in Gerald Pomper (ed.), *The Election of 1988: Reports and Interpretations* (Chatham, N.J.: Chatham House, 1989), 196.

16. Ibid., 198–200.

17. Wilson Carey McWilliams, "The Meaning of the Election" in Gerald Pomper (ed.), *The Election of 1992*, 191.

18. Ibid., 205.

19. James Ceaser and Andrew Busch, *Upside Down and Inside Out: The 1992 Elections and American Politics* (Lanham, Md.: Littlefield Adams, 1993), 181.

20. Walter Dean Burnham, "The Legacy of George Bush: Travails of an Incumbent" in Pomper, *The Election of 1992*, 28.

21. Ibid., 32.

22. Tom Rosenstiel, "The Road To Here," in Sabato, *Toward the Millennium*, 15.

23. Ibid., 16.

24. Wilson Carey McWilliams, "Conclusion—The Meaning of the Elections," in Gerald Pomper (ed.), *The Election of 1996: Reports and Interpretations* (Chatham, N.J.: Chatham House, 1997), 243.

25. Gerald Pomper, "The Presidential Election" in *The Election of 1996*, 196.

26. See Paul Lazarsfeld, Bernard Berelson, and Hazel Gaudet, *The People's Choice*, 1st ed. (New York: Duel, Sloan, and Pearce, 1944) and Bernard Berelson, Paul Lazarsfeld, and William McPhee, *Voting* (Chicago: University of Chicago Press, 1954).

27. See Angus Campbell, Gerald Gurin, and Warren Miller, *The Voter Decides* (Chicago: RowPeterson, 1959), and Campbell, Converse, Miller, and Stokes, *The American Voter*.

28. Angus Campbell, Philip Converse, Warren Miller, and Donald Stokes, *Elections and the Political Order* (New York: Wiley, 1966), 2.

29. Philip Converse, "Religion and Politics: The 1960 Election," 9–24, and "Stability and Change in 1960: A Reinstating Election," 78–95, in *Elections and the Political Order*.

30. Warren Miller, "Party Identification, Realignment, and Party Voting: Back to the Basics," *American Political Science Review* vol. 85 (June 1991), 565.

31. Ibid., 564.

32. Ibid., 565.

33. V. O. Key Jr., "A Theory of Critical Elections," *Journal of Politics*, vol. 17 (February 1955), 3.

34. Ibid., 4.

35. V. O. Key Jr., "Secular Realignment and the Party System," Vol. 21 (

36. Ibid., 209.

37. Edward Carmines and James Stimson, *Race and the Transformation of American Politics* (Princeton: Princeton University Press, 1989), 47.

38. Robert Huckfeldt and Carol Kohfeld, *Race and the Decline of Class in American Politics* (Urbana: University of Illinois Press, 1989), 10–11, and Hanes Walton Jr., "Review of 'Race and the Decline of Class in American Politics'" in *Journal of American History* (December 1990), 1097–1098.

39. Katherine Tate, *From Protest to Politics: The New Black Voter in American Elections* (Cambridge: Harvard University Press, 1993), 52.

40. Michael C. Dawson, *Behind the Mule: Race and Class in African American Politics* (Chicago: University of Chicago Press, 1994), 106.

41. Lucius Barker and Mark Jones, *African Americans and the American Political System*, 3d ed. (Englewood Cliffs, N.J.: Prentice Hall, 1994), 220.

42. Dan T. Carter, *From George Wallace to Newt Gingrich: Race in the Conservative Counterrevolution, 1963–1994* (Baton Rouge: Louisiana State University Press, 1996), 40.

43. Ibid., 102.

44. Steven Rosenstone, Roy Behr, and Edward Lazarus, *Third Parties in America* 2d ed. (Princeton: Princeton University Press, 1996), 110–116.

45. Harold Stanley and David Castle, "Partisan Changes in the South: Making Sense of Scholarly Dissonance" in Robert Swansbrough and David Brodsky (eds.), *The South's New Politics: Realignment and Dealignment* (Columbia: University of South Carolina Press, 1988), 238.

46. Ibid.

47. Charles Bullock III, "Creeping Realignment in the South," in Swansbrough and Brodsky, *The South's New Politics*, 220–237.

48. David Brodsky, "Partisan Change: An Overview of a Continuing Debate," in Swansbrough and Brodsky, *The South's New Politics*, 9.

49. Quoted in Joe Silbey, "Beyond Realignment and Realignment Theory: American Political Eras, 1789–1989" in Byron Shafer (ed.), *The End of Realignment: Interpreting American Electoral Eras* (Madison: University of Wisconsin Press, 1991), 4. See also James Sundquist, "The 1984 Election: How Much Realignment?" *Brookings Review* vol. 3 (Winter 1985), 15.

50. Warren Miller, "The Election of 1984 and the Future of American Politics," in Kay Lehman Schlozman (ed.), *Elections in America* (Boston: Allen and Unwin, 1987), 293–310. Miller advances the unique argument that an ideological realignment occurred with the 1984 election.

51. Silbey, "Beyond Realignment and Realignment Theory," 17.

52. Jeff Fishel (ed.), *Parties and Elections in an Anti-Party Age* (Bloomington: Indiana University Press, 1978), 1–24.

53. David Broder, *The Party's Over: The Failure of Politics in America* (New York: Harper and Row, 1972), 3–18.

54. Kay Lawson and Peter Merkl (eds.), *When Parties Fail: Emerging Alternative Organizations* (Princeton: Princeton University Press, 1988), 3–37.

55. Martin Wattenberg, *The Decline of American Political Parties, 1952–1992* 2d ed. (Cambridge: Harvard University Press, 1992). See also William Crotty and Gary Jackson, *American Parties in Decline* (Boston: Little, Brown, 1980).

56. Karen O'Connor and Larry Sabato, *American Government: Continuity and Change* (Boston: Ally and Bacon, 1997), 453.

57. Ibid., 455.

58. Rosenstone, Behr, and Lazarus, *Third Parties in America* 2d ed., 121.

59. V. O. Key Jr., "The Future of the Democratic Party," *Virginia Quarterly Review* vol. 28 (Spring 1952), 161.

60. Ibid., 163.

61. Lorenzo Morris, "Race and the Rise and Fall of the Two-Party System," in Lorenzo Morris (ed.), *The Social and Political Implications of the 1984 Jesse Jackson Presidential Campaign* (New York: Praeger, 1990), 78.

62. Robert Cherny, "The Democratic Party in the Era of William Jennings Bryan," 171–202, and John Cooper Jr., "Wilsonian Democracy," 203–228, in Peter Kovler (ed.), *Democrats and the American Idea: A Bicentennial Appraisal* (Washington, D.C.: Center for National Policy Press, 1992).

63. Hanes Walton Jr., *Black Politics* (Philadelphia: J. B. Lippincott, 1972), 119.

64. Donald Kinder and Lynn Sanders, *Divided by Color: Racial Politics and Democratic Ideas* (Chicago: University of Chicago Press, 1996).

65. Letter from Democratic Congressman Arthur Mitchell to President Franklin Delano Roosevelt, January 1935.

66. Malcolm Moss, *Hats in the Ring* (New York: Random House, 1960), 14–15.

67. Dan T. Carter, *The Politics of Rage: George Wallace, the Origins of the New Conservatism, and the Transformation of American Politics* (Baton Rouge: Louisiana State University Press, 1995), 11.

68. Dan T. Carter, *From George Wallace to Newt Gingrich*, xii.

69. Ibid.

70. Barry Goldwater, *The Conscience of a Conservative* (Shepherdsville, Kentucky: Victor Publishing, 1960).

71. Carter, *The Politics of Rage*, 221.

72. Carter, *From George Wallace To Newt Gingrich*, 15–16.

73. Rosenstone, Behr, and Lazarus, *Third Parties in America*, 113.

74. Ibid., 111.

75. Walton, *The Native Son Presidential Candidate*, 75–79.

76. Louis Harris, *Is There a Republican Majority?* (New York: Harper, 1954); and Andrew Hacker, "Is there a New Republican Majority?" in Louise Howe (ed.), *The White Majority: Between Poverty and Affluence* (New York: Random House, 1970).

77. Carter, *From George Wallace To Newt Gingrich*, xiv. See also Gary Wills, "Newt Gingrich's Revolution," *The New York Review of Books* vol. 42 (23 March 1995), 4–8.

78. Nicol Rae, *Southern Democrats* (New York: Oxford University Press, 1994), 114.

79. Ibid., 120.

80. Ibid., 129.

81. Ibid., 151.

82. O'Connor and Sabato, *American Government*, "African Americans, Political Context, and the Clinton Presidency: The Legacy of the Past in the Future," 469.

83. Hanes Walton, Jr. and William Generette, Jr., *African American Power and Politics: The Political Context Variable* (New York: Columbia University Press, 1997), 373–376.

84. Ibid., 474.

85. Ibid., 467.

86. Ibid., 474.

87. Lorenzo Morris, "Race and the Rise and Fall of the Two-Party System," in *The Social and Political Implications of the 1984 Jesse Jackson Presidential Campaign*, 87.

88. Ibid.

Part 1. Epistemology and the Native-Son Candidate

1. Donald Kinder and Thomas Palfrey, "On Behalf of an Experimental Political Science," in Donald Kinder and Thomas Palfrey (eds.), *Experimental Foundations of Political Science* (Ann Arbor: University of Michigan Press, 1993), 3–5.

2. V. O. Key Jr., "Interpreting the Election Results" in Paul David (ed.), *The Presidential Election and Transition* (Washington, D.C.: Brookings Institution, 1961), 174.

3. Ibid., 175.

4. Philip Converse, "Religion and Politics" in Campbell, et al. (eds.), *Elections and the Political Order*, 96–124.

5. Ibid., 101.

6. Philip Converse, Angus Campbell, Warren Miller, and Donald Stokes, "Stability and Change in 1960" in *Elections and the Political Order*, 88.

7. Ruth Silva, *Rum, Religion, and Votes*, 1–17.

8. On this point see Hanes Walton Jr. and Robert Smith, *American Politics and the African American Quest for Universal Freedom* (Needham Heights, Mass.: Allyn and Bacon, 2000), chapter 8.

2. Theory

1. *Guide to U.S. Elections* (Washington, D.C.: Congressional Quarterly, 1975), 78.

2. Ralph Goldman, *The National Party Chairman and Committees: Factionalism of the Top* (New York: M. E. Sharpe, 1990), 321.

3. Ruth Silva, *Rum, Religion, and Votes*; Edmund Moore, *A Catholic Runs for President: The 1928 Campaign* 2d ed. (New York: Ronald Press, 1956); Roy Peel and Thomas Donnelly, *The 1928 Campaign: An Analysis* (New York: Smith, 1931); and Donald Lisio, *Hoover, Blacks, and Lily-Whites: A Study of Southern Strategies* (Chapel Hill: University of North Carolina Press, 1985).

4. Key, "The Future of the Democratic Party," 161.

5. Harold Gosnell, *Grass Roots Politics: National Voting Behavior of Typical States* (New York: Russell and Russell, 1970), 13.

6. V. O. Key Jr., *Southern Politics in State and Nation: A New Edition* (Knoxville: University of Tennessee Press, 1977), 37.

7. See Earl Black and Merle Black, "The Wallace Vote in Alabama: A Multiple Regression Analysis," *Journal of Politics* vol. 35 (August 1973), 730–736, and Raymond Tatlovich, "Friend and Neighbors Voting: Mississippi, 1943–1973" *Journal of Politics* vol. 37 (August 1975), 807–814.

8. Michael Lewis-Beck and Tom Rice, "Localism in Presidential Elections: The Home State Advantage," *American Journal of Political Science* vol. 27 (August, 1983), 548–549.

9. Ibid., 548.

10. Key, *Southern Politics*, 179–180, n39.

11. Lewis-Beck and Rice, 549.

12. Steven Rosenstone, *Forecasting Presidential Elections* (New Haven: Yale University Press, 1983).

13. Ibid., 45.

14. Ibid., 128.

15. Ibid., 88.

16. Walton, *The Native Son Presidential Candidate*, 132.

17. Hanes Walton Jr. and Daniel Brantley, "Black Southern Politics: A Look at the Tradition and the Future" in Walton (ed.), *Black Politics and Black Political Behavior*, 294.

18. Ibid.

19. Ibid., 296.

20. Ibid., 296–297.

21. Robert F. Burks, *The Eisenhower Administration and Black Civil Rights* (Knoxville: University of Tennessee Press, 1984), 15.

22. Ibid., 6.

23. Ibid., 15.

24. Ibid., 92.

25. Ibid., 17.

26. Ibid.

27. Dan T. Carter, *The Politics of Rage*, 89.

28. Ibid., 86.

29. Taylor Branch, *Parting the Waters: America in the King Years, 1954–1963* (New York: Simon and Schuster, 1988), 191.

30. Ibid.

31. Burks, *The Eisenhower Administration and Black Civil Rights*, 168–9.

32. Ibid.

33. Hanes Walton Jr., *The Political Philosophy of Martin Luther King Jr.* (Westport, Conn.: Greenwood, 1971), chap. 2.

34. April 1985 interview with George Dalley at the Howard University Political Science department session on Jesse Jackson's 1984 presidential race.

35. "Andrew Young Attacks Mondale Staff with Racial Slur," *Reuters North European Service* 18 August 1984, 1; Colin Bessonette, "Q & A on the News," *Atlanta Journal Constitution* 4 May 1995, 2A; and Walter Shapiro and Howard Fineman, "Can Mondale Come Back?" *Newsweek* 3 September 1984, 24.

36. June 1989 interview with Congressman Mervyn Dymally at his office.

37. McWilliams, "The Meaning of the Election" in Gerald Pomper (ed.), *The Election of 1992*, 203.

38. Louis Koenig, *Bryan: a Political Biography* (New York: Putnam's, 1971), 9–18.

39. McWilliams, "Conclusion—The Meaning of the Election" in Pomper, *The Election of 1996*, 262.

40. Samuel DuBois Cook, "Political Movements and Organizations," *Journal of Politics* vol. 26 (February 1964), 143.

41. Ibid.

42. Alice V. McGillivray and Richard M. Scammons, *America at the Polls: A Handbook of Presidential Election Statistics, 1920–1956 Harding to Eisenhower, 1960–1996 Kennedy to Clinton*, (Washington, D.C.: Congressional Quarterly, 1998) 42.

43. Walton, *Black Republicans*, 45–47.

44. McGillivray and Scammons, 36.

45. Ibid., 30.

46. Cook, "Political Movements and Organizations," 142–143.

47. Quoted in Raymond Arsenault, *The Wild Ass of the Ozarks: Jeff Davis and the Social Bases of Southern Politics* (Knoxville: University of Tennessee Press, 1988), 48–49.

48. *Guide to U.S. Elections*, 78.

49. Goldman, *The National Party Chairman and Committees*, 345.

50. Walton, *The Native Son Presidential Candidate*, 101–147.

51. Carter, *From George Wallace To Newt Gingrich*, 46.

52. Ibid., 53.

53. Ibid., 93–94, 122.

3. *Methodology*

1. Richard P. McCormick, *The Presidential Game: The Origins of American Presidential Politics* (New York: Oxford University Press, 1982), 4.

2. Ibid., 74.

3. Ibid., 4.

4. Rae, *Southern Democrats*, 156.

5. Dennis Kavanagh, *Political Science and Political Behavior* (Boston: George Allen and Universal, 1983), 9.

6. Herbert Tingsten, *Political Behavior: Studies in Election Statistics*, in translation (Totowa, N.J.: Bedminister, 1963). See also John Sprague, "On Warren Miller's Longest Footnote: The Vote in Context" in Jennings and Mann (eds.), *Elections at Home and Abroad*, 210–214.

7. Gosnell, *Grass Roots Politics*, 13.

8. Key, *Southern Politics*, 3–27.

9. Ibid., 298–316.

10. J. Morgan Kousser, *The Shaping of Southern Politics: Suffrage Restrictions and the Establishment of the One Party South, 1880–1910* (New Haven: Yale University Press, 1974), 124–130.

11. Gerald Gaither, *Blacks and the Populist Revolt: Ballots and Bigotry in the "New South"* (Tuscaloosa: University of Alabama Press, 1977).

12. Arsenault, *The Wild Ass of the Ozarks*, 11.

13. Ibid., 18.

14. For a different categorization of Arkansas counties into an ecological structure see Thomas Pettigrew and Ernest Campbell, "Faubus and Segregation: An Analysis of Arkansas Voting," *Public Opinion Quarterly* vol. 24 (Fall 1960), 400–442. For a critical rejoinder which stresses the limitation of this categorization see Robert Savage and Richard Gallagher, "Politicocultural Regions in a Southern State: An Empirical Topology of Arkansas Counties," *Regions* vol. 7 (1977), 91–105.

15. President Clinton was born in Hope, Arkansas, in Hempstead county, and grew up in Hot Springs, in Garland county.

16. Walton, *The Native-Son Presidential Candidate*, 29.

17. Diane Blair, *Arkansas Politics and Government: Do the People Rule?* (Lincoln: University of Nebraska Press, 1988), 300, n7.

18. Walton, *The Native Son Presidential Candidate*, 29–30.

19. Blair, *Arkansas Politics and Government*, 60.

10. Arsenault, *The Wild Ass of the Ozarks*, 18.

21. Gary Wekkin, "Arkansas: Electoral Competition in the 1990s" in Charles Bullock III and Mark Rozell (eds.) *The New Politics of the Old South: An Introduction to Southern Politics* (Lanham, Md.: Rowman and Littlefield, 1998), 185.

22. Ibid., 186.

23. Ibid., 190.

24. For a complete discussion of these statistical data see the Appendix.

Part 2. The Political Context of a Native-Son Candidate

1. Blair, *Arkansas Politics and Government*, 212.

2. Randy Finley, *From Slavery To Uncertain Freedom: The Freedmen's Bureau in Arkansas, 1865–1869* (Fayetteville: University of Arkansas Press, 1966), 1.

3. Ibid., 2.

4. Ibid., 163–164.

5. Ibid., 165.

6. Daisy Bates, *The Long Shadow of Little Rock: A Memoir* (New York: David McKay, 1962), 2–3.

7. Ibid., 3–4.

8. Ibid., 221.

9. Lani Guinier, *Lift Every Voice* (New York: Simon and Schuster, 1998), 25.

10. Lani Guinier, *The Tyranny of the Majority* (New York: Free Press, 1994), 11–12.

11. Ibid., 10–11.

12. Ibid., 11.

13. *Whitfield* v. *Democratic Party* 686 F. Supp. 1365 (E.D. Ark. 1988); *Whitfield* v. *Democratic Party* 890 F. 2d, 1423 (8th Cir. 1889); *Whitfield* v. *Democratic Party* 902 F. 2d 15 (9th Cir. 1990); *Whitfield* v. *Bill Clinton* 498 U.S. 1126, 112 L. Ed. 2nd., 1193.

14. Stephen Carter, "Foreword" in Guinier, *The Tyranny of the Majority*, vii.

15. Guinier, *Lift Every Voice*, 278.

16. *Smith* v. *Clinton*, 687 F. Supp. 1310 (E.D. Ark. 1988).

17. *M.C. Jeffers et al.,* v. *Bill Clinton*, F. Supp. 585, 1990 U.S. District, 26.

18. Ronald Smothers, "Arkansas Plan to Promote Election of Black Judges Brings a Familiar Challenge," *New York Times* (8 April 1996), 10.

19. For the initial legal brief filed in 1930 by African American Democrats in Arkansas to participate in the all-white primary, see *Robinson* v. *Hohman*, 181 Ark. 428 (1930) and 26 S.W. 2d 66.

20. Bill Clinton, "State Initiatives to increase Citizen Participation," in Karen Arrington and William Taylor (eds.), *Voting Rights in America: Continuing the Quest for Full Participation* (Washington, D.C.: Leadership Conference Education Find/Joint Center for Political and Economic Studies, 1992), 143–151.

21. Matthew Holden Jr., *The President, Congress, and Race Relations* (Boulder: Ernest Patterson Memorial Lecture, University of Colorado, April 1986), 59.

4. The Arkansas Electorate

1. Key, *Southern Politics*, 183.

2. Diane Blair and Robert Savage, "The Appearances of Realignment and Dealignment in Arkansas," in Swansbrough and Brodsky (eds.), *The South's New Politics*, 126–127.

3. Ibid., 127.

4. Ibid., 139.

5. Robert H. Swansbrough, "Future Directions in Southern Politics" in *The South's New Politics*, 289.

6. Robert Scher, *Politics in the New South: Republicanism, Race, and Leadership in the Twentieth Century* 2d ed. (New York: M.E. Sharpe, 1997), 53–76.

7. Brian Walton, "How Many Voted in Arkansas Elections Before the Civil War," *Arkansas Historical Quarterly* vol. 40 (1980), 72.

8. The median turnout is 47 percent.

9. Key, *Southern Politics*, 493–502 and fig. 64.

10. Stuart Towns, "A Louisiana Medicine Show: The Kingfish Elects An Arkansas Senator," *Arkansas Historical Quarterly* vol. 20 (1966), 117–127. See also Herman Deutsch, "Hattie and Huey," *Saturday Evening Post* (15 October 1932), 7.

11. Alexander Heard, *A Two-Party South?* (Chapel Hill: University of North Carolina Press, 1952), 58, table 6 "Southern Elections Contested By Republicans, Selected Offices."

12. This is 93 percent of the total number of elections.

13. Heard, *A Two-Party South?*, 40.

14. Walton, *The Native Son Presidential Candidate*, 19. The simple correlation between the Wallace vote and the Carter vote is r=.50, while the r2=.25.

15. Heard, *A Two-Party South?*, 58.

18. Diane Blair, *Arkansas Politics and Government*, 86, 217–218. See also Richard Yates, "Arkansas: Independent and Unpredictable" in William Havard (ed.), *The Changing Politics of the South* (Baton Rouge: Louisiana State University Press, 1972), 233–293.

5. The African American Electorate

1. Heard, *A Two-Party South?*, 86.

2. James Farr, Johnson Dryzek, and Stephen Leonard, "Introduction" in James Farr, Johnson Dryzek, and Stephen Leonard (eds.), *Political Science in History: Research Programs and Political Traditions* (New York: Cambridge University Press, 1995), 2.

3. Ibid., 6.

4. Ibid., 17.

5. Hanes Walton Jr., *The Study and Analysis of Black Politics: A Bibliography* (New York: Scarecrow Press, 1975), 2.

6. Key, *Southern Politics*, 517.

7. Ibid., 521.

8. For such studies see Luther Jackson, "Race and Suffrage in the South Since 1940," *New South* (June/July 1948); Margaret Price, *The Negro Voter in the South* (Atlanta: Southern Regional Council, 1957) and her *The Negro and the Ballot in the South* (Atlanta: Southern Regional Council, 1959).

9. Chandler Davidson and Bernard Grofman (eds.), *Quiet Revolution in the South* (Princeton: Princeton University Press, 1994).

10. Ibid., 3–17.

11. Bill Clinton, "State Initiatives to Increase Citizen Participation" in *Voting Rights in America*, 143–151.

12. For a critique see Hanes Walton Jr., "Review of 'Quiet Revolution in the South'," *Georgia Historical Quarterly* vol. 79 (Summer 1995), 516–518. For an exception to the Key legacy see Hugh D. Price, *The Negro and Southern Politics: A Chapter of Florida History* (New York: New York University Press, 1957).

13. Ann D. Gordon, et al. (eds), *African American Women and the Vote: 1837–1965* (Amherst: University of Massachusetts Press, 1997).

14. Alexander Heard and Donald Strong, *Southern Primaries and Elections 1920–1949* (Tuscaloosa: University of Alabama Press, 1950), 23.

15. Hanes Walton Jr., *Black Republicans: The Politics of the Black and Tans* (Metuchen, N.J.: Scarecrow Press, 1975), 123–128. See also David Lisio, *Hoover, Blacks, and Lily-Whites*.

16. Walton, *Black Republicans*, 127.

17. Heard and Strong, *Southern Primaries and Elections 1920–1949*, 224.

18. Ibid., 23.

19. Walton and Generette, "African Americans, Political Context, and the Clinton Presidency: The Legacy of the Past in the Future," 373–376.

20. Hanes Walton Jr., "Black Southern Politics: The Influence of Bunche, Martin, and Key" in Walton (ed.), *Black Politics and Black Political Behavior*, 19–38.

21. The single correlation coefficient is $r = .17$.

22. The single correlation coefficient squared, $r^2 = .02$.

23. For a comprehensive view, see Pat Waters and Reese Cleghorn, *Climbing Jacob's Ladder: The Arrival of Negroes in Southern Politics* (New York: Harcourt, Brace, and World, 1967).

24. Lorn Foster (ed.), *The Voting Rights Act: Consequences and Implications* (New York: Praeger, 1985), 3–9.

25. V. O. Key Jr., *A Primer of Statistics for Political Scientists* (New York: Thomas Y. Crowell, 1969), 189–192 for good sources.

26. The Census Bureau data on estimated voting is quite conservative and underestimates the actual number. Blair places the 1982 number at 90,000. Blair, *Arkansas Politics and Government*, 300.

27. Jerome Clubb, William Flanigan, and Nancy Zingale (eds.), *Analyzing Electoral History: A Guide to the Study of American Voter Behavior* (Beverly Hills: Sage, 1981), 48.

28. Paul Riverie, *1976 Arkansas Election Data* (Little Rock: Secretary of State, May 1980), 1.

29. Erik Austin, Jerome Clubb, and Michael Traugott, "Aggregate Units of Analysis," in *Analyzing Electoral History*, 81–104.

30. William Flanigan, *Political Behavior of the American Electorate* 4th ed. (Boston: Allyn and Bacon, 1979) and S. A. Rice, *Quantitative Methods in Politics* (New York: Alfred Knopf, 1928). See also Ronald P. Fairmisano, "Analyzing American Voting, 1830–1860: Methods" in Joel Sibley and Samuel McSeveney (eds.), *Voters, Parties, and Elections* (Massachusetts: Xerox College Publishing, 1972), 46–56.

31. Gaither, *Blacks and the Populist Revolt*, 186–188.

32. Walton, *The Native Son Presidential Candidate*, 55–71.

33. Arsenault, *The Wild Ass of the Ozarks*, 40–43.

34. Brian Walton, "How Many Voted in Arkansas Elections Before the Civil War," *Arkansas Historical Quarterly* vol. 40 (1980), 72.

35. Ibid., 73.

36. Tom Dillard, "To the Back of the Elephant: Racial Conflict in the Arkansas Republican Party," *Arkansas Historical Quarterly* vol. 33 (1974), 3.

37. Ibid. See also Willard B. Gatewood Jr., "Negro Legislators in Arkansas, 1891: A Document," *Arkansas Historical Quarterly* vol. 31 (Autumn 1972), 222–223.

38. Heard, *A Two-Party South?*, 227–238.

39. John William Graves, "Negro Disfranchisement in Arkansas," *Arkansas Historical Quarterly* vol. 26 (1967), 203.

40. Ibid., 209.

41. Ibid., 210.

42. Ibid., 216–220.

43. Arsenault, *The Wild Ass of the Ozarks*, 3. See also Richard Niswonger, "A Study in Southern Demagoguery: Jeff Davis," *Arkansas Historical Quarterly* vol. 39 (1980), 114–124; Cal Ledbetter, Jr. "Jeff Davis and the Politics of Combat," *Arkansas Historical Quarterly* vol. 33 (1974), 15–37.

44. Key, *Southern Politics*, 598.

45. Ibid., 579.

46. Ibid., 602.

47. Ibid., 618.

48. Tilman C. Cothran and William M. Phillips, "Expansion of Negro Suffrage in Arkansas," *Journal of Negro Education* vol. 26 (Summer 1957), 289.

49. Ibid., 292.

50. Ibid., 293–296. For more on the poll tax see R. Grann Lloyd, *White Supremacy in the United States* (Washington, D.C.: Public Affairs Press, 1952); Rayford Logan (ed.), *The Attitudes of the Southern White Press Toward Negro Suffrage, 1932–1940* (Washington, D.C.: Public Affairs Press, 1940); and Frederick Ogden, *The Poll Tax in the South* (Tuscaloosa: University of Alabama Press, 1958).

6. The Congressional Vote for Clinton

1. Walton, *The Native Son Presidential Candidate*, 40–51.

2. James E. Carter, *Why Not the Best* (New York: Bantam Books, 1976), 88–89.

3. Walton, *The Native Son Presidential Candidate*, 35–52.

4. Letter from Bill Clinton to President Gerald Ford, 6 October 1974, in the Gerald R. Ford Presidential Library, Ann Arbor, Mich. The author would like to thank Supervisory Archivist David A. Horrocks for bringing this letter to his attention and sending me a copy. This letter is not mentioned in any of the current biographies on President Clinton.

5. Richard Scammon (ed.), *America Votes: 1966* (Washington, D.C.: Congressional Quarterly, 1968), 37–38.

6. Heard, *A Two-Party South?*, 38–40, 111.

7. Michael Barone, Grant Ujifusa, and Douglas Matthews, *The Almanac of American Politics: 1974* (Boston: Gambit, 1974), 47.

8. Ibid., 48.

9. Ibid., 47.

10. Institute of Politics in Arkansas, *Arkansas Votes: 1974* (Conway, Ark.: Institute of Politics in Arkansas, Hendrix College, 1975), 5.

11. J. Morgan Kousser, "The Voting Rights Act and the Two Reconstructions," in Bernard Grofman and Chandler Davidson (eds.), *Controversies in Minority Voting: The Voting Rights Act in Perspective* (Washington, D.C.: Brookings Institution, 1992), 135–176.

12. Key, *Southern Politics*, 37–41 and 302.

13. Institute of Politics in Arkansas, *Arkansas Votes: 1974*, 4.

14. Ibid.

15. David Maraniss, *First in His Class: A Biography of Bill Clinton* (New York: Simon and Schuster, 1995), 340.

16. Barone, Ujifusa, Matthews, *The Almanac of American Politics: 1974*, 43.

17. Ibid.

18. Maraniss, *First in His Class*, 337.

19. Blair, *Arkansas Politics and Government*, 62.

20. Key, *Southern Politics*, chap. 14.

7. The Attorney General Vote for Clinton

1. Maraniss, *First in His Class*, 340.

2. Ibid., 356.

3. James MacGregor Burns, W. W. Patterson, Thomas Covin, and David Magleby, *State and Local Politics: Government by the People* 8th ed. (Englewood Cliffs, N.J.: Prentice Hall, 1996), 141.

4. Blair, *Arkansas Politics and Government*, 146.

5. Maraniss, *First in His Class*, 340.

6. Martin Walker, *The President We Deserve: Bill Clinton—His Rise, Falls, and Comebacks* (New York: Crown Publishers, 1996), 82.

7. Maraniss, *First in His Class*, 346.

8. Ibid., 347.

9. Walker, *The President We Deserve*, 83

10. Key, *Southern Politics*, 189.

11. Ibid.

12. Ibid., 186.

13. Maraniss, *First in His Class*, 296–297.

14. Ibid.

15. Numan Bartley and Hugh D. Graham, *Southern Politics and the Second Reconstruction* (Baltimore: Johns Hopkins University Press, 1975), 184–200.

16. Ibid., 148.

17. Ibid., 188. See also Roy Reed, "Progressive Politics in the Dogpatch," in Ernest Dumas (ed.), *The Clintons of Arkansas* (Fayetteville: University of Arkansas Press, 1993), 148–160.

18. Stephen Smith, "Compromise, Consensus, and Consistency," in *The Clintons of Arkansas*, 9 and Meredith Oakley, *On the Make: The Rise of Bill Clinton* (Washington, D.C.: Regnery Publishing, 1994), 159–161.

8. *The Gubernatorial Vote for Clinton*

1. On the way in which Clinton's 1980 reelection bid influenced his strategic plans see Maraniss, *First in His Class*, 384–404; Walker, *The President We Deserve*, 93–96; Dumas, *The Clintons of Arkansas*, 13–14, 67–68, 92–94; and Oakley, *On the Make*, 256–279.

2. Walton, *The Native Son Presidential Candidate*, 52–53.

3. Maraniss, *First in His Class*, 351.

4. Walker, *The President We Deserve*, 82.

5. Ibid., 84.

6. Martin Wattenberg, *The Rise of Candidate Centered Politics: Presidential Elections of the 1980s* (Cambridge: Harvard University Press, 1991), 4–20.

7. Walker, *The President We Deserve*, 85.

8. Maraniss, *First in His Class*, 352.

9. Ibid., 353.

10. Arsenault, *The Wild Ass of the Ozarks*, 78–203.

11. J. Morgan Kousser, *The Shaping of Southern Politics*. For discussion of Arkansas parties see 82, 124–130, and 240–246.

12. Roy Reed, *Faubus: The Life and Times of an American Prodig*al (Fayetteville: University of Arkansas Press, 1997), 338.

13. Ibid., 339.

14. Ibid., 342.

15. Walker, *The President We Deserve*, 91; Maraniss, *First in His Class*, 379.

16. Maraniss, *First in His Class*, 402.

17. Walker, *The President We Deserve*, 97.

18. Ibid.

19. Ibid., 98.

20. Maraniss, *First in His Class*, 403.

21. Charles Allen and Jonathan Portis, *The Comeback Kid: The Life and Career of Bill Clinton* (New York: Birch Lane Press, 1992), 11, 55, 72–81.

22. Blair, *Arkansas Politics and Government*, 80; Ernest Dumas, "Black Vote is the Key to Clinton's Victory," *Arkansas Gazette* (11 November 1982); and John Brummet, "Clinton's Appeal to Blacks Rests on Record, Skill," *Arkansas Gazette* (5 December 1982).

23. Bruce Brown and Herbert Weisberg, *An Introduction to Data Analysis* (San Francisco: Freeman and Company, 1980), 69.

24. Key, *Southern Politics*, 50–51, 66, 104, 109, 175, 188.

25. Warren Miller, "Party Identification, Realignment, and Party Voting," *American Political Science Review* vol. 85 (June 1991), 557–566.

26. Soren Holmberg, "Party Identification Compared Across the Atlantic," in Jennings and Mann, *Elections at Home and Abroad*, 93–122; and Morris, "Race and the Rise and Fall of the Two Party System," in *The Social and Political Implications of the 1984 Jesse Jackson Presidential Campaign*, 95–98.

27. William J. Clinton, "Foreword" in Timothy Donovan and Willard Gatewood

Jr. (eds.), *The Governors of Arkansas: Essays in Political Biography* (Fayetteville: University of Arkansas Press, 1981), ix.

28. Donovan and Gatewood, "Preface," *The Governors of Arkansas*, iii.

Part 4. The Native-Son Presidential Candidate

1. Gerald Pomper, "The Presidential Election," in Pomper (ed.), *The Election of 1992*, 140.

2. McWilliams, "The Meaning of the Election," Ibid., 206.

3. Anthony J. Corrado, "The 1992 Presidential Election: A Time for Change," in L. Sandy Maisel (ed.), *The Parties Respond* 2d ed. (Boulder, Colo.: Westview Press, 1994), 214.

4. Walter Dean Burnham, "Introduction: Bill Clinton—Riding the Tiger" in Pomper (ed.), *The Election of 1996*, 3.

5. Bob Woodward, *The Agenda: Inside the Clinton White House* (New York: Simon and Schuster, 1994), 53.

6. One group of election analysts saw class as the key variable in the 1976 Carter election, and not his southerness. For example, James Sundquist wrote: "the swing to Carter was evidently less because he was a southerner than because he was a Democrat. The significant aspect of the 1976 presidential contest in the South was that the class basis of voting . . . reappeared in that subregion." Sundquist, *Dynamics of the Party System: Alignment and Realignment of Political Parties in the United States* rev. ed. (Washington, D.C.: Brookings, 1983), 370. For his evidence Sundquist uses Paul Abramson, "Class Voting in the 1976 Presidential Election," *Journal of Politics* vol. 40 (November 1978). However, this class variable has not endured.

7. McWilliams, "Conclusion: The Meaning of the Election, *The Election of 1996*, 259.

8. Maraniss, *First in His Class*, 305.

9. Bill Clinton, *Between Hope and History: Meeting America's Challenges for the 21st Century* (New York: Times Books, 1996), 118–119.

9. The Presidential Vote for Clinton

1. Walker, *The President We Deserve*, 78.

2. Woodward, *The Agenda*, 22.

3. Walton, *The Native Son Presidential Candidate*, 73–74.

4. Walker, *The President We Deserve*, 109.

5. Maraniss, *First in His Class*, 438.

6. Walker, *The President We Deserve*, 111.

7. Maraniss, *First in His Class*, 462.

8. Barbara Norrander, *Super Tuesday: Regional Politics and Presidential Primaries* (Lexington: University Press of Kentucky, 1992), 1–2.

9. Ibid., 27–28.

10. Ibid., 28.

11. Walton, *The Native Son Presidential Candidate*, 133.

12. V. O. Key Jr., *The Responsible Electorate* (Cambridge: Harvard University Press, 1966), 30.

13. Charles Erichner and John Maltese, "The Electoral Process" in Michael Nelson (ed.), *Guide to the Presidency* vol. 1, 2d ed. (Washington, D.C.: Congressional Quarterly, 1996), 299.

14. Ceaser and Bush, *Upside Down and Inside Out*, 55.

15. Susan Tolchin, *The Angry American: How Voter Rage is Changing the Nation* (Boulder: Westview Press, 1996), 43.

16. Heard, *A Two-Party South?*, 38–39, 40.

17. See Louis Bolic, Gerald DeMaio, and Douglass Muzzio, "Blacks and the Republican Party: The 20 Percent Solution," *Political Science Quarterly* vol. 107 (Spring 1992), 63–79, and their "The 1992 Republican Tent: No Blacks Walked In," *Political Science Quarterly* vol. 108 (Spring 1993), 255–270.

18. Walton, *The Native Son Presidential Candidate*, 5–12.

19. Hanes Walton Jr., "African Americans, H. Ross Perot, and Image Politics: The Nature of African American Third Party Politics," in Hanes Walton Jr., *African American Power and Politics: The Political Context Variable* (New York: Columbia University Press, 1996), 282–293.

20. Hanes Walton Jr., "Black Female Presidential Candidates: Bass, Mitchell, Chisholm, Wright, Reid, Davis, and Fulani" in Walton (ed.), *Black Politics and Black Political Behavior*, 251–274.

21. In the Republican primary, 42,976 votes were cast and Senator Robert Dole got 76.2 percent (32,759 votes), Pat Buchanan 23.4 percent (10,067 votes), and uncommitted 0.3 percent (150 votes).

22. Walton, *The Native Son Presidential Candidate*, 84.

23. Carter's uncommitted voters never reached the one percent mark in the Democratic primaries in Georgia.

24. Walton, *The Native Son Presidential Candidate*, 92, table 4.14.

25. Walton, "Black Female Presidential Candidates," 251–274.

26. Walton, *The Native Son Presidential Candidate*, 98–99.

10. The Regional Vote: Clinton and Carter

1. Rosenstone, *Forecasting Presidential Elections*, 45–88.

2. Walton, *The Native Son Presidential Candidate*, 126.

3. Ibid., 128.

4. Ibid., 127.

5. Walton and Brantley, "Black Southern Politics: A Look at the Tradition and the Future," in Walton (ed.), *Black Politics and Black Political Behavior*, 294–297.

6. Diane Clark Hine, *Black Victory: The Rise and Fall of the White Primary in Texas* (New York: KTO Press, 1979).

7. Heard, *A Two-Party South?*, 194–195. See also *Robinson et al. v. Holman*, 181 Ark. 428 (1930) 26 S.W. 2d 66.

8. Walton, *The Native Son Presidential Candidate*, 129.

9. Hanes Walton Jr., "The Democrats and African Americans: The American Idea," in Peter Kovler (ed.), *Democrats and the American Idea: A Bicentennial Appraisal* (Washington, D.C.: Center For National Policy Press, 1992), 339–340.

10. Ibid. See also "Quo Vadis," *The Crisis* (November 1912), 45 and "Editorial: Politics," *The Crisis* (August 1912), 181.

11. Walton, *The Native Son Presidential Candidate*, 129.

12. Barry Goldwater, *The Conscience of a Conservative*, 24–37.

13. Samuel DuBois Cook, "Political Movements and Organizations," 130–131.

14. Ceaser and Busch, *Upside Down and Inside Out*, 176.

15. Walker, *The President We Deserve*, 144.

16. Paul Abramson, "Measuring the Southern Contribution to the Democratic Coalition," *American Political Science Review* vol. 81 (June 1987), 567–570.

17. For a full length discussion of Wallace's diminished physical capacity in the 1976 primaries see Dan T. Carter, *The Politics of Rage*, 437–458.

18. Maraniss, *First in His Class*, 376–377.

19. Ibid, 379.

20. Ibid. On August 9, 1999 President Clinton flew to Atlanta and awarded the former President and his wife the Presidential Medal of Freedom. Maybe this was a gesture of reconciliation. Two days later he gave the same award to former President Ford.

21. Ibid., 379–380.

22. Ibid., 377.

23. Walton, *The Native-Son Presidential Candidate*, 139.

24. Ibid., 142.

25. For an extensive discussion of the impact of Vice President Gore on the region's electoral behavior see Walton and Brantley, "Black Southern Politics" in *Black Politics and Black Political Behavior*, 294–297.

26. Leslie McLemore and Mary Coleman, "The Jesse Jackson Campaign and the Institutionalization of Grass-Roots Politics: A Comparative Perspective" in Walton, *Black Politics and Black Political Behavior*, 49–60.

27. Walton and Brantley, "Black Southern Politics," 296–297.

Part 5. The Native-Son Candidate and Democratic Elections

1. Key, "The Future of the Democratic Party," 171.

2. Ibid., 172.

3. Corrado, "The 1992 Presidential Election," in Maisel (ed.), *The Parties Respond*, 208.

4. Jon Hale, "The Democratic Leadership Council: Institutionalizing Party Faction," in Daniel Shea and John Green, (eds.), *The State of the Parties: The Changing Role of Contemporary American Parties* (New York: Rowman and Littlefield, 1994), 251.

5. Ibid., 251–252.

6. Ibid., 257.

7. Ibid., 259.

8. L. Sandy Maisel, "The Platform Writing Process: Candidate-Centered Plat-

forms in 1992" in Green and Shea (eds.), *The State of Parties* 2d ed. (New York: Rowman and Littlefield, 1996), 312.

9. Hanes Walton Jr., "African Americans and the Clinton Presidency: Political Appointments as Social Justice," in Walton, *African American Power and Politics*, 313–322.

10. Woodward, *The Agenda*, 40.

11. Ibid., 41.

12. Maraniss, *First in His Class*, 10.

13. James Ceaser and Andrew Busch, *Losing To Win: The 1996 Elections and American Politics*, (Lanham, Md.: Rowman and Littlefield, 1997), 48.

14. Ibid.

15. Ibid.

16. Key, "The Future of the Democratic Party," 171.

17. Manning Marable, "What Clinton Owed Us—And Why He Didn't Pay Up," and "Presidential Politics, Race, and the 1996 Election: Beyond Liberalism," in Manning Marable (ed.), *Black Liberation in Conservative America* (Boston: South End Press, 1997), 129–135 and 151–156.

11. The Democratic Party in Presidential Elections: The Native-Son Theory Revised

1. David Shribman, "Reconstructing Bill Clinton's Victory," in L. Sandy Maisel (ed.), *The Parties Respond*, 369.

2. Walton and Generette, "African Americans, Political Context, and the Clinton Presidency: The Legacy of the Past in the Future," 373–376.

3. L. Sandy Maisel, "Prologue," *The Parties Respond*, xv–xviii.

4. Ibid., xv. See also Peter Kellogg, "Civil Rights Consciousness in the 1940s," *The Historian* vol. 42 (November 1979), 4–8, and Denton L. Watson, "Assessing the Role of the NAACP in the Civil Rights Movement," *The Historian* vol. 55 (Spring 1993), 453–468.

5. Clayborne Carson, "Civil Rights, Reform, and the Black Freedom Struggle," in Charles Eagle (ed.), *The Civil Rights Movement in America* (Jackson, Miss.: University Press of America, 1986), 19–32.

6. Ibid.

7. Desmond King, *Separate and Unequal: Black Americans and the U.S. Federal Government* (New York: Oxford University Press, 1995). See also Hanes Walton Jr., "Review of 'Separate and Unequal: Black Americans and the U.S. Federal Government'," *Journal of American History* (March 1997), 1425–1426.

8. Warren E. Miller, "Party Identification and the Electorate of the 1990s" in Maisel, *The Parties Respond*, 118.

9. Ibid.

10. V. O. Key Jr., *Politics, Parties, and Pressure Groups* 5th ed. (New York: Thomas Y. Crowell, 1964), ix–xiii.

11. See Paul Allen Beck, *Party Politics in America* 8th ed. (New York: Longman, 1997).

12. Matthew Holden, "Editor's Introduction," *National Political Science Review* vol. 4 (1994), 1–6.

13. V. O. Key Jr., *Politics, Parties, and Pressure Groups* 1st ed. (1942), 18.

14. Ibid., 28–29.

15. Key, *Southern Politics* 5th ed., 229.

16. Ibid., 230.

17. Ibid., 238–239.

18. Ibid., 240.

19. Walter J. Stone, Ronald Rapport, and Alan Abramowitz, "Party Polarization: The Reagan Revolution and Beyond," in Maisel, *The Parties Respond*, 69–102.

20. Carter, *The Politics of Race*, 396–400.

21. Colin Campbell and Bert Rockman (eds.), *The Bush Presidency: First Appraisals* (Chatham, N.J.: Chatham House, 1991).

22. Maraniss, *First in His Class*, 454.

23. Bartley and Graham, *Southern Politics and the Second Reconstruction*, 184–200.

24. Ibid. On Arkansas, see Blair, *Arkansas Politics and Government*, 272–273.

25. James McKee, *Sociology and the Race Problem* (Urbana: University of Illinois Press, 1993), 222–255.

26. Scher, *Politics in the New South*, 331.

27. Walton, *The Native Son Presidential Candidate*, 120–130.

28. See Betty Glad, *Jimmy Carter: In Search of the Great White Hope* (New York: W. W. Norton, 1980).

29. Walton, *The Native Son Presidential Candidate*, xxiv. See also David Alsobrook, "Resources for Recent Alabama History in the Jimmy Carter Library: A Preliminary Summary." *The Alabama Review* (April 1990).

30. Blair, *Arkansas Politics and Government*, 272.

31. Allen and Portis, *The Comeback Kid*, 270–271.

32. Ibid., 272.

33. Ibid., 273.

34. Ibid.

35. Maraniss, *First in His Class*, 337.

36. Gary Orren and Nelson Polsby, *Media and Momentum: The New Hampshire Primary and Nomination Politics* (Chatham, N.J.: Chatham House, 1987), 1–8.

37. Walton, *The Native Son Presidential Candidate*, 129.

38. Allen and Portis, *The Comeback Kid*, 243.

39. These African American homegrown activists from Clinton's previous campaigns include Rodney Slater, Carol Willis, and Bob Nash, who were appointed to subcabinet posts in 1992. In the second term, Rodney Slater was appointed transportation department secretary.

40. Gerald Pomper, "The Presidential Election" in Pomper (ed.), *The Election of 1996*, 182.

41. Ibid., 175.

42. Ibid.

43. Because President Clinton's percentage in the District of Columbia stood at 84.6 percent in 1992 and 85.2 percent in 1996, such high percentages were dropped so as not to distort the results.

44. Pomper, "The Presidential Election," in *The Election of 1996*, 175.

45. Maraniss, *First in His Class*, 45.

46. Walton and Generette, *African American Power and Politics*, 313–322.

47. Hanes Walton Jr., "Public Policy Responses to the Million Man March," *The Black Scholar* vol. 28 (Fall 1995), 217–23.

48. Elsa Walsh, "Kennedy's Hidden Campaign," *The New Yorker* (31 March 1997), 66.

49. Ibid.

50. Ibid.

51. Robert Smith, *We Have No Leaders: African Americans in the Post-Civil Rights Era* (Albany: State University of New York Press, 1996), 271–272.

52. The table in chapter 11 presents testable propositions emanating from this evolving variable.

12. Epilogue: Scandal, Public Support, and the Native-Son Variable

1. Arnold Herdenheimer (ed.), *Political Corruption* (New York: Holt, Rinehart, Winston, 1970), 4–27, and John Gardiner and David Olson (eds.), *Theft of the City: Readings on Corruption in Urban America* (Bloomington: Indiana University Press, 1974), 3–38, 349–439.

2. On this matter see Arthur Schlesinger, *The American As Reformer* (Cambridge: Harvard University Press, 1950) and Richard Hofstadter, *The Age of Reform* (New York: Vintage Books, 1955).

3. Max Lerner, *America as a Civilization: Life and Thought in the United States* (New York: Henry Holt, 1987), 28–51.

4. Robert Speel, *Changing Patterns of Voting in the Northern United States: Electoral Realignment, 1952–1996* (University Park: Pennsylvania State University Press, 1998), 204.

5. Ibid., 169.

6. Courtney Brown, *Serpents in the Sand: Essays on the Nonlinear Nature of Politics and Human Destiny* (Ann Arbor: University of Michigan Press, 1995), 65.

7. Speel, 165.

8. Nelson Polsby and Aaron Wildavsky, *Presidential Elections* 7th ed. (New York: Free Press, 1987), 210–211.

9. Jack Anderson, *The Washington Exposé* (Washington, D.C.: Public Affairs Press, 1967), and Drew Pearson and Jack Anderson, *The Case Against Congress* (New York: Simon and Schuster, 1968).

10. On the role of personal morality as a character issue in Congressman Powell's career see a book written by a member of the committee that voted to unseat him: Andy Jacobs, *The Powell Affair: Freedom Minus One* (New York: Bobbs-Merrill, 1973). Also see Kent Weeks, *Adam Clayton Powell and the Supreme Court* (New York: Dunellen Publishing, 1971); Charles Hamilton, *Adam Clayton Powell Jr.: The Political Biography of an American Dilemma* (New York: Atheneum, 1991); Wil Haygood, *King of the Cats: The Life and Times of Adam Clayton Powell Jr.* (New York: Houghton Mifflin, 1993); and Neil Hickey and Ed Edwin, *Adam Clayton Powell and the Politics of Race* (New York: Fleet Publishing, 1965).

11. McWilliams, "The Meaning of the Election," in Pomper (ed.), *The Election of 1976*, 155.

12. Ibid.

13. McWilliams, "The Meaning of the Election," in Pomper (ed.), *The Election of 1988*, 180.

14. Karen Foerstel, "Voters' Plea for Moderation Unlikely to be Heeded," *Congressional Quarterly Weekly Report* (7 November 1998), 2980.

15. Jeffrey Katz, "Shakeup in the House," *Congressional Quarterly Weekly Report* (7 November 1998), 2989–2992.

16. Ibid., 3001.

17. Keating Holland, "Election Day '98 Voters Did Not Punish Clinton Democrats" in *Polls and Scandal From Nixon to Clinton: A Resource for Journalists* (New York: Media Studies Center and American Association for Public Opinion Research, 1998), 12.

18. Ibid.

19. Ibid., 13.

20. Kathleen Frankovic, "1998 Public Praises the Leader, not the Man," in *Polls and Scandal from Nixon to Clinton*, 6.

21. Ibid., 7.

22. Cliff Zukin, "Move On, Scandal-Weary Public Urges Then and Now," in *Polls and Scandal from Nixon to Clinton*, 10–11.

23. Carol Cannon, "What Hath Bill Wrought?" *National Journal* (7 November 1998), 2622.

24. Walton, *African American Power and Politics*, 1–31.

Appendix

1. Gary King and Lyn Ragsdale, *The Elusive Executive: Discovering Statistical Patterns in the Presidency* (Washington, D.C.: Congressional Quarterly Press, 1988), 3.

2. Walter Dean Burnham, "Printed Sources" in Jerome Clubb, William Flanigan, and Nancy Zingale, *Analyzing Electoral History* (Beverly Hills, Cal.: Sage, 1981), 46.

3. Arsenault, *The Wild Ass of the Ozarks*, 260.

4. Idella Swisher, "Election Statistics in the United States," *American Political Science Review* vol. 27 (June 1933), 423–424.

5. Ibid., 428.

6. Ibid., 423.

7. David Young, "The Initiative and Referendum in Arkansas Come of Age," *American Political Science Review* vol. 27 (February 1933), 75.

8. Riviere, 1980, 1.

9. Letter, John L. Ferguson, Arkansas History Commission, to Hanes Walton Jr., (11 March 1997), 1.

10. Walton, *The Native Son Presidential Candidate*, 149–156.

11. U.S. Bureau of the Census, Current Population Reports Series 23 No. 168, *Studies in the Measurement of Voter Turnout* (Washington, D.C.: Government Printing Office, 1990).

Books and Chapters

Allen, Charles and Jonathan Portis. *The Comeback Kid: The Life and Career of Bill Clinton*. New York: Birch Lane Press, 1992.

Arsenault, Raymond. *The Wild Ass of the Ozarks: Jeff Davis and the Social Bases of Southern Politics*. Knoxville: University of Tennessee Press, 1984.

Barker, Lucius and Mark Jones. *African Americans and the American Political System* 3d edition. Englewood Cliffs, N.J.: Prentice Hall, 1994.

Barone, Michael, Grant Ujifusa, and Douglas Matthews. *The Almanac of American Politics: 1974*. Boston: Gambit, 1974.

Bartley, Numan. *From Thurmond To Wallace: Political Tendencies in Georgia (1948–1968)*. Baltimore: John Hopkins University Press, 1970.

—— and Hugh D. Graham. *Southern Politics and the Second Reconstruction*. Baltimore: Johns Hopkins University Press, 1975.

Bates, Daisy. *The Long Shadow of Little Rock: A Memoir*. New York: David McKay, 1962.

Beck, Paul Allen. *Party Politics in America* 8th edition. New York: Longman, 1997.

Bennett Jr., Lerone. "Swifter Than Eagles, Stronger Than Lions." In F. Thomas Trotter, ed., *Politics, Morality, and Higher Education: Essays in Honor of Samuel DuBois Cook*. Tennessee: Providence House Publishers, 1997.

Berelson, Bernard, Paul Lazarsfeld, and William McPhee. *Voting*. Chicago: University of Chicago Press, 1954.

Blair, Diane. *Arkansas Politics and Government: Do the People Rule?* Lincoln: University of Nebraska Press, 1988.

———— and Robert Savage. "The Appearances of Realignment and Dealignment in Arkansas." In Robert Swansbrough and David Brodsky, eds., *The South's New Politics: Realignment and Dealignment*. Columbia: University of South Carolina Press, 1988.

Brown, Bruce and Herbert Weisberg. *An Introduction to Data Analysis*. San Francisco, Cal.: Freeman and Company, 1980.

Branch, Taylor. *Parting the Waters: America in the King Years: 1954–1963*. New York: Simon and Schuster, 1988.

Broder, David. *The Party's Over: The Failure of Politics in America*. New York: Harper and Row, 1972.

Burdick, Eugene and Arthur Brodbeck, eds., *American Voting Behavior*. Glencoe, Ill.: Free Press, 1959.

Burks, Robert F. *The Eisenhower Administration and Black Civil Rights*. Knoxville: University of Tennessee Press, 1984.

Burnham, Walton Dean. "Printed Sources." In Jerome Clubb, William Flanigan, and Nancy Zingale, eds., *Analyzing Electoral History*. California: Sage, 1981.

————. "The Legacy of George Bush: Travails of an Incumbent." In Pomper, *The Election of 1992*.

Burns, James MacGregor, W. W. Patterson, Thomas Covin, and David Magleby. *State and Local Politics: Government by the People* 8th edition. Englewood Cliffs, N.J.: Prentice Hall, 1996.

Campbell, Angus, Philip Converse, Gerald Gurin, and Warren Miller. *The Voter Decides*. Chicago: RowPeterson, 1959.

Campbell, Angus, Philip Converse, Warren Miller, and Donald Stokes. *The American Voter*. New York: Wiley, 1960.

————. *Elections and the Political Order*. New York: Wiley, 1966.

Campbell, Colin and Bert Rockman, eds., *The Bush Presidency: First Appraisals*. Chatham, N.J.: Chatham House, 1991.

Carmines, Edward and James Stimson. *Race and the Transformation of American Politics*. Princeton: Princeton University Press, 1989.

Carson, Clayborne. "Civil Rights, Reform, and the Black Freedom Struggle." In Charles Eagle, ed., *The Civil Rights Movement in America*. Jackson: University Press of America, 1986.

Carter, Dan T. *From George Wallace to Newt Gingrich: Race in the Conservative Counterrevolution 1963–1994*. Baton Rouge: Louisiana State University Press, 1996.

————. *The Politics of Rage: George Wallace, the Origins of the New Conservatism, and the Transformation of American Politics*. Baton Rouge: Louisiana State University Press, 1995.

Carter, James E. *Why Not the Best*. New York: Bantam Books, 1976.

Carter, Stephen. "Foreword." In Lani Guinier, *The Tyranny of the Majority*. New York: Free Press, 1994.

Ceaser, James and Andrew Busch. *Upside Down and Inside Out: The 1992 Elections and American Politics*. Lanham, Md.: Littlefield Adams, 1993.

———. *Losing to Win: The 1996 Elections and American Politics*. Lanham, Md.: Rowman and Littlefield, 1997.

Cherny, Robert. "The Democratic Party in the Era of William Jennings Bryan." In Peter Kovler, ed., *Democrats and the American Idea: A Bicentennial Appraisal*. Washington, D.C.: Center for National Policy Press, 1992.

Clinton, Bill. *Between Hope and History: Meeting America's Challenges for the 21st Century*. New York: Times Books, 1996.

———. "State Initiatives to Increase Citizen Participation." In Karen Arrington and William Taylor, eds., *Voting Rights in America: Continuing the Quest for Full Participation*. Washington, D.C.: Leadership Conference Education Foundation/Joint Center for Political and Economic Studies, 1992.

———. "Foreword." In Timothy Donovan and Willard Gatewood Jr., eds., *The Governors of Arkansas: Essays in Political Biography*. Fayetteville: University of Arkansas Press, 1981.

Clinton, Bill and Al Gore, *Putting People First: How We Can All Challenge America* (New York: Times Books, 1992).

Clubb, Jerome, William Flanigan, and Nancy Zingale, eds., *Analyzing Electoral History: A Guide to the Study of American Voter Behavior*. Beverly Hills: Sage, 1981.

Congressional Quarterly. *Guide to Elections*. Washington, D.C.: Congressional Quarterly, 1975.

Converse, Philip. "Religion and Politics: The 1960 Election." In Angus Campbell, Philip Converse, Warren Miller, and Gerald Gurin, eds., *Elections and the Political Order*. New York: John Wiley, 1960.

Crotty, William and Gary Jackson. *American Parties in Decline*. Boston: Little, Brown, 1980.

Davidson, Chandler and Bernard Grofman, eds., *Quiet Revolution in the South*. Princeton: Princeton University Press, 1994.

Dawson, Michael C. *Behind the Mule: Race and Class in African American Politics*. Chicago: University of Chicago Press, 1994.

Erichner, Charles and John Maltese. "The Electoral Process." In Michael Nelson, ed., *Guide to the Presidency* vol. I, 2d edition. Washington, D.C.: Congressional Quarterly, 1996.

Farr, James, Johnson Dryzek, and Stephen Leonard, "Introduction." *Political Science in History: Research Programs and Political Traditions*. New York: Cambridge University Press, 1995.

Finley, Randy. *From Slavery To Uncertain Freedom: The Freedmen's Bureau in Arkansas, 1865–1869*. Fayetteville: University of Arkansas Press, 1996.

Fishel, Jeff, ed. *Parties and Elections in an Anti-Party Age*. Bloomington: Indiana University Press, 1978.

Flanigan, William. *Political Behavior of the American Electorate* 4th ed., New York: Alfred Knopf, 1928.

Foirmisano, Ronald P. "Analyzing American Voting, 1830–1860: Methods." In Joel

Sibley and Samuel McSeveney, eds., *Voters, Parties, and Elections*. Massachusetts: Xerox College Publishing, 1972.

Foster, Lorn, ed. *The Voting Rights Act: Consequences and Implications*. New York: Praeger, 1985.

Gaither, Gerald. *Blacks and the Populist Revolt: Ballots and Bigotry in the "New South."* Tuscaloosa: University of Alabama Press, 1977.

Glad, Betty. *Jimmy Carter: In Search of the Great White Hope*. New York: W.W. Norton, 1980.

Goldman, Ralph. *The National Party Chairman and Committees: Factionalism of the Top*. New York: M.E. Sharpe, 1990.

Goldwater, Barry. *The Conscience of a Conservative*. Kentucky: Victor Publishing, 1960.

Gordon, Ann D., Bettye Collier-Thomas, John Bracey, Arlene Avakian, and Joyce Berkman, eds. *African American Women and the Vote: 1837–1965*. Amherst: University of Massachusetts Press, 1997.

Gosnell, Harold. *Grass Roots Politics: National Voting Behavior of Typical States*. New York: Russell and Russell, 1970.

Hacker, Andrew. "Is There a New Republican Majority?" In Louise Howe, ed., *The White Majority: Between Poverty and Affluence*. New York: Random House, 1970.

Hale, Jon. "The Democratic Leadership Council: Institutionalizing Party Faction." In Daniel Shea and John Green, eds., *The State of the Parties: The Changing Role of Contemporary American Parties*. New York: Rowman and Littlefield, 1994.

Harris, Louis. *Is There a Republican Majority?* New York: Harper, 1954.

Heard, Alexander. *A Two-Party South?* Chapel Hill: University of North Carolina Press, 1952.

——— and Donald Strong. *Southern Primaries and Elections, 1920–1949*. Tuscaloosa: University of Alabama Press, 1950.

Hine, Diane Clark. *Black Victory: The Rise and Fall of the White Primary in Texas*. New York: KTO Press, 1979.

Holden Jr., Matthew. *The President, Congress, and Race Relations*. Boulder: Ernest Patterson Memorial Lecture, University of Colorado, April 1986.

Huckfeldt, Robert and Carol Kohfeld. *Race and the Decline of Class in American Politics*. Urbana: University of Illinois Press, 1989.

Institute of Politics in Arkansas. *Arkansas Votes, 1974*. Conway, Ark.: Institute of Politics in Arkansas, Hendrix College, 1975.

———. *Arkansas Votes, 1972*. Conway, Ark.: Institute of Politics in Arkansas, Hendrix College, 1973.

Jennings, M. Kent and Thomas E. Mann. "Warren Miller and the Study of Elections." In M. Kent Jennings and Thomas E. Mann, eds., *Elections at Home and Aboard: Essays in Honor of Warren E. Miller*. Ann Arbor: University of Michigan Press, 1994.

Kavanagh, Dennis. *Political Science and Political Behavior.* Boston: George Allen and Universal, 1983.

Key Jr., V. O. *Politics, Parties, and Pressure Groups* 5th ed. New York: Thomas Y. Crowell, 1964.

——. "Interpreting the Election Results: 1960." In Paul David, ed., *The Presidential Election and Transition.* Washington, D.C.: Brookings Institution, 1961.

——. *Politics, Parties, and Pressure Groups.* New York: Thomas Y. Crowell, 1942.

——. *A Primer of Statistics for Political Scientists.* New York: Thomas Y. Crowell, 1969.

——. *The Responsible Electorate.* Cambridge: Harvard University Press, 1966.

——. "Social Determinism and Electoral Decision: The Case of Indiana." In Burdick and Brodbeck, *American Voting Behavior.*

——. *Southern Politics in State and Nation,* a new edition. Knoxville: University of Tennessee Press, 1977.

Kinder, Donald and Thomas Palfrey. "On Behalf of an Experimental Political Science." *Experimental Foundations of Political Science.* Ann Arbor: University of Michigan Press, 1993.

—— and Lynn Sanders. *Divided by Color: Racial Politics and Democratic Ideas.* Chicago Press, 1996.

King, Desmond. *Separate and Unequal: Black Americans and the U.S. Federal Government.* New York: Oxford University Press, 1995.

King, Gary and Lyn Ragsdale. *The Elusive Executive: Discovering Statistical Patterns in the Presidency.* Washington, D.C.: Congressional Quarterly Press, 1988.

Koenig, Louis. *Bryan: a Political Biography.* New York: Putnam's, 1971.

Kousser, J. Morgan. *The Shaping of Southern Politics: Suffrage Restrictions and the Establishment of the One Party South, 1880–1910.* New Haven: Yale University Press, 1974.

——. "The Voting Rights Act and the Two Reconstructions." In Bernard Grofman and Chandler Davidson, eds., *Controversies in Minority Voting: The Voting Rights Act in Perspective.* Washington, D.C.: Brooking Institution, 1992.

Lawson, Kay and Peter Merkl, eds. *When Parties Fail: Emerging Alternative Organizations.* Princeton: Princeton University Press, 1988.

Lazarsfeld, Paul, Bernard Berelson, and Hazel Gaudet. *The People's Choice* 1st ed. New York: Duel, Sloan, and Pearce, 1944.

Lisio, Donald. *Hoover, Blacks, and Lily-Whites: A Study of Southern Strategies.* Chapel Hill: University of North Carolina Press, 1985.

Lloyd, R. Grann. *White Supremacy in the United States.* Washington, D.C.: Public Affairs Press, 1952.

Logan, Rayford, ed. *The Attitudes of the Southern White Press Toward Negro Suffrage, 1932–1940.* Washington, D.C.: Public Affairs Press, 1940.

MacLeans, Nancy. *Behind the Mask of Chivalry: The Making of the Second Ku Klux Klan.* New York: Oxford University Press, 1994.

Maisel, L. Sandy, ed. *The Parties Respond* 2d ed. Boulder, Colo.: Westview Press, 1994.

———. "The Platform Writing Process: Candidate-Centered Platforms in 1992." In John Green and Daniel Shea, eds., *The State of Parties: The Changing Role of Contemporary American Parties* 2d ed. New York: Rowman and Littlefield, 1966.

Marable, Manning. "Presidential Politics, Race, and the 1996 Election: Beyond Liberalism." *Black Liberation in Conservative America.* Boston: South End Press, 1997.

———. "What Clinton Owed Us—And Why He Didn't Pay Up." In Manning Marable, ed., *Black Liberation in Conservative America.* Boston: South End Press, 1997.

Maraniss, David. *The Clinton Enigma.* New York: Simon and Schuster, 1998.

———. *First in His Class: A Biography of Bill Clinton.* New York: Simon and Schuster, 1995.

Mays, Benjamin E. *Born to Rebel.* New York: Charles Scribner, 1971.

McCormick, Richard P. *The Presidential Game: The Origins of American Presidential Politics.* New York: Oxford University Press, 1982.

McGillivray, Alice V. and Richard M. Scammons. *America at the Polls: A Handbook of Presidential Election Statistics, 1920–1956 Harding to Eisenhower, 1960–1996 Kennedy to Clinton.* Washington, D.C.: Congressional Quarterly Press, 1998.

McKee, James. *Sociology and the Race Problem.* Urbana: University of Illinois Press, 1993.

McWilliams, Wilson Carey. "The Meaning of the Election." In Gerald Pomper, ed., *The Election of 1976: Reports and Interpretation.* New York: David McKay, 1977.

———. "The Meaning of the Election." In Gerald Pomper, ed., *The Election of 1980: Reports and Interpretation.* New York: Chatham House, 1980.

———. "The Meaning of the Election." In Gerald Pomper, ed., *The Election of 1984: Report and Interpretations.* Chatham, N.J.: Chatham House, 1985.

———. "The Meaning of the Election." In Gerald Pomper, ed., *The Election of 1988: Reports and Interpretations.* Chatham, N.J.: Chatham House, 1989.

———. "The Meaning of the Election." In Gerald Pomper, ed., *The Election of 1992.* Chatham, N.J.: Chatham House.

———. "Conclusion—The Meaning of the Elections." In Gerald Pomper, ed., *The Election of 1996: Reports and Interpretations.* Chatham, N.J.: Chatham House, 1997.

Miller, Warren. "The Election of 1984 and the Future of American Politics," in Kay Lehman Schlozman (ed.), *Elections in America* (Boston: Allen & Unwin, 1987).

Moore, Edmund. *A Catholic Runs for President: The 1928 Campaign* 2nd ed. (New York: Ronald Press, 1956).

Morris, Lorenzo. "Race and the Rise and Fall of the Two-Party System," in his (ed.). *The Social and Political Implications of the 1984 Jesse Jackson Presidential Campaign* (New York: Praeger, 1990).

Moss, Malcolm. *Hats in the Ring* (New York: Random House, 1960).

Niswronger, Richard. "A Study in Southern Demagoguery: Jeff Davis," *Arkansas Historical Quarterly* Vol. 39 (1980), pp. 114–124.

Oakley, Meredith. *On the Make: The Rise of Bill Clinton* (Washington, DC: Regnery Publishing, 1994).

O'Connor, Karen & Larry Sabato, *American Government: Continuity and Change* (Boston: Allyn and Bacon, 1997).

Odgen, Frederick. *The Poll Tax in the South* (Alabama: University of Alabama Press, 1958).

Oreen, Gary & Nelson Polsby, (eds.). *Media & Momentum: The New Hampshire Primary and Nomination Politics* (New Jersey: Chatham House, 1987).

Peel, Roy & Thomas Donnelly, The *1928 Campaign - An Analysis* (New York: Smith, 1931).

Pomper, Gerald. "The Presidential Election" in his (ed.), *The Election of 1996: Reports and Interpretation* (New Jersey: Chatham House Publishers, 1997), p. 182.

Price, Hugh D. *The Negro and Southern Politics: A Chapter of Florida History* (New York: New York University Press, 1957).

Price, Margaret . *The Negro and the Ballot in the South* (Atlanta: Southern Regional Council, 1959).

———. *The Negro Voter in the South* (Atlanta: Southern Regional Council, 1957)

Rae, Nicol. *Southern Democrats* (New York: Oxford University Press, 1994).

Reed, Roy. "Progressive Politics in the Dogpatch," in Ernest Dumas, (ed.), *The Clintons of Arkansas* (Fayetteville: University of Arkansas Press, 1993).

Rice, S. A. *Quantitative Methods in Politics* (New York: Alfred Knopf, 1928).

Rosenstone, Steven. *Forecasting Presidential Elections* (New Haven: Yale University Press, 1983).

———, Roy Behr, Edward Lazarus. *Third Parties in America* 2nd edition (Princeton: Princeton University Press, 1996).

Sabato, Larry . "The November Vote: A Status Quo Election," in Larry Sabato (ed.) Toward the Millennium: The Elections of 1996 (Boston: Allyn & Bacon, 1997).

Sundquist, James. *Dynamics of the Party System: Alignment and Realignment of Political Parties in the Untied States* rev. ed. (Washington, DC: Brookings, 1983).

Scammon, Richard. (ed.), *America Votes: 1966* (Washington, DC: Congressional Quarterly, 1968).

Scher, Robert . *Politics in the New South: Republicanism Race and Leadership in the Twentieth Century* 2nd ed. (New York: M. E. Sharpe, 1997).

Schneider, William. "The November 4 Vote for President: What Did It Mean? In Austin Ranney (ed.), *The American Elections of 1980* (Washington, D.C.: American Enterprise Institute, 1982), p. 218.

Seagull, Louis. *Southern Republicans* (Cambridge: Schenkeman Publishing Company, 1975).

Shribman, David. "Reconstructing Bill Clinton's Victory," in L. Sandy Maisel, (ed.), *The Parties' Respond* 2nd ed. (Colorado: Westview Press, 1994).

Silbey, Joe. "Beyond Realignment and Realignment Theory: American Political Eras, 1789–1989" in Byron Shafer (ed.), *The End of Realignment: Interpreting American Electoral Eras* (Madison: University of Wisconsin Press, 1991).

Silva, Ruth. *Run, Religion. and Votes: 1928 Reexamined* (University Park: Pennsylvania State University Press, 1962).

Smith, Robert. *We Have No Leaders: African Americans in the Post-Civil Rights Era* (Albany: State University of New York Press, 1996).

Sprague, John. "On Warren Miller's Longest Footnote: The Vote in Context in M. Kent Jennings & Thomas Mann (eds.), *Elections at Home and Abroad: Essay in Honor of Warren E. Miller* (Ann Arbor: University of Michigan Press, 1994).

Stanley, Harold & David Castle. "Partisan Changes in the South: Making Sense of Scholarly Dissonance" in Robert Swansbrough & David Brodsky, (eds.). *The South's New Politics: Realignment and Dealignment* (Columbia: University of South Carolina Press, 1988).

Talmadge, Herman. *Talmadge: A Political Legacy: A Politician's Life: A Memoir* (Atlanta: Peachtree Publishers, Ltd., 1987).

———. *You and Segregation* (Birmingham: Vulcan, 1955).

Tate, Katherine. *From Protest to Politics: The New Black Voter in American Elections* (Cambridge: Harvard University Press, 1993).

Thompson, C. & F. Shattuck. *The 1956 Presidential Campaign* (Washington, DC: Brooking Institution, 1960).

Tingsten, Herbert. *Political Behavior: Studies in Election Statistics.* Translated (Totowa, New Jersey: Bedminister, 1963).

Tolchin, Susan. *The Angry American: How Vote Rage is Changing the Nation* (Boulder: Westview Press, 1996).

Hanes Walton, Jr. *African American Power & Politics: The Political Context Variable* (New York: Columbia University Press, 1997).

———. "African Americans and the Clinton Presidency: Political Appointments as Social Justice, Hanes Walton, Jr. *African American Power and Politics: The Political Context Variable* (New York: Columbia University Press, 1997).

———. "African Americans, H. Ross Perot and the Image Politics: The Nature of African American Third Party Politics," Hanes Walton, Jr., *African American Power & Politics: The Political Context Variable* (New York: Columbia University Press, 1996).

———. *Black Politics* (Philadelphia: J. B. Lippincott, 1972).

———. "Black Female Presidential Candidates: Bass, Mitchell, Chisholm, Wright, Reid, Davis and Fulani," Hanes Walton, Jr. (ed.), *Black Politics and Black Political Behavior: A Linkage Analysis* (Connecticut: Praeger Publishers, 1994).

———. "Black Southern Politics: The Influence fo Bunche, Martin, and Key" (ed.), *Black Politics and Black Political Behavior: A Linkage Analysis* (Connecticut: Praeger Publishers, 1994).

———. *Black Republicans: The Politics of the Black and Tans* (New Jersey: Scarecrow Press, 1975).

———. "Black Southern Politics: A Look at the Tradition and the Future," in Walton (ed..), *Black Politics and Black Political Behavior: A Linkage Analysis* (Connecticut: Praeger, 1994).

——— "Black Voting Behavior in the Segregation Era: 1944–1964." *Black Politics and Black Political Behavior: A Linkage Analysis* (Connecticut: Praeger, 1994).

———. "The Democrats and African Americans: The American Idea," in Peter Kovler (ed.), *Democrats and the American Idea: A Bicentennial Appraisal* (Washington, DC: Center For National Policy Press, 1992).

———. *The Political Philosophy of Martin Luther King. Jr.* (Connecticut: Greenwood, 1971), Chapter 2.

———. *The Study and Analysis of Black Politics: A Bibliographv* (New York: Scraecrow Press, 1975).

——— & Daniel Brantley. "Black Southern Politics: A Look at the Tradition and the Future," Hanes Walton, Jr., (ed.). *Black Politics and Black Political Behavior: A Linkage Analysis* (Connecticut: Praeger Publishers, 1994).

——— & William Generette. *African American Power & Politics: The Political Context Variable* (New York: Columbia University Press, 1997).

——— & Robert Smith, *American Politics: And the African American Ouest for Universal Freedom* (Massachusetts: Allyn & Bacon, 1999), Chapter

Waters, Pat & Reese Cleghorn. *Climbing Jacob's Ladder: The Arrival of Negroes in Southern Politics* (New York: Harcourt, Brace, and World, 1967).

Wattenberg, Martin. *The Decline of American Political Parties. 1952–1992* 2nd ed. (Cambridge: Harvard University Press, 1992.

———. *The Rise of Candidate Centered Politics: Presidential Elections of the 1980's* (Cambridge: Harvard University Press, 1991).

Woodward, Bob. *The Agenda: Inside the Clinton White House* (New York: Simon & Schuster, 1994), p. 53.

Yates, Richard. "Arkansas: Independent and Unpredictable" in William Havard, (ed.), *The Changing Politics of the South* (Baton Rouge: Louisiana State University Press, 1972).

Articles

"Editorial: Politics," *The Crisis* (August, 1912), p. 181.

"Quo Vadis," *The Crisis* (November, 1912), p. 45.

Abraman, Paul, "Class Voting in the 1976 Presidential Election," *Journal of Politics* Vol. 40, (November, 1978).

———, "Measuring the Southern Contribution to the Democratic Coalition," *American Political Science Review* Vol. 81, (June, 1987), pp. 567–570.

Alsobrook, David Alsobrook, "Resources for Recent Alabama History in the Jimmy Carter Library: A Preliminary Summary." *The Alabama Review* (April, 1990).

Bass, Jr., Harold & Andrew Westmoreland, "Parties and Campaigns in Contemporary Arkansas Politics" *Arkansas Political Science Journal* Vol. 5 (1984), pp. 42–45.

Black, Earl & Merle Black, "The Wallace Vote in Alabama: A Multiple Regression Analysis," *Journal of Politics* Vol. 35 (August, 1973), pp. 730–736.

Bolic, Louis, Gerald DeMaio and Douglass Muzzio, "Blacks and the Republican Party: The 20 Percent Solution," *Political Science Quarterlv* Vol. 107, (Spring, 1992), pp. 63–79,

———, "The 1992 Republican Tent: No Blacks Walked in," *Political Science Quarterlv* Vol. 108 (Spring, 1993), pp. 255–270.

Brummet, John, "Cinton's Appeal to Blacks, Rests on Record, Skill," *Arkansas Gazette* (December 5, 1982).

Cook, Samuel DuBois, "Political Movements and Organizations" *Journal of Politics* Vol. 26 (February, 1964), pp. 130–131.

Cothran, Tilman C. And William M. Phillips. Expansion of Negro Suffrage in Arkansas." *Journal of Negro Education* Vol 26 (Summer, 1957), p. 289.

Deutsch, Herman, "Hattie and Huey," *Saturday Evening Post* (October 15, 1932), p. 7.

Dillard, Tom, "To the Back of the Elephant: Racial Conflict in the Arkansas Republican Party," *Arkansas Historical Ouarterlv* Vol. 33 (1974), p. 3.

Duman, Ernest, "Black Vote is the Key Clinton's Victory," in *Arkansas Gazette* (November 11, 1982).

Gatewood, Jr., Willard B., "Negro Legislators in Arkansas, 1891: A Document," *Arkansas Historical Ouarterly* Vol. 31 (Autumn, 1972), pp. 222–223.

Graves, John William, "Negro Distranchisement in Arkansas," *Arkansas Historical Quarterly* Vol. 26 (1967), p. 203.

Holden, Mathew, "Editor's Introduction," *National Political Science Review* Vol. 4 (1994), pp. 1–6.

Kellogg, Peter, "Civil Rights Consciousness in the 1940s," *The Historian* Vol. 42 (November 1979).

Key, Jr, V. O. "The Future of the Democratic Party, *The Virginia Ouarterlv Review* Vol. 28 (Spring, 1952).

———, "The Political Relevant in Surveys," *Public Opinion Ouarterlv* Vol. 24 (Spring, 1960), pp. 55–56.

———, "A Theory of Critical Elections," *Journal of Politics* Vol. 17 (February, 1955), p. 3.

Lewis-Beck, Michael & Tom Rice, "Localism in Presidential Elections: The Home State Advantage," *American Journal of Political Science* Vol. 27 (August 1983), 548–556.

Miller, Warren, "Party Identification, Realignment, and Party Voting: Back To the Basics," *American Political Science Review* Vol. 85 (June, 1991), pp. 557–566.

Pettigrew, Thomas and Ernest Campbell, "Faubus and Segregation: An Analysis of Arkansas Voting," *Public Opinion Ouarterlv* Vol. 24 (Fall, 1960), pp. 400–442.

Savage, Robert and Richard Gallagher, "Politico Cultural Regions in a Southern State: An Empirical Topology of Arkansas Counties," *Regions* Vol. 7. (1977), pp. 91–105.

Sundquist, James. "The 1984 Election: How Much Realignment?" *Brookings Review* Vol. 3 (Winter, 1985).

Swicher, Idella. "Election Statistics in the United States." *American Political Science Review* Vol. (June, 1933), pp. 423–424.

Tatlovich, Raymond, "Friend and Neighbors, Voting: Mississippi, 1943–1973" *Journal of Politics* Vol. 37 (August, 1975), pp. 807–814.

Towns, Stuart, "A Louisiana Medicine Show: The Kingfish Elects An Arkansas Senator," *Arkansas Historical Ouarterly* Vol. 20 (1966), pp. 117–127.

Walton, Brian, "How Many Voted in Arkansas Elections Before the Civil War," *Arkansas Historical Ouarterly* Vol. (1980), p. 72.

Walton, Jr., Hanes, "Public Policy Responses to the Million Man March," *The Black Scholar* Vol. 28 (Fall, 1995), pp. 217–23.

———, "Review of Quiet Revolution in the South," *Georgia Historical Quarterly* Vol. 79 (Summer, 1995), pp. 516–518.

———, "Review of Race and the Decline of Class in American Politics." *Journal of American Historv* (December, 1990).

———, "Review of Separate and Unequal: Black Americans and the U.S. Federal Government, *Journal of American History* (March, 1997), pp. 1425–1426.

Watson, Denton L.,"Assessing the Role of the NAACP in the Civil Rights Movement," *The Historian* Vol. 55 (Spring, 1993), pp. 453–468.

Wills, Gary, "Newt Gingrich's Revolution," *The New York Review of Books* (March 23, 1995), Vol. 42, pp. 4–8.

Walsh, Elsa, "Kennedy's Hidden Campaign," *The New Yorker* (March 31, 1997), p. 66.

Young, David. "The Initiative and Referendum in Arkansas Come of Age." *American Political Science Review* Vol. (February, 1933), p. 75.

Cases

Robinson, et. al. v. *Holman* 181 Ark 428 (1930) 26 SW 2nd 66.

Perkins v. *City of West Helena. Arkansas* 675 F. 2d 201 1982).

Smith v. *Clinton* 687 F. Supp. 1310 (E.E. Ark., 1988).

Whitfield v. *Democratic Party* 686 F. Supp. 1365 (E.E. Ark, 1988); *Whitfield* v. *Democratic Party* 890 F. 2d, 1423 (8 Cir. 1889)

Whitfield v. *Democratic Party* 902 F. 2d 15 (9th Cir. 1990); *Whitfield* v. *Bill Clinton* 498 U.S. 1126, 112 L. Ed 2nd., 1193.

Robinson v. *Hohman* 181 Ark. 428(1930) and, 26 SW. 2nd. 66.

Election Data

Campbell, et. Ar., V. Lee County Election Committee (No. H.C. - 48–86.

Paul Riverie, 1976, 1978, 1980, 1982, Arkansas Election Data (Arkansas: Secretary of State, May, 1976–82).

William "Bill" McCuen, *1984, 1986, 1988, 1990, 1992 Arkansas Election Data* (Arkansas: Secretary of State, 1984–1992)..

Sharon Priest, *1994, 1996 Arkansas Election Data* (Arkansas: Secretary of State, 1994–1996).

Government Publications

U.S. Bureau of the Census, Current Population Reports Series P. 23 No. 168, *Studies in the Measurement of Voter Turnout* (Washington, DC: Government Printing Office, 1990).

Interviews, Letters & Memoranda

Interview with Dalley, at the Howard University Political Science Department Session on Jesse Jackson's 1984 Presidential Race.

Interview with Congressman Mervyn Dymally, at office in June, 1989.

Letter, Democratic Congressman Arthur Mitchell, to President Franklin Delaneo Roosevelt.

Letter, John L. Ferguson, Arkansas History Commission, to Hanes Walton, Jr., November 18, 1996.

Letter, John L. Ferguson to Hanes Walton, Jr., (March 11, 1997), p. 1.